The Nationality and Statelessness of Nomadic Peoples under International Law

The Nationality and Statelessness of Nomadic Peoples under International Law

HEATHER JEAN ALEXANDER

Lead Researcher, Center for the Future of Citizenship, Montreal, Canada

OXFORD
UNIVERSITY PRESS

OXFORD
UNIVERSITY PRESS

Oxford University Press is a department of the University of Oxford. It furthers the University's objective of excellence in research, scholarship, and education by publishing worldwide. Oxford is a registered trade mark of Oxford University Press in the UK and in certain other countries.

Published in the United States of America by Oxford University Press
198 Madison Avenue, New York, NY 10016, United States of America.

Library of Congress Cataloging-in-Publication Data
Names: Alexander, Heather Jean, 1977– author.
Title: The nationality and statelessness of nomadic peoples under international law / Heather Jean Alexander.
Description: New York : Oxford University Press, 2025. | Includes bibliographical references and index.
Identifiers: LCCN 2025002403 (print) | LCCN 2025002404 (ebook) | ISBN 9780197772331 (hardback) | ISBN 9780197772348 (epub) | ISBN 9780197772355 (updf)| ISBN 9780197772362 (online)
Subjects: LCSH: Nomads—Legal status, laws, etc. | Citizenship. | Stateless persons. | Statelessness.
Classification: LCC KI290 .A94 2025 (print) | LCC KI290 (ebook) | DDC 341.4/85—dc23/eng/20250121
LC record available at https://lccn.loc.gov/2025002403
LC ebook record available at https://lccn.loc.gov/2025002404

DOI: 10.1093/9780197772362.001.0001

Printed by Integrated Books International, United States of America

The manufacturer's authorized representative in the EU for product safety is Oxford University Press España S.A., Parque Empresarial San Fernando de Henares, Avenida de Castilla, 2 – 28830 Madrid (www.oup.es/en).

Note to Readers

This publication is designed to provide accurate and authoritative information in regard to the subject matter covered. It is based upon sources believed to be accurate and reliable and is intended to be current as of the time it was written. It is sold with the understanding that the publisher is not engaged in rendering legal, accounting, or other professional services. If legal advice or other expert assistance is required, the services of a competent professional person should be sought. Also, to confirm that the information has not been affected or changed by recent developments, traditional legal research techniques should be used, including checking primary sources where appropriate.

(Based on the Declaration of Principles jointly adopted by a Committee of the American Bar Association and a Committee of Publishers and Associations.)

For Cyrus

Contents

Acknowledgments

Some of the material for this book is taken from my PhD dissertation, 'The Nationality and Statelessness of Nomads under International Law: With a Comprehensive Examination of the Nationality and Statelessness of Former Bedouin in Kuwait, Tuareg in Mali and Sama Dilaut (Bajau Laut) in Malaysia' (Tilburg University 2020), available online. I would like to thank my thesis advisers at Tilburg University, Dr. Laura van Waas, Co-Director of the Institute on Statelessness and Inclusion, and Professor Willem van Genugten. I would also like to thank the members of my committee, Professor Ernst Hirsch Ballin, Professor Gerard-René de Groot, Dr. Bronwen Manby, Professor Cornelis Flinterman, and Professor Morag E. A. Goodwin. I would also like to thank the team at Oxford University Press, as well as the other individuals and organizations who provided their invaluable expertise, including, but not limited to, the *Association des Femmes Juristes* in Côte d'Ivoire, UNHCR Côte d'Ivoire, the Peter McMullin Centre on Statelessness, Professor Michelle Foster, Professor Christoph Sperfeldt, Dr. Anthony Toth, Professor Dawn Chatty, Dr. Helen Brunt, Professor Mohammad Al-Wuhaib, Professor Arsène Brice Bado, and Professor Jonathan Simon. I would also like to thank artist Laura-Anne Passarello for her help with the maps in this book. Special thanks to members of the Fulani community who shared their insights and expertise with me.

Table of Cases

Table of Treaties

Table of Legislation

Other International and Regional Instruments

1
Introduction

1.1 Why Research Nomadic Peoples and Statelessness?

It is indisputable that the twentieth and twenty-first centuries have been filled with tension and conflict between many nomadic communities and the governments of the nation-states in which they live. In 1980, anthropologist Dan Aronson noted that nomadic pastoralists "are almost by definition marginal in most countries, especially where the state has risen and is based primarily in settled agricultural population."[1] As the examples cited in this book will show, since Aronson made this observation, conflict and tension between nation-state governments and nomadic peoples have only worsened in many parts of the world. Two of the examples highlighted in this book are pastoral communities in the Sahel, whose way of life is often viewed by their governments in apocalyptic terms. As experts Baz Lecocq and Amy Niang put it, governments in Africa see pastoralists as "a challenge to the order and stability of the postcolonial state, if not a threat to the territorial integrity of the countries concerned."[2] Conflict and tension between nomadic communities and the governments of nation-states threaten nomadic human rights, fueling their marginalization, and contributing in some cases to armed conflict and grave violations of international law.

A vast literature exists on the causes of this tension and conflict, some of which will be cited in this book. Experts have pointed to many causes, including colonization, modernization, globalization, the shift to a wage economy, the growing, global dominance of large-scale agriculture, resource extraction, the expansion of centralized government, increased urbanization, armed conflict, and climate change and the destruction of natural

[1] Dan Aronson, 'Must Nomads Settle? Some Notes toward Policy on the Future of Pastoralism' in Philip Salzman (ed), *When Nomads Settle: Processes of Sedentarization as Adaptation and Defense* (Praeger 1980) 180.

[2] Baz Lecocq and Amy Niang, 'Identités sahéliennes en temps de crise: histoires, enjeux et Perspectives' in Baz Lecocq and Amy Niang (eds), *Identités sahéliennes en temps de crise: Histoires, enjeux et perspectives* (LIT Verlag 2019) 10.

The Nationality and Statelessness of Nomadic Peoples Under International Law. Heather Jean Alexander, Oxford University Press. © Oxford University Press 2025. DOI: 10.1093/9780197772362.003.0001

ecosystems.[3] This book will fill a gap in this literature on nomadic-state tension and conflict by looking at statelessness, a well-documented cause and consequence of marginalization for minority groups, but one which is largely missing from the literature on nomadic peoples and their relationships with nation-state governments.

While the word "statelessness" may conjure a host of psychological, political, and cultural references for the reader,[4] this book will mostly examine the problem of nomadic statelessness from a legal perspective. Under international law, stateless persons are those individuals who are not considered nationals by any state under the operation of its laws.[5] While there is a widely recognized right to a nationality under international law, many nomadic peoples have struggled to enjoy this right, a fact this book will explore.
It is impossible to overstate the devastating effects of statelessness on the lives of stateless people.[6] Nationality in a nation-state is critical to having standing with governments, access to the courts, health care, and employment, and, in many countries, own land. For nomadic communities in particular, nationality is necessary in many countries to advocate for culturally appropriate schooling, the legalization of nomadic livelihoods, freedom of movement, and to combat assimilation.[7] As indigenous rights experts Van Genugten, Meijknecht, and Rombouts put it, "The right to a nationality (is) a 'gateway' to the recognition of a plurality of other rights."[8]

[3] For some examples, see Thomas Arkell, 'The Decline of Pastoral Nomadism in the Western Sahara' (1991) 76 Geo 162, 163 (on the Sahrawis); Angela Manderscheid, 'Decline and Re-emergence of Nomadism: Tibetan Pastoralists Revive a Nomadic Way of Life and Production' (2001) 53 GeoJournal 173 (on revival and decline among Lapland and Tibetan pastoralists); Anja Fischer, 'Research and Nomads in the Age of Globalization' in Anja Fischer and Ines Kohl (eds), *Tuareg Society within a Globalized World: Saharan Life in Transition* (I B Tauris 2010) 13–14 (on the Tuareg).

[4] Jérémie Gilbert, *Nomadic Peoples and Human Rights* (Routledge 2014) 160.

[5] Convention Relating to the Status of Stateless Persons (adopted 28 September 1954, entered into force 6 June 1960) 360 UNTS 117, art 1 (when together with the 1961 Convention, "Statelessness Conventions").

[6] For some examples, see Amal De Chickera, 'Unravelling Anomaly: Detention, Discrimination and the Protection Needs of Stateless Persons' (Equal Rights Trust 2010); The Salam for Democracy and Human Rights and the Institute on Statelessness and Inclusion, 'Nothing but a Pen and a Word: Voices from the Stateless Bidoon Community in Kuwait during the COVID-19 Pandemic' (2023); Global COVID19 Consortium and Institute on Statelessness and Inclusion, 'Malaysia, Together We Can: The COVID-19 Impact on Stateless People and a Roadmap for Change' (2023).

[7] See for example Steinar Pedersen, 'The Coastal Sámi of Norway and Their Rights to Traditional Marine Livelihood' (2012) 3 Arctic Rev L Pol 51 (on the use of the courts by Sámi fishermen); Heather Alexander, 'The Open Sky or a Brick and Mortar School? Statelessness, Education and Nomadic Children' in Institute on Statelessness and Inclusion (ed), *The World's Stateless Children* (Wolf 2017) (on the importance of nationality to protecting the right to not only access school but advocate for culturally appropriate schooling).

[8] Willem van Genugten, Anna Meijknecht and Bas Rombouts, 'Stateless Indigenous People(s): The Right to a Nationality, Including Their Own' (2014) 19 Tilburg L Rev 98, 98.

This book acknowledges, however, that nation-state nationality has often had negative consequences for some nomadic peoples. As this book will explore, there is a complex relationship between nationality law and the assimilation of marginalized groups. Experts like Lindsey Kingston[9] have rightly questioned the usefulness of nationality in existing nation-states to nomadic peoples. As expert Tendayi Bloom observes, discussing indigenous peoples, "[i]t can sometimes be difficult for theorists in the liberal tradition to examine citizenship divorced from the mythology of emancipation surrounding its development . . . the indigenous peoples discussed here did not share this history."[10]

The problem of nomadic statelessness, however, remains a grave violation of international law that should be addressed by nation-states and the international community, which are the subjects of this book. The seriousness of nomadic statelessness raises the question of solutions. The United Nations High Commissioner for Refugees (UNHCR) and other experts promote several generalized solutions to statelessness, most of which invoke various principles and norms under international law, including the right to be registered at birth, antidiscrimination in the granting of nationality, and identifying statelessness for the purposes of facilitated naturalization.[11] This book will interrogate the appropriateness and usefulness of these solutions for nomadic peoples as a specific class of persons and a unique type of community.[12]

This book makes a timely and important contribution to the field of statelessness studies, which has been historically marginalized within academia.[13] The topic of nomadic statelessness has received even less attention, though the UNHCR, the agency mandated at the global level to prevent and resolve statelessness, the Council of Europe, and others have noted that many

[9] Lindsey N Kingston, *Fully Human: Personhood, Citizenship, and Rights* (OUP 2019) 149. See also Lindsey N Kingston, 'Statelessness as a Lack of Functioning Citizenship' (2014) 19 Tilburg L Rev 133; Tendayi Bloom, 'Members of Colonized Groups, Statelessness and the Right to Have Rights' in Tendayi Bloom (ed), *Understanding Statelessness* (Routledge 2017) 158.

[10] Bloom (n 9) 161.

[11] See for example the international norms invoked in the UNHCR, 'Global Action Plan to End Statelessness 2014-2024' (Div of Int'l Protection 2014) 18; the UNHCR, Global Alliance web page <https://www.unhcr.org/ibelong/the-new-global-alliance-to-end-statelessness/> accessed 1 September 2024); and the work of nomadic rights expert Jérémie Gilbert.

[12] Such an analysis has been the subject of at least one unpublished, internal UN study in which the author of this book took part.

[13] Lindsey N Kingston, 'Conceptualizing Statelessness as a Human Rights Challenge: Framing, Visual Representation, and (Partial) Issue Emergence' (2019) 11 J H R Prac 52 (on statelessness and issue emergence).

nomadic peoples are stateless and have cited the serious violations of international law that may occur as a result.[14] Many individual studies also exist on stateless nomadic communities, some of which are mentioned in this book. This book will draw on information from four nomadic communities that previous studies have documented as stateless or at risk of statelessness: former Bedouin nomadic peoples in Kuwait, Sama Dilaut (Bajau Laut) in Malaysia, Tuareg in Mali, and Fulani in Côte d'Ivoire.

Most of the information available on nomadic communities comes from the fields of anthropology and history. To tackle the subject of nomadic statelessness, an area of law that is underresearched, this book draws on the work of experts from these fields, as well as sociology, political science, geography, and philosophy, to provide background information on the four groups used as examples in this book. This book is not, however, an interdisciplinary study or a comparative study. The selected examples are not intended to be representative of all nomadic peoples. Rather, the information that is compiled in this book from outside of the field of law is used to inform and contextualize a discussion of the effectiveness of international law in providing solutions to stateless nomadic communities and individuals. This approach is also an acknowledgement of the complexity and multifaceted nature of statelessness, adopting the advice of statelessness experts Mark Manly and Laura van Waas, who argue for a comprehensive approach.[15]

As a work of international law, this book adopts a broad and progressive approach to legal analysis by looking at treaty law, case law, soft law, the opinions of experts and advisory bodies, regional laws and mechanisms, and, where appropriate, national laws. This book will sometimes apply norms and laws in the hypothetical case of full-state adoption. It will also consider soft law and regional law to look at emerging developments in the law, and it will propose reforms where necessary. While adopting a progressive approach, however, this book will also acknowledge the specific obligations of the four states examined here, Kuwait, Mali, Côte d'Ivoire, and Malaysia.

[14] Council of Europe: Committee of Ministers, Recommendation No. R (83) 1 of the Committee of Ministers to Member States on Statelessness Nomads and Nomadic peoples of Undetermined Nationality, 22 February 1983, 1. See also Mark Manly, 'UNHCR's Mandate and Activities to Address Statelessness' in Alice Edwards and Laura van Waas (eds), *Nationality and Statelessness under International Law* (CUP 2014) 108, citing 'UNHCR, Action to Address Statelessness: A Strategy Note' March 2010, para 35; UNHCR, 'Global Action Plan to End Statelessness 2014-2024' (Div of Int'l Protection 2014); UNHCR IBelong Campaign, 'This is Our Home: Stateless Minorities and Their Search for Citizenship' (UNHCR 2017).

[15] Mark Manly and Laura van Waas, 'The State of Statelessness Research' (2014) 19 Tilburg L Rev 3, 5.

This book is divided into six chapters. Chapters 1 and 2 are background chapters, providing context for the substantive analysis in chapters 3 through 6. Chapter 1 introduces the subject matter, including the nomadic communities used as examples, and defines key terms. Chapter 2 discusses the bias against nomadic peoples that exists in academia and explores the representation of nomadic peoples in the literature on nomadic rights. The themes of bias and representation will reoccur throughout the book and chapter 2 provides important context to the writing of the book itself and some of the weaknesses of the source material.

Drawing on a wide variety of sources, chapters 3 through 6 begin by identifying a root cause of statelessness of one or more of the four groups used as examples: the Bedouin in Kuwait, the Tuareg in Mali, the Fulani in Côte d'Ivoire, and the Sama Dilaut in Malaysia. Each chapter then discusses areas of international law that might provide a solution to the identified cause of nomadic statelessness. Causes of nomadic statelessness covered by these chapters include the right to be registered at birth, the protections against discrimination in granting nationality, the rights of indigenous peoples to a nationality, and the prohibitions against statelessness. Each chapter identifies gaps in the existing framework and recommends reforms. The chapters build on one another, but some areas of possible intersection between topics and concepts have been pared down to preserve the clarity of the book's structure and to provide an easier reading experience. As this book is intended to be a jumping-off point for further research and analysis, it is hoped that some of the intersections that are not discussed in this book will be explored in future books and articles, and potential intersections are flagged as worthy of future study.

Chapter 3 looks at the international laws regarding civil registration, including the right to be registered at birth. It draws from the experiences with civil registration of the four nomadic groups used as examples in this book to highlight some of the ways in which the question of their civil registration intersects with their nationality and statelessness. Chapter 3 summarizes some of the ways in which civil registration, including birth registration, but also other forms of documents and registries contribute to statelessness for nomadic peoples, and examines the extent to which international law may provide solutions for some nomadic peoples, including by prohibiting discrimination in birth registration, while also identifying gaps and proposing areas of law that should be strengthened to better protect the rights of nomadic peoples to a nationality.

Chapter 4 looks at the prohibitions in international law against discrimination in the granting of nationality. Discrimination may be defined as "[t]reating one or more members of a specified group unfairly as compared with other people."[16] Chapter 4 first examines the extent to which there is discrimination against the Bedouin in the nationality laws of Kuwait, against the Tuareg in the nationality laws of Mali, against the Fulani in the nationality laws of Côte d'Ivoire, and against the Sama Dilaut in the nationality laws of Malaysia. It next analyzes how international law addresses this discrimination and identifies gaps where international law could better assist nomadic peoples to combat it.

Chapter 5 looks at the right to a nationality for indigenous peoples, exploring how the indigenous rights framework might form part of a solution to statelessness for the Bedouin, the Tuareg, the Fulani, and the Sama Dilaut. It explores how indigenous rights intersect with land rights and the right to be nomadic, as well as with the right to a nationality under international law. It also interrogates the concept of indigeneity for nomadic peoples and examines how this concept has impacted nomadic nationality rights. Finally, it looks at the related right of nomadic peoples to self-determination as a solution to statelessness.

Building on the material in the preceding chapters, Chapter 6 looks at the prohibitions against statelessness under international law, examining the usefulness of solutions to statelessness that are predicated on identifying individual nomadic people as stateless and providing a facilitated solution. Chapter 6 also discusses some of the reasons such a pathway to a solution may do more harm than good, touching upon the broader, and often problematic, relationship between nomadic peoples and the concept of statelessness.

1.2 Key Terms and Concepts

This section defines the key terms and concepts used throughout this book and explains how they will be used. It is designed to be a reference for the rest of the book. Some of these terms and concepts are legal terms with precise definitions, while others are terms in general use.

[16] This definition is taken from the *Oxford Reference Dictionary* <https://www.oxfordreference.com/view/10.1093/oi/authority.20110803095721450> accessed 7 October 2024.

1.2.1 Nomadic Peoples

This book uses the term "nomadic peoples," which is not a legal term and has no definition in law but is a term frequently employed by anthropologists, governments, and settled peoples to describe certain communities that practice lifestyles of frequent or continuous mobility as a way of life, including long-distance trade, traveling performance, pastoralism, seasonal hunting, and gathering.[17] Self-identification is often a key factor of nomadic people's identity, in part because colonial attitudes have colored and distorted the historical record in ways that are still being uncovered and discussed, and in part because nomadism encompasses a wide variety of different practices that are hard to define and classify. The *Dana Declaration on Mobile Peoples and Conservation* defines these communities as

> a subset of indigenous and traditional peoples whose livelihoods depend on extensive common property use of natural resources over an area, who use mobility as a management strategy for dealing with sustainable use and conservation, and who possess a distinctive cultural identity and natural resource management system.[18]

The 2007 Segovia Declaration of Nomadic Peoples and Transhumant Pastoralists defines pastoral nomadism as "seasonal mobility and common property of natural resources (particularly rangelands), regulated by customary law and practices, customary institutions, and leadership, all making use of local and indigenous knowledge."[19]

Nomadism is also a mutable and changeable characteristic, with many populations moving in and out of nomadism over time.[20] Experts have defined the term "nomad" in different ways.[21] It often has negative connotations,

[17] See Philip Carl Salzman, 'Introduction' in Philip Carl Salzman (ed), *When Nomads Settle: Processes of Sedentarization as Adaptation and Response* (Praeger 1980) 10, where he defines nomadism as the 'movement of the household during the annual round of productive activities.' For an overview of the origins and meaning of the term nomad, see Youssouf Diallo, *Nomads des espaces interstitiels: Pastoralisme, identité, migrations (Burkina Faso-Cote d'Ivoire)* (Rüdiger Köppe Verlag 2008) 23–28.

[18] *Dana Declaration on Mobile Peoples and Conservation* (2002) <http://www.danadeclaration.org/> accessed 7 October 2024.

[19] Segovia Declaration of Nomadic Peoples and Transhumant Pastoralists (La Granja, Segovia, Spain, 14 September 2007).

[20] Dawn Chatty, *Mobile Pastoralists: Development Planning and Social Change in Oman* (Columbia UP 1996) 3–8. See also Diallo (n 17) 27–33, where he discusses 'episodes' of nomadism.

[21] André Bourgeot, *Les sociétés touarègues; Nomadism, identité, résistances* (Karthala 1995) 154–156, citing to the definitions of nomadism of A Bernard, N Lacroix, J Berque and R Capot-Rey. See

and many experts, including anthropologist Dawn Chatty, and nomadic communities prefer the term "mobile peoples." The term "nomad" may impose an imagined ideology on otherwise disparate groups or create a false dichotomy between nomadic peoples and the rest of society. This book will use the term "nomadic peoples" because it is often used by governments that, along with international law, are the primary subjects of this book, but it will use other terms where appropriate in quotations or in specific cases. As a work primarily focused on governments, international institutions, and the law, what is missing from this book are many of the opinions and views of nomadic peoples themselves on the topic of nationality and the problem of statelessness. Chapter 2 discusses these questions of representation and voice in more detail.

Some, but not all, nomadic peoples may also self-identify as indigenous peoples.[22] The *Oxford English Dictionary* defines indigenous as "inhabiting or existing in a land from the earliest times or from before the arrival of colonists,"[23] though there is no fixed definition of indigenous status.[24] Chapter 5 discusses the intersection between nomadism and indigenous status.

1.2.2 Statelessness and Risk of Statelessness

As the introduction explained, governments and international law are the primary subjects of this book. This is because statelessness is a problem that is largely the direct result of government laws and policies and is bad for states and the international system. Everyone on earth has links to at least

also Anatoly Khazanov, *Nomads and the Outside World* (2nd edn, U Wisconsin P 1994) 15–16 (on the problems with the term nomadism as a way of life distinct from settlement). But see contra Frank Hole, 'Pastoral Mobility as an Adaptation' in Jeffrey Szuchman (ed), *Nomads, Tribes, and the State in the Ancient Near East: Cross-disciplinary Perspectives* (Chicago UP 2009) 269–270 (arguing that mobility and settlement are distinct ways of life).

[22] See generally Joshua Castellino and Cathal Doyle, 'Who Are "Indigenous Peoples"? An Examination of Concepts Concerning Group Membership in the United Nations Declaration on the Rights of Indigenous Peoples' in Jessie Hohmann and Marc Weller (eds), *The UN Declaration on the Rights of Indigenous Peoples: A Commentary* (OUP 2018) 8–37, particularly 25.

[23] Indigenous, n. Oxford English Dictionary online, accessed 3 October 2024, <https://www.oed.com/dictionary/indigenous_adj?tl=true>.

[24] For one example, see the discussion of indigenous status and the Tuareg in Jeremy Keenan, *The Lesser Gods of the Sahara: Social Change and Contested Terrain amongst the Tuareg of Algeria* (Routledge 2004) 7–8.

one state, both through birth and through connections established during their lives, like residence, education, family ties, military service, and many others. Resolving statelessness by formalizing these links through nationality laws and procedures is clearly within the ambit of governments and is, in fact, one of their primary functions.

According to the 1954 Convention Relating to the Status of Stateless Persons, Article 1, a stateless person, or *apatride*, is a "person who is not considered as a national by any state under the operation of its law."[25] Statelessness occurs for many reasons, including because of discriminatory nationality laws, discrimination in how nationality laws are applied, gaps between the nationality laws of the same state, gaps between the nationality laws of different states, and multiple generations lacking civil registration and, therefore, the ability to prove that they qualify under the law. Statelessness is also a typical result of the breakup of states and the decolonization process. Statelessness may also be caused by denationalization or by the renunciation of nationality.[26]

It is important to understand what is meant by "under operation of its law" in the definition of statelessness. The operation of law may take the form of court decisions, statutes, administrative rules, procedural rules, and treaties and custom. Nationality can be conferred either automatically, when the requirements of the law are met, or following a formal procedure. Sources of law may vary depending on the legal system used in a country. When determining statelessness, therefore, it is necessary to look at all points at which nationality is determined, from the procedures used at local registration offices in issuing documents to relevant court cases to changes made to the laws by legislatures, to the actions of embassies. "The reference to 'law' in Article 1(1) should be read broadly to encompass not just legislation, but also ministerial decrees, regulations, orders, judicial case law (in countries with a tradition of precedent) and, where appropriate, customary practice."[27]

It is important to note that persons at risk of statelessness may also be considered stateless for the purposes of finding a solution. As statelessness expert Gabor Gyulai puts it, "[e]stablishing statelessness is often a cumbersome

[25] Convention Relating to the Status of Stateless Persons (adopted 28 September 1954, entered into force 6 June 1960) 360 UNTS 117.

[26] Laura van Waas, *Nationality Matters: Statelessness under International Law* (Intersentia 2008) 49–93.

[27] UNHCR, 'Handbook on the Protection of Stateless Persons under the 1954 Convention Relating to the Status of Stateless Persons' (Geneva 2014).

exercise and if the evidentiary rules are too strict, this can easily undermine the protection objective of the 1954 Convention."[28]

As Lindsey Kingston points out, a "legalistic focus" can often ignore the "subtle realities" of statelessness.[29] As a normative concept, statelessness poses a challenge because it is the absence of a status, yet it can also be a status in and of itself.[30] At the same time, there are often serious problems with applying the term "stateless" to vulnerable groups, as will be discussed at length in chapter 6.

As chapter 3 notes, the mere fact that an individual lacks identity documents does not mean that person is stateless.[31] However, persons with no identity documents and whose parents have no identity documents may be at risk of statelessness. A lack of registration can have many of the same consequences as statelessness, such as making it impossible for children to attend school or for an individual to return home from abroad. If the problem of a lack of registration is not resolved after multiple generations, it can become statelessness, particularly in places where biometric registration is becoming more prevalent.[32]

While this book focuses mainly on the causes of nomadic statelessness and the possible solutions offered under international law, it is important to reiterate the seriousness of the problem and the devastating effects of statelessness on individuals, communities, and states. In addition to the crisis it presents to individuals as mentioned in the introduction, statelessness can be a driver of political, economic, and social unrest and makes it more difficult for states to address crime, poverty, and other social problems. Nationality remains both vital and irreplaceable for communities to enforce their rights and unite to participate in the political process.

While today, basic human rights are assured by international law regardless of nationality status, it remains true, as the introduction mentioned, that

[28] Gabor Gyulai, 'The Determination of Statelessness and the Establishment of a Statelessness-specific Protection Regime' in Alice Edwards and Laura van Waas (eds), *Nationality and Statelessness under International Law* (CUP 2014) 137.

[29] Lindsey N Kingston, 'Worthy of Rights: Statelessness as a Cause and Symptom of Marginalisation' in Tendayi Bloom, Katherine Tonkiss and Phillip Cole (eds), *Understanding Statelessness* (Routledge 2017), 17.

[30] See the discussion of statelessness and noncitizenship as types of status under Indian law in Anubhav Dutt Tiwari, Ali Johar and Jessica Field, 'The Illegalisation of Rohingya Refugees in India: A (Non)Citizenship Crisis Promoted by Law and Policy' (2024) 50 J Eth Mig Stud 1.

[31] Amal de Chickera and Laura van Waas, 'Unpacking Statelessness' in Tendayi Bloom (ed), *Understanding Statelessness* (Routledge 2017) 65.

[32] Bronwen Manby, 'Who Belongs? Statelessness and Nationality in West Africa' (Migration Policy Institute 2016) (on West Africa).

many vital civil rights, such as the power to petition one's government, access to the courts, and the right to vote, often require nationality. Statelessness is also bad for the nation-state system, as displaced stateless persons raise tensions with neighboring states. Arendt called statelessness an "element of (state) disintegration."[33] Nevertheless, as this book will explore, statelessness can sometimes be useful for states to exclude so-called problematic groups.

1.2.3 Nationality and Citizenship

The study of statelessness must be accompanied by a survey of nationality law, for the concepts are intertwined.[34] Despite the fact that it is a core component of the nation-state system, it is not easy to formulate a clear definition of nationality as a concept in law.[35] Some experts argue that nationality as a concept in law must have some minimum content of rights and duties, such as the right to enter a country and reside there, while others view nationality as an identifier to which rights and duties may or may not attach.[36] In the modern period, nationality often guarantees basic civil rights, including, in many countries, voting, holding office, and access to the courts.

Under colonization, however, governments often treated colonized populations as subjects, rather than nationals, and subjected peoples often lacked rights.[37] Colonial systems of tiers of nationality produced deeply unequal and divided societies along race, gender, and religious lines. It is also necessary to say a few words about the term "citizenship." This book will use the term "nationality" throughout, in part for simplicity, and in part because the former is often, though not always, preferred by international

[33] Hannah Arendt, *The Origins of Totalitarianism* (Houghton Mifflin Harcourt 1973) 269.

[34] Manly and van Waas (n 15) 5.

[35] Engin Isin and Peter Nyers, 'Introduction: Globalizing Citizenship Studies' in Engin Isin and Peter Nyers (eds), *Routledge Handbook of Global Citizenship Studies* (Routledge 2014) 1.

[36] Paul Weis, *Nationality and Statelessness in International Law* (Brill 1979) 60–62; Kingston, 'Statelessness as a Lack of Functioning Citizenship' (n 9) 127; Alice Edwards, 'The Meaning of Nationality in International Law in an Era of Human Rights: Procedural and Substantive Aspects' in Alice Edwards and Laura van Waas (eds), *Nationality and Statelessness under International Law* (CUP 2014) 30–38; Gerard-Rene De Groot and Oliver Willem Vonk, *International Standards on Nationality Law: Texts, Cases and Materials* (Wolf Legal 2015) 36; Heather Alexander and Jonathan Simon, 'No Port, No Passport: Why Submerged States Can Have No Nationals' (2016) 26 Wash Intl L J 307.

[37] See generally Maximilian Koessler, 'Subject, Citizen, National and Permanent Allegiance' (1946) 56 Yale L J 58. See also David Scott FitzGerald, 'The History of Racialized Citizenship' in A Shachar and others (eds), *The Oxford Handbook of Citizenship* (OUP 2017) 132–135.

experts.[38] This book will use citizenship where it occurs in original quotes or documents and in certain specific cases.

As well as being a concept under the law, nationality is also a social and cultural construct. Nationality as a social or cultural construct has long been a topic of academic study in the work of John Stuart Mill, Hannah Arendt, David Miller, and many others. To be a national in the social or cultural sense is commonly understood as being a member of a community of people sharing a common way of life that is rooted in a particular territory and has the right to exclude outsiders.[39] Nationality as a social or cultural construct is relevant to nationality as a legal concept because the former often provides a moral justification for the latter.[40] For example, nationality as a cultural concept justifies the legal concept of *jus sanguinis*, or nationality by descent, or, in another example, the principle of self-determination under international law.

1.2.4 Civil Registration and Legal Identity

Legal identity is the recognition of a person under the law. At the same time, civil registration is defined as the continuous, permanent, compulsory, and universal recording of the occurrence and characteristics of vital events pertaining to the population, as provided through decree or regulation in accordance with the legal requirements in each country.[41]

In countries practicing nationality via *jus soli*, or birth in the territory of the state, the birth certificate is the key document establishing nationality, as is required under international law. Birth certificates and other forms of

[38] De Groot and Vonk (n 36) 3. See also Jonkheer Haro and Frederik van Panhuys, *The Role of Nationality in International Law* (A W Sijthoff 1959) 38; Marc Verwilghen, *Conflits de nationalités, Plurinationalité et apatridie* (Brill 1999) 88.

[39] Will Kymlicka, *Multicultural Citizenship: A Liberal Theory of Minority Rights* (OUP 1995) 1, 54, 124. See also David Miller, *On Nationality* (OUP 1995) 24–27; Jürgen Habermas, *The Postnational Constellation: Political Essays* (MIT Press 2001), 9–10, 63–64; Zygmunt Bauman, 'Soil, Blood and Identity' (2008) 40 Sociol Rev 675, 683–684.

[40] Jacques Maury, 'Nationalité. Théorie générale du français' in Albert de La Pradelle and Jean-Hippolyte-Paulin Niboyet (eds), *Répertoire de droit international* (Sirey 1931). See also the discussion in Phillip Cole, 'Introduction: 'Border Crossings'—The Dimensions of Membership' in Gideon Calder, Phillip Cole and Jonathan Seglow (eds), *Citizenship Acquisition and Natural Belonging Migration, Membership and the Liberal Democratic State* (Palgrave Macmillan 2010) 1–23; Costica Dumbrava, 'Bloodlines and Belonging: Time to Abandon Ius Sanguinis?' in Rainer Bauböck (ed), *Debating Transformations of National Citizenship* (SpringerLink 2018) 73.

[41] UNDESA, 'Principles and Recommendations for a Vital Statistics System, Statistical Papers' (2014) Series M N. 19/Rev3 (2014) 65.

registration also provide evidence of nationality. Besides birth certificates, widely used documents to establish or prove nationality include certificates of nationality, national IDs, and passports.

Other documents, however, such as title to land, registration of the payment of taxes, licenses issued by the state, and school registration, may serve as evidence of habitual or long-term residence or serve to establish a legal identity, including place of birth or descent from a national, which may be crucial to establishing nationality in some cases. Habitual residence is a common way to establish nationality during the succession of states and, at decolonization, to establish what this book will call the "first body of nationals" of postcolonial states.

1.2.5 The Right to a Nationality

Today, there is a widely recognized, though not universally agreed upon, right to a nationality under international law. Still, during the nineteenth and early twentieth centuries, nationality was widely thought to be the exclusive domain of sovereign states and was therefore largely exempted from the realm of international law, unless as stipulated by treaty.[42] The twentieth century saw the emergence of a framework of norms limiting state sovereignty over nationality, mainly to prevent states from infringing on the sovereignty of one another.[43] In 1955, the International Court of Justice handed down an opinion in the *Nottebohm* case on nationalities where the individual did not have an adequate "link" or was not "closely connected" to the state.[44]

During the twentieth century, international law also acknowledged the critical role of nationality in the individual's life as part of an emerging body

[42] Edwards (n 36) 14–16. See also the discussion in Ruth Donner, *The Regulation of Nationality in International Law* (2nd edn, Brill 1994) 10 and De Groot and Vonk (n 36) 41–46.

[43] Ian Brownlie, 'Relations of Nationality in Public International Law' (1963) 39 Brit YB of Intl L 284, 285–289, 387. See also Carol Batchelor, 'Statelessness and the Problem of Resolving Nationality Status' (1998) 10 Intl J Ref L 156; Donner (n 42) 45–67; Maury (n 40) 9–10, 20, 74; James Crawford, *Brownlie's Principles of Public International Law* (9th edn, Oxford University Press 2019) 495–503; Jan Hendrik Willem Verzijl, *International Law in Historical Perspective. Vol 5: Nationality and Other Matters relating to Individuals* (Martinus Nijhoff 1998), 21, 23–24; Malcolm Shaw, *International Law* (9th edn, CUP 2021) 567–571; van Waas (n 26) 37. See also for example cases before the American-Mexican Mixed Claims Commission as well as the Convention on Certain Questions relating to the Conflict of Nationality Law (signed 12 April 1930, entered into force 1 July 1937) 179 LNTS 89, though the Convention was ratified by only twenty states and the League of Nations ceased operations in 1946.

[44] *Nottebohm Case (Liechtenstein v Guatemala)* (Second Phase) [1955] ICJ Rep 4, 23.

of human rights law. Of foremost importance to the development of a right to a nationality was the nonbinding Universal Declaration of Human Rights, which guarantees the right to a nationality in Article 15.[45] Other international treaties that support the right to a nationality include the International Covenant on Civil and Political Rights,[46] the Convention on the Rights of the Child,[47] and the Convention on the Elimination of All Forms of Racial Discrimination,[48] which are binding on states parties. The Declaration on the Rights of Indigenous Peoples[49] also supports the right to a nationality for indigenous peoples, though it is non-binding.

Regional treaties also establish the right to a nationality, including the Arab Charter on Human Rights of 2004, Article 29,[50] the African Charter on the Rights and Welfare of the Child, Article 6,[51] and the Covenant on the Rights of the Child in Islam, Article 7,[52] the American Convention on Human Rights, Article 20,[53] the American Declaration of the Rights and Duties of Man of 1948, Article 19,[54] the Strasbourg Convention of 1963 on the Reduction of Cases of Multiple Nationality,[55] and the 1973 Convention to Reduce the Number of Cases of Statelessness in Europe, and the European Convention on Nationality of 1997.[56] The African Charter on Human and Peoples' Rights[57] guarantees the right to freedom of movement and to enter and exit one's country in Article 12, rights adjacent to nationality.

[45] Universal Declaration of Human Rights (adopted 10 December 1948, UNGA Res 217 A (III)), art 15.

[46] International Covenant on Civil and Political Rights (adopted 16 December 1966, entered into force 23 March 1976) 999 UNTS 171, with 173 state parties.

[47] Convention on the Rights of the Child (adopted 20 November 1989, entered into force 2 September 1990) 1577 UNTS 3, with 196 state parties.

[48] International Convention on the Elimination of All Forms of Racial Discrimination (adopted 21 December 1965, entered into force 4 January 1969) 660 UNTS 195, with 182 state parties.

[49] United Nations Declaration on the Rights of Indigenous Peoples (adopted 13 September 2007, UNGA Res 61/295), adopted by 144 states.

[50] Arab Charter on Human Rights, League of Arab States, 12 IHRR 893 (2005) (adopted 22 May 2004, came into force 15 March 2008), with twenty-two state parties.

[51] African Charter on Human and Peoples' Rights (1982) 21 ILM 58 (African Charter) (adopted 27 June 1981, entered into force 21 October 1986).

[52] Covenant on the Rights of the Child in Islam (adopted 6 June 2005, entered into force 28 November 2005).

[53] American Convention on Human Rights, Pact of San José, Costa Rica, 1144 UNTS 123 (adopted 18 July 1978), with twenty-five state parties.

[54] American Declaration of the Rights and Duties of Man, OAS Res XXX (adopted by the Ninth International Conference of American States 1948), repr. Basic Documents Pertaining to Human Rights in the InterAmerican System OEA/Ser L V/II.82 Doc 6 Rev 1 at 17 (1992).

[55] Convention on the Reduction of Cases of Multiple Nationality and on Military Obligations in Cases of Multiple Nationality, ETS 43 (signed 6 May 1963, entered into force 28 March 1968).

[56] European Convention on Nationality, CETS No 166 (adopted 6 November 1997, entered into force 1 March 2000), with ten ratifications.

[57] African [Banjul] Charter on Human and Peoples' Rights, 21 ILM 58 (came into force on 27 June 1981), with fifty-four state parties.

The Statelessness Conventions,[58] binding on states parties, support the right to a nationality, but they also provide protection for stateless people and a pathway to a solution for statelessness, as well as a framework to prevent statelessness. The Statelessness Conventions may, therefore, be seen as adding more specificity to the right to a nationality by mandating the conditions under which nationality is established in some circumstances and by creating a duty on the part of states to identify, prevent, and resolve statelessness, as well as protect stateless people.

Treaty bodies and courts have issued dicta indicating that states have a general duty not to adopt laws that create statelessness[59] and prohibiting the discriminatory withdrawal of nationality.[60] Soft law has also played an important role in guiding state practice. Perhaps the most important guidance on statelessness in recent years is the *UNHCR Handbook on the Protection of Stateless Persons*, which provides guidance for identifying stateless persons in a migratory situation.[61] It marks a vital step in bringing rigor to the identification of statelessness as a formal category under international law and protections for stateless migrants.

It should be noted, however, that there is no international tribunal tasked with adjudicating cases of statelessness, as would have been created by Article 11 of the 1954 *Draft Convention on the Elimination of Future Statelessness*. As a result, identifying statelessness in a migratory situation falls to national governments, with guidance from UNHCR. As well, cases of *in situ* statelessness, or persons who are stateless "in their own country," are not expressly covered by the *Handbook*, as Chapter 6 will discuss in more detail. While international law mandates the prevention of statelessness, as van Waas points out, the 1961 Convention "stops short of prescribing obligations that will decisively eliminate statelessness in all circumstances."[62] For example, denaturalization was widely acknowledged to be a threat to the rights of

[58] Convention Relating to the Status of Stateless Persons, 360 UNTS 117 (adopted 28 September 1954, entered into force 6 June 1960); Convention on the Reduction of Statelessness, 989 UNTS 175 (signed 30 August 1961, entered into force 13 December 1975).

[59] *Case of the Girls Yean and Bosico v Dominican Republic, Oliven Yean and Bosico Cofi v Dominican Republic* (Preliminary Objections, Merits, Reparations and Costs) (2005) Inter-American Commission on Human Rights.

[60] Human Rights Council, Twenty-fifth session, 'Human Rights and Arbitrary Deprivation of Nationality' Report of the Secretary-General (19 December 2013).

[61] UNHCR, 'Handbook on the Protection of Stateless Persons under the 1954 Convention Relating to the Status of Stateless Persons' (Geneva 2014) 17–28.

[62] Laura van Waas, 'The U.N. Statelessness Conventions' in Alice Edwards and Laura van Waas (eds), *Nationality and Statelessness under International Law* (CUP 2014) 75.

neighboring states in the wake of World War II, but though limited, it has not, even today, been completely prohibited.[63]

This book will focus on the right to a nationality and the duty to prevent statelessness, including how these intersect with other human rights and international law frameworks, focusing on four key areas of law: (1) the right to be registered at birth and the international laws relating to civil registration, (2) the prohibitions in international law against discrimination in the granting of nationality, (3) the right to nationality under the indigenous rights framework, including the right to self-determination for indigenous persons under international law, and (4) the international laws to identify, prevent, and resolve statelessness. Other relevant human rights treaties and frameworks will be discussed where appropriate.

1.3 The International Commitments of Kuwait, Mali, Côte d'Ivoire, and Malaysia

Nonratification of treaties and difficulties in enforcing international law are general problems to the entire field and should not impede a substantive discussion of gaps and flaws in both individual laws and the international law system. While this book considers international law in its entirety, including soft law and regional approaches, and adopts a progressive approach, it here notes that individual states have specific obligations. This section briefly summarizes some of the most relevant international obligations of the four states used as examples in this book: Kuwait, Mali, Côte d'Ivoire, and Malaysia. These obligations will also be noted where appropriate in future chapters.

All four countries are parties to several binding conventions and treaties relevant to nomadic statelessness, including, perhaps most importantly, the Convention on the Rights of the Child, though Malaysia has a reservation to Article 7 on the right to a nationality. Kuwait, Côte d'Ivoire, and Mali are also parties to the International Convention on the Elimination of All Forms of Racial Discrimination.[64] Côte d'Ivoire and Mali[65] are party to

[63] Donner (n 40) 150–159.

[64] The International Convention on the Elimination of All Forms of Racial Discrimination was ratified by Kuwait 15 October 1968, by Mali, 16 July 1974, and by Côte d'Ivoire on 4 January 1973.

[65] Information on Mali's and Côte d'Ivoire's treaty status can be found at Claiming Human Rights, Guide to International Procedures Available in Cases of Human Rights Violations in Africa at UNESCO, 'Guide to International Procedures Available in Cases of Human Rights Violations in Africa' (2024) <http://www.claiminghumanrights.org> accessed 27 May 2024.

the Statelessness Conventions, but Kuwait is not, though it is a party to the International Covenant on Civil and Political Rights and the Arab Charter on Human Rights.[66]

Malaysia is also not a party to the Statelessness Conventions, though it is a party to the International Covenant on Economic, Social and Cultural Rights and the International Covenant on Civil and Political Rights.[67] The Constitution of Malaysia, however, provides for the nationality of otherwise stateless persons in its Second Schedule.[68] Mali and Côte d'Ivoire are also members of ECOWAS (the Economic Community of West African States), though Mali has recently announced it is leaving the community. ECOWAS has issued the nonbinding Abidjan Declaration of Ministers of ECOWAS Member States on Eradication of Statelessness.[69] This section provided an overview of the international commitments of Kuwait, Mali, Côte d'Ivoire, and Malaysia. Future chapters will mention other commitments where relevant.

1.4 The Nomadic Communities Used as Examples in this Book

This book uses four examples to highlight how a diverse set of governments applied nationality laws to nomadic peoples, as well as to expose some of the experiences nomadic communities have had with statelessness, in order to inform an analysis of the solutions to statelessness that are available under international law. This book selected these four nomadic communities as examples because (1) they have all been identified by experts as being stateless or at risk of statelessness, (2) they live in diverse locations and regions, (3) they practice diverse types of nomadism, and (4) they had diverse experiences with colonial legal systems. This book is not a comparative

[66] UNHCR, 'States Party to the Statelessness Conventions as of 1st October 2017' <http://www.refworld.org/pdfid/54576a754.pdf> accessed 7 October 2024. See also United Nations Human Rights Office of the High Commissioner <http://tbinternet.ohchr.org/_layouts/TreatyBodyExternal/Countries.aspx?CountryCodeK̄WT&LangĒN> accessed 7 October 2024 for the reporting status of Kuwait on various treaties.

[67] See the website for the Office of the High Commissioner for Human Rights, 'Ratification Status for Malaysia' <http://tbinternet.ohchr.org/_layouts/TreatyBodyExternal/Treaty.aspx?CountryID92&LangĒN> accessed 27 May 2024.

[68] Malaysian Const, Second Schedule, pt 2 (1957) art 1(c).

[69] Abidjan Declaration of Ministers of ECOWAS Member States on Eradication of Statelessness, 25 February 2015, Regional Treaties, Agreements, Declarations and Related.

study, however, and the information on these communities is neither exhaustive nor comprehensive. It provides examples of some of the challenges nomadic communities have faced in accessing nationality and some of the ways in which they experience statelessness to inform a discussion of solutions. While many of the experiences highlighted in this book will be depressingly familiar to other nomadic communities around the world, the examples are not intended to be representative. Where controversy about these communities exists in the literature, it will be noted.

1.4.1 The Bedouin

The first example selected for this book is the Bedouin of the Gulf region. According to experts, while nomadism is no longer practiced in Kuwait, many people living in the Gulf region, including in Kuwait, are descendants of nomadic Bedouin, or Bedu, and much previous scholarship has documented their statelessness in Kuwait, where they make up the majority of the *bidoon*, or those without status.[70]

For thousands of years, the Bedouin practiced nomadic pastoralism and trade across the Arabian Peninsula, living alongside and intermingled with settled oases and coastal communities.[71] Bedouin society was hierarchical, with camel-herding tribes at the top of the social structure. The area today known as Kuwait has always been very dry,[72] making pastoralism an ideal use of land away from oases and coastal areas. Bedouin also served as guides and protection for the caravan trade that drove the regional economy. The desert came to be dominated by noble Bedouin tribes, either nomadic or semi-settled and often practicing long-distance trade, and semi-nomadic tribes employed in sheep, camel, or goat pastoralism and centered around oases or coastal towns. Information on Bedouin comes from academic sources, reports, interviews with experts, and newspaper articles.

[70] Much of the information on the Bedouin in this book is taken from the work of Claire Beaugrand, Dawn Chatty, Anthony Toth, and others. On the topic of the origins of Bedouin tribes in Kuwait, see particularly the work of Claire Beaugrand, *Stateless in the Gulf: Migration, Nationality and Society in Kuwait* (I B Tauris 2018) and Claire Beaugrand, 'Statelessness and Transnationalism in Northern Arabia: Biduns and State Building in Kuwait, 1959-2009' (London School of Economics 2010). It is important to here note the complexity of the history of Bedouin tribes in Kuwait, much of which has been simplified here.

[71] Chatty (n 20) 5–8.

[72] Michael Casey, *The History of Kuwait* (Greenwood 2007) 4–5.

1.4.2 The Tuareg

The Tuareg, or *Kel Tamasheq*, are a pastoral nomadic group living in the Sahel region of Africa whose territories are split across multiple countries, primarily in Libya, Niger, Mali, and Algeria.[73] Though the extent to which the Tuareg are stateless is unknown, expert interviews and UNHCR data confirm that they are at risk of statelessness due to conflict, displacement, and intergenerational, low levels of civil registration.

Historically, Tuareg society was divided between urban and pastoral communities, with pastoral communities organized into a loose federation of drum groups headed by an *Amanokal*, and urban communities such as the Ayar Sultanate governed by a Sultan. The line between pastoralists and agriculturalists in the Sahel was fluid, however.[74] Pastoral Tuareg nobles often occupied positions of high status, controlling political, religious, and economic life.[75] In exchange for military protection, noble Tuareg families levied taxes on grain and other agricultural products, called *tiwse*, against their sedentary vassals, and taxed the trading caravans that traveled north through the Sahara.[76] Each drum group occupied a particular region of the Sahel and had many vassal clans, slaves, and servant (*haratin*) families under their protection, though conflict in northern Mali in recent decades has greatly disrupted Tuareg life. Much of the information on the Tuareg in this book comes from academic sources, reports, newspaper articles, and interviews with experts.

[73] Much of the information on the Tuareg for this book is taken from the work of experts Boilley, Lecocq, Bourgeot, and others. See for example Attilio Gaudio, *Le Mali* (2nd edn, Karthala 1988) 183; Pierre Boilley, *Les Touaregs Kel Adagh : dépendances et révoltes : du français au Mali contemporain* (Karthala 1999); Jeremy Keenan, 'Resisting Imperialism: Tuareg Threaten US, Chinese and Other Foreign Interests' in Anja Fischer and Ines Kohl (eds), *Tuareg Society within a Globalized World: Saharan Life in Transition* (I B Tauris 2010); Baz Lecocq, *Disputed Desert: Decolonisation, Competing Nationalisms and Tuareg Rebellions in Northern Mali* (Brill 2010); Baz Lecocq, 'Tuareg City Blues—Cultural Capital in a Global Cosmopole' in Ines Kohl and Anja Fischer (eds), *Tuareg Society Within a Globalized World: Saharan Life in Transition* (Bloomsbury Press 2010) 41; André Bourgeot, '*Les sociétés touarègues: nomadism, identité, résistances*' (Karthala 1995); André Bourgeot, 'Sahara: espace géostratégique et enjeux politiques (Niger)' (2014) 31 NAQD: Revue d'Etudes et de Critique Sociale 153.

[74] Victor Azarya, 'Pastoralism and the state in Africa: Marginality or incorporation?' (1996) 38 Nom Peoples 11, 15–16 (on the Fulani).

[75] Bruce Hall, *A History of Race in Muslim West Africa, 1600-1960* (CUP 2011) 186. See also Boilley (n 73) 28–31.

[76] See generally Anatoly M. Khazanov, 'Nomads in the History of the Sedentary World' in Anatoly Khazanov and Andre Wink (eds), *Nomads in the Sedentary World* (Curzon 2001).

1.4.3 The Fulani

The Fulani, also known as the *Fulbe, Peul, Fula*, or *Foulbé*, are a community living throughout and across West Africa and practicing both pastoralism and trade. Urban sultans and emirs of several important empires during the precolonial period, including the Maasina Emirate and Sokoto Caliphate, were founded by Fulani nobles, with Fulani pastoralists as their vassals.

According to anthropologists Thomas Bassett and Youssouf Diallo, the modern migration of pastoral Fulani first came to Côte d'Ivoire at independence due to draught, a lack of good pastorage in Burkina Faso, and political problems with the Malian government. In contrast, other Fulani came in the early 1970s to look after the cattle of Senufo chiefs, who were the local authorities in the region.[77] According to Bassett, Fulani had been present in northern Côte d'Ivoire since at least the turn of the last century, however. Many Fulani were also drawn to Côte d'Ivoire by welcoming government policies under former Ivoirian president Houphouët-Boigny. Most Fulani in Côte d'Ivoire have origins in what are today Burkina Faso and Mali, though they also come from Nigeria, Benin, Mali, Guinea, and Senegal. Long-distance, cross-border, regional movement is a common feature of Fulani pastoralism,[78] and as with all the nomadic groups used as examples for this book, the line is blurry between mobility across borders for pastoralism and migration.

Many Fulani today transit through northern Côte d'Ivoire, having shifted their seasonal transhumance routes to the south in response to conflict and climate change. Others practice sedentary forms of herding, while others live in towns and cities, such as Korhogo, Kong, and Bouna. Pastoral and sedentary Fulani form one community, however, and pastoral Fulani rely on sedentary members to negotiate with local landowners for grazing rights. The Fulani are widely acknowledged as critical to Ivorian beef production, but pastoralism relies on access to communal lands during industrial agriculture and urbanization. During the precolonial and colonial periods, both Fulani and many Tuareg lived in the Sahel, so future chapters will sometimes discuss the two communities together. Information on the Fulani comes

[77] Thomas J Bassett, 'Fulani Herd Movements' (1986) 76 Geo Rev 233, 234, 237. See also Diallo (n 17) 185–204 (citing Michel Benoît).

[78] Mirjam de Bruijn and Han van Dijk, 'Changing Population Mobility in West Africa: Fulbe Pastoralists in Central and South Mali' (2003) 102 Afr Affairs 285, 290–291.

primarily from interviews with experts and members of the Fulani community, academic sources, reports, and newspaper articles.[79]

1.4.4 The Sama Dilaut

The fourth group is the Sama Dilaut/Bajau Laut,[80] who live in the Sulu Sea between what is now Malaysia, Indonesia, and the Philippines, a zone of contested borders. The Sama Dilaut are one of several "sea nomadic" groups who used to live primarily on boats and practice a hunter/gatherer lifestyle, though a large percentage of Sama Dilaut are now settled. Sabah, Malaysia was chosen as the country of consideration due to the well-documented problem of statelessness in Sabah by UNHCR and other experts.[81] While some scholars argue that the Sama Dilaut are not nomadic peoples because they do not practice pastoralism, this book will refer to them as nomadic peoples because this is how the Malaysian government and many outsiders view them.[82]

In the precolonial period, boat nomadism could be found scattered throughout Southeast Asia and there is evidence of sea nomadism off the coast of what is now Sabah, Malaysia going back as far as three thousand

[79] Some of this information is based on focus group discussions with male members of the Fulani (Foulbé) community, as well as individual interviews with representatives of local governments, agents of consular offices of Burkina Faso and Mali, NGO and United Nations staff, officials of the government of Côte d'Ivoire in Abidjan, and professors from the University of Abidjan. All interviews were confidential. The discussions and interviews took place from November to December 2018 in various locations in Cote d'Ivoire: Korhogo and environs (including the villages of Napie and Komborodougou) (Savanes district), a Fulani camp north of Kouloukorosso (Savanes district), Kong (Savanes district), Bouna (Zanzan district), and Abidjan. It was not possible to interview Fulani women.

I thank the participants and the Association des Femmes Juristes for their contributions. This research was carried out under the auspices of the Peter McMullin Centre on Statelessness at the University of Melbourne and received ethics approval from the University of Melbourne Human Research Ethics Committee (Ethics ID: 1852661.1). Some of this research has also been cited in Christoph Sperfeldt, 'Statelessness and Governance at the Periphery: 'Nomadic' Populations and the Modern State in Thailand, Côte d'Ivoire, and Lebanon' in Tendayi Bloom and Lindsey N Kingston (eds), *Statelessness and Governance: Rights, Identity, Citizenship* (Manchester UP 2021) and Heather Alexander, 'Identité juridique et préservation du nomadisme comme mode de vie: les hommes Foulbé en Côte d'Ivoire' (available online 2023).

[80] The Sama Dilaut are also sometimes called the Bajau Laut. On the advice of anthropologist Helen Brunt, this book will refer to them as Sama Dilaut.

[81] Helen Brunt, 'Stateless Stakeholders: Seen but Not Heard? The Case of the Sama Dilaut in Sabah, Malaysia,' University of Sussex 2013). See also Helen Brunt, Greg Acciaoli and Julian Clifton, 'Foreigners Everywhere, Nationals Nowhere: Exclusion, Irregularity, and Invisibility of Stateless Bajau Laut in Eastern Sabah, Malaysia' (2017) 15 J Imm Ref Stud 232.

[82] Lioba Lenhart, 'Recent Research on Southeast Asian Sea Nomadic Peoples' (1995) 36 Nom Peoples 245, 245.

years. Until the mid-1950s, the Sama Dilaut lived almost exclusively in boats, hunting and fishing, and following a seasonal pattern throughout the Sulu Sea between what is now Malaysia, Indonesia, and the Philippines. The Sama Dilaut had a close relationship with communities on shore, trading in sea products. Information on the Sama Dilaut comes from academic sources,[83] reports, newspapers, and interviews with experts.

[83] James Warren, *The North Borneo Chartered Company's Administration of the Bajau, 1878-1909; the Pacification of a Maritime, Nomadic People* (Ohio UP 1971) 65–66; Clifford Sather, 'Sulu's Political Jurisdiction over the Bajau Laut' (1971) 3 Borneo Research Bulletin 43; James Warren, *The Sulu Zone: 1768-1898* (Singapore UP 1981); James Warren, 'Looking Back on "The Sulu Zone": State Formation, Slave Raiding and Ethnic Diversity in Southeast Asia' (1996) 69 J Malaysian Branch Royal Asiatic Soc 21; Clifford Sather, *The Bajau Laut: Adaptation, History, and Fate in a Maritime Fishing Society of South-eastern Sabah* (OUP 1997); Carol Warren, 'Consciousness in Social Transformation: The Sama Dilaut of East Malaysia' (1980) 5 Dialectical Anthro 227; Barbara Watson Andaya and Leonard Y Andaya, *A History of Malaysia* (2nd edn, Palgrave Macmillan 2001); Clifford Sather, 'Commodity, Trade, Gift Exchange, and the History of Maritime Nomadism in Southeastern Sabah' (2002) 6 Nom Peoples 14.

2

Antinomadic Bias and Nomadic Perspectives in Academia

2.1 Introduction

The main subjects of this book are the legal systems and government policies relating to nationality and statelessness in Kuwait, Mali, Côte d'Ivoire, and Malaysia, and the international laws relating to nationality and statelessness, including how they are applied, or not applied, to nomadic peoples, using sources from municipal and international law. By using four examples of stateless nomadic communities, or those at risk of statelessness, to inform the discussion, this book also relies on sources from anthropology, history, sociology, and other disciplines. This book, therefore, mostly relies on nonnomadic sources, perspectives, and types of knowledge, including colonial-era sources, that may be biased against nomadism as a way of life.

Chapter 2 acknowledges the pervasive and sometimes all-encompassing presence of a bias against nomadism in academia. This bias has only begun to be addressed and contextualized by more recent scholarship and by centering the perspectives of nomadic peoples themselves. Chapter 2 will summarize some aspects of this bias that are most important to discussions of nomadic nationality and statelessness in later chapters. This chapter is far from exhaustive on the topic of antinomadic bias, but it summarizes some key areas that provide context for the rest of the book.

2.2 A Lack of Nomadic Perspectives

This book, like all books, is a product of the academic environment in which it was written, and this section acknowledges this fact. Academia on nomadic peoples remains dominated by nonnomadic experts. Therefore, this book must rely on sources that may be biased or inaccurate because they were written by nonnomadic persons in a climate of antinomadic bias. This is particularly true for sources from the colonial period. One prominent example is

The Nationality and Statelessness of Nomadic Peoples Under International Law. Heather Jean Alexander, Oxford University Press. © Oxford University Press 2025. DOI: 10.1093/9780197772362.003.0002

J. Spencer Trimingham's "Islam in West Africa."[1] While subsequent scholars have criticized Trimingham's book as being "outdated," it remains an important work in the literature.[2] Scholarship on nomadic peoples is also often contested by nomadic and nonnomadic experts and between and among nonnomadic experts. Views of colonial-era sources have evolved. For example, received wisdom on the origins of Bedouin tribes in the Gulf region or the role of the Sama Dilaut in Sabah society during the precolonial period, much of which was based on colonial sources, has more recently been called into question.

This book is also a product of the bias against nomadism in academia and the lack of nomadic voices and perspectives. For example, the decision to discuss nomadic statelessness and international law in the form of a book written in English is itself deeply informed and influenced by a bias in academia in general against nonwritten forms of knowledge and noncolonial languages. Without allowing the entire exercise of scholarship to collapse beneath the weight of a meta-discussion, it is worth acknowledging here some of how bias influences this book and inviting others to comment and critique this book's approach in future scholarship.

This book presents nomadic scholarship and voices wherever possible while acknowledging the enormous work remaining. When nomadic perspectives are presented in this book, they are often filtered through the work of nonnomadic peoples, including interviews conducted by the author of this book with Fulani pastoralists in northern Côte d'Ivoire, as well as the work of Dawn Chatty, Bruce Hall, Pierre Boilley, and Baz Lecocq. More recently, there has been the entry into the academic canon of more nomadic voices and perspectives. For example, in 2019, Ekuru Aukot, a nomadic pastoralist from the Ateker nation, asked in an essay in *Forced Migration Review*, "Am I stateless because I am a nomad?" discussing the profound disconnect between his sense of belonging to his nomadic community and the realities of belonging to the nation-state system.[3] Such nomadic perspectives in academia, however, remain relatively rare. Where possible, they are included. The next sections will explore antinomadic bias in certain areas of academia that are particularly relevant to this book.

1 J Spencer Trimingham, *Islam in West Africa* (Clarendon 1959).

2 Rex Sean O'Fahey, 'Islamic Hegemonies in the Sudan: Sufism, Mahdism and Islamism' in Louis Brenner (ed), *Muslim Identity and Social Change in Subsaharan Africa* (Indiana UP 1994) 21.

3 Ekuru Aukot, 'Am I Stateless because I Am a Nomad?' (2009) 32 Forced Migration Rev 18.

2.3 Antinomadic Bias in Academia on Statehood and State Formation

The lack of nomadic voices in academia is not an isolated problem but is indicative of what is arguably a broader climate of antinomadic bias in academia that colors the entire area of scholarship on statehood and state formation. It is beyond the scope of this book to fully explore the contours and extent of this bias, but this section will briefly summarize some key points that provide important context to chapters 3 through 6. This bias, or stigma, against nomadic forms of social and political organization in the academic literature on statehood and state formation has been documented by experts such as Jérémie Gilbert,[4] Youssouf Diallo,[5] Robert Sack,[6] and Marco Moretti[7] and takes several common forms. It includes the view that nomadic peoples cannot form states but are instead members of "tribes," the idea that nomadic peoples do not own their lands but only pass over them, and the idea of nomadism as an earlier phase of social organization that is in opposition to supposedly modern life.[8] Anthropologist Hilary Gilbert, for example, notes that "[p]astoralism, constructed as rooted in a primitive, pre-agricultural past,

[4] Jérémie Gilbert, 'Still No Place to Go: Nomadic Peoples Territorial Rights in Europe' (2004) 4 Eur YB on Minority Issues 141, 145, 159; Jérémie Gilbert, 'Nomadic Territories: A Human Rights Approach to Nomadic Peoples' Land Rights' (2007) 7 Hum Rts L Rev 681, 685–692; Jérémie Gilbert, *Nomadic Peoples and Human Rights* (Routledge 2014) 154–155.

[5] See his discussion of academic views of West African nomadism and land use in Youssouf Diallo *Nomades des espaces interstitiels : pastoralisme, identité, migrations (Burkina Faso-Cote d'Ivoire)* (Rüdiger Köppe Verlag 2008) 23–31,

[6] Robert Sack, *Human Territoriality: Its Theory and History* (Cambridge UP 1986) 132–133 (discussing early colonial perspectives and theories on nomadic land use and statehood).

[7] M Moretti, *Le Droit international public et les peuples nomades* (Publibook 2006) 119–124.

[8] For a summary, see Gilbert, *Nomadic Peoples* (n 4) 63–67. See also the discussion by Jeffery Szuchman in his introduction to his collection, 'Integrating Approaches to Nomads, Tribes, and the State in the Ancient Near East' in Jeffery Szuchman (ed), *Nomads, Tribes, and the State in the Ancient Near East: Cross-disciplinary Perspectives* (Chicago UP 2009) 2 (discussing the problems with the term "nomad" in academia and the "myth of the stateless nomad"). For examples of theories of nomadism as a way of life and its relationship to sedentarization, see Jacques Maury, 'Nationalité. Théorie générale du français' in A G De LaPradelle and J-H-P Niboyet (eds), *Répertoire de droit international* (Sirey 1931) 71; William J Foltz, *From French West Africa to the Mali Federation* (Yale UP 1965), 1–2 (presenting the West African deserts and jungles, occupied by nomadic peoples, as unsuitable for civilization); P C Salzman, 'Introduction' in P C Salzman (ed), *When Nomads Settle: Processes of Sedentarization as Adaptation and Response* (Praeger 1980).

11–14 (discussing various theories of the process of sedentarization of nomadic peoples); Samuel N Dicken and Forrest R Pitts, *Introduction to Cultural Geography: A Study of Man and His Environment* (Ginn 1970) 40–43 (on the shift from "backward" nomadism to "civilization" with the shift to agriculture); Anatoly M. Khazanov, *Nomads and the Outside World* (2nd edn, U Wisconsin P 1994) 198–200 (on the process of nomadic sedentarization). For a more on the European idea that civilization is progressing toward an ideal, see also the classic text, John B Bury, *The Idea of Progress: An Inquiry into Its Origin and Growth* (Macmillan 1932).

affronts the linear narratives of 'progress' and 'modernity' adopted by many states."[9]

The view of nomadic society as naturally stateless, however, was not limited to Europeans or European thought. Diallo notes, writing of the Fulani peoples in the Sahel. In precolonial times, settled rulers sometimes viewed nomadic communities as a cause of destabilization.[10] Anthony Toth, an expert on Bedouin in Kuwait, explains that Ibn Saud, the powerful ruler of the region that would become Saudi Arabia, saw Bedouin nomadism and political independence as a problem and sought to limit their "historical hegemony" through sedentarization and religious conversion, with limited success.[11]

Since at least the fifteenth century, much of European philosophical and political thought held that land ownership and, critically, productive use and improvement of land were essential to state formation and territorial sovereignty, a view that to many European philosophers and thinkers excluded nomadic peoples from the possibility of state formation.[12] While this view of nomadic peoples as naturally stateless was particularly popular in Europe, the idea of nomadic, or pastoral, society as tribal and, therefore, in opposition to civilization also existed in the Middle East. John C. Wilkinson, an expert on Islamic studies, argues that

> [t]he distinction that must be drawn is that between two social structures, those which Ibn Khaldun labelled *badw* and *hadar*. Hadar is the organization of a *central government system* operating through an urban network and controlling a rural hinterland from which derives most of its wealth. It is the system which operated in the conquered lands and the values of its *urban-based elite* constitute hadar'iya, *civilization*. Badw is not bedu

[9] Hilary Gilbert, '"This Is Not Our Life, It's Just a Copy of Other Peoples": Bedouin and the Price of "Development" in South Sinai' (2011) 15 Nom Peoples 7, 7.

[10] Diallo (n 5) 27.

[11] Anthony Toth, 'Last Battles of the Bedouin and the Rise of Modern States in Northern Arabia: 1850-1950' in Dawn Chatty (ed), *Nomadic Societies in the Middle East and North Africa: Entering the 21st Century* (Brill 2006) 66–67 (citing, among others, Al-Fahad, Al-Rasheed, and Kostiner).

[12] For an overview of these views, see James Crawford, *The Creation of States in International Law* (2nd edn, OUP 2006) 257–267 (on indigenous statehood and territory). See also M Shaw, *International Law* (9th edn, CUP 2021) 23–24; R Sack, *Human Territoriality: Its Theory and History* (CUP 1986) 15, 66–71 (discussing how territoriality influences the supposed social organization of nomadic peoples); Gilbert, *Nomadic Peoples* (n 4) 60.

> but *tribally organized society* whose elite operates from *oasis settlement* and whose power derives from manipulating kinship principles to regulate marriage, social interaction and the redistribution of power, force, wealth.[13]

The idea that nomadic peoples were incapable of forming states, however, was far from universally accepted among academics and experts during the colonial period and has frequently been challenged since.[14] It was a dominant and very influential view in academia during colonization, and its influence can still be seen today. It contributed to the concept of *terra nullius*, whereby nomadic lands were deemed unoccupied and could be legitimately seized by others.[15] According to the related theory *mare liberum*, no one could own the oceans because they could not be improved upon or settled, and, therefore, by implication, boat nomadism could not be the foundation for a state.[16] These concepts had a major impact on colonial-era views that nomadic peoples could not form states because they didn't occupy their lands, with enormous repercussions for the status of nomadic leaders under colonization.[17] In some cases not discussed in this book, nomadic peoples were subjected to elimination and genocide. Nomadic rights expert Jérémie Gilbert notes, "[A]cts of elimination and mass killing were based on a racist bias against nomadic peoples, not only because of their race or ethnicity but because they were nomads."[18]

[13] John C Wilkinson, 'Traditional Concepts of Territory in Southeast Arabia' (1983) 149 Geo J 306, 313 (my italics). Note that the distinction between Badu and Hadar is contested throughout the region.

[14] See for example Kojo Yelpaala, 'Western Anthropological Concepts in Stateless Societies: A Retrospective and Introspective Look at the Dagaaba' (1992) 17 Dialectical Anthro 431 (on the Dagaaba in West Africa); but see contra Michal Tymowski, 'The Origins and Structures of Political Institutions' in Michal Tymowski and Henri J M Claessen (eds), *Pre-Colonial Black Africa; Dynastic Monarchy, Taxes and Tributes, War and Slavery, Kinship and Territory* (Edwin Mellen 2009) 5 (where they argue in favor of preserving the distinction between states and stateless societies, citing to Evans-Pritchard and Fortes).

[15] Gilbert, *Nomadic Peoples* (n 4) 90–100. See also Gilbert, 'Nomadic Territories' (n 4) 686; Moretti (n 7) 40, 134–136.

[16] Hugo Grotius, *Mare Liberum Sive De Jure Quod Batavis Competit Ad Indicana Commercia Dissertatio* (Elsevier 2014).

[17] Gilbert, *Nomadic Peoples* (n 4) 59–70. See also Diallo (n 5) 28.

[18] Gilbert, *Nomadic Peoples* (n 4) 31.

2.4 Antinomadic Bias in Academia on Development and Conservation

Antinomadic bias influenced academia not only on nomadic peoples and state formation but also on economic development and environmental policy, a view now being questioned by a new generation of environmental experts. This topic is largely beyond the scope of this book, but some general points summarized here will help to inform and provide context to the discussions in chapters 3 through 6. For example, oil extraction in the Gulf has coincided with both governments and international experts throughout the region holding negative views of nomadism as somehow bad for the desert environment.[19] With Kuwait and other Gulf states now pumping millions of barrels of oil and building large infrastructure projects, including pipelines, the opinions of outside experts about the supposed environmental harms of nomadism, a form of land management practiced in the region for centuries, has provided another rationale for Gulf State governments to remove Bedouin nomadic peoples from the desert and place them in public housing in urban areas.[20]

International experts have also lent credence to concerns over pastoralism's supposedly negative environmental impact in Mali. Despite pastoralism being used as a land management system in fragile environments in West Africa for centuries,[21] both the Malian government and the international aid community have pushed for the settlement of the Tuareg to supposedly prevent desertification.[22] Pastoral Charters enacted across the West African region contain language linking pastoralism to environmental degradation,[23]

[19] See generally Dawn Chatty and Michael Colchester, 'Introduction' in Dawn Chatty and Michael Colchester (eds), *Conservation and Mobile Indigenous Peoples: Displacement, Forced Settlement and Sustainable Development* (Berghan 2002) 1–15 (on the common view that conservation requires the removal of indigenous peoples).

[20] For an overview of this process in multiple countries in the Gulf region, see Riccardo Bocco, 'The Settlement of Pastoral Nomads in the Arab Middle East: International Organizations and Trends in Development Policies, 1950-1990' in Dawn Chatty (ed), *Nomadic Societies in the Middle East and North Africa: Entering the 21st Century* (Brill 2006) 302–328.

[21] James McDougall, 'Frontiers, Borderlands, and Saharan/World History' in James McDougall and Judith Scheele (eds), *Saharan Frontiers: Space and Mobility in Northwest Africa* (Indiana UP 2012) 79, 83.

[22] Anatoly Khazanov, 'Pastoralists in the Contemporary World: The Problem of Survival' in J Ginat and A Khazanov (eds), *Changing Nomads in a Changing World* (Sussex 1998) 7–23.

[23] Charte Pastorale du Mali, Loi No 01-004 (27 February 2001) Article 7. See also Claire Oxby, 'Will the 2010 'Code Pastoral' Help Herders in Central Niger? Land Rights and Land Use Strategies in the Grasslands of Abalak and Dakoro Departments' (2011) 15 Nom Peoples 53, 53 (on Niger).

even as large-scale, industrial farming has increased throughout much of the region.

Questionable claims that nomadism is bad for the environment are not limited to pastoralists. Although the Malaysian government allows large-scale, commercial fishing, Sama Dilaut artisanal fishing has also been framed as bad for the environment.[24] While the Malaysian government pumps thousands of barrels of oil through pipelines in the area, a new generation of experts notes that both the government and conservationist groups accuse Sama Dilaut communities, which have practiced artisanal fishing in the Sulu Sea for generations, of being, in the words of experts Greg Acciaoli, Helen Brunt, and Julian Clifton, "associated with illegal and destructive practices such as blast fishing, cyanide fishing, coral mining, and the harvesting of protected species . . ., as well as over-exploiting individual fisheries to the point of collapse."[25]

2.5 Conclusion

This chapter discussed nomadic representation in academia, a topic that impacts the sources used in this book. It summarized how antinomadic bias has impacted academia in terms of nomadism, statehood, and environmental policy. This chapter was not a summary of all forms of antinomadic bias; rather, it highlighted a few examples particularly relevant to this book. While modern scholarship and better inclusion of nomadic voices in academia have helped to address this bias, much work remains to be done, and a perhaps unavoidable reliance on colonial-era and nonnomadic sources remains a weakness of this book.

[24] Jonny Langenheim, 'Blast Fishing in Borneo: Bombs Are Quick, but They Kill the Coral Reefs' <https://www.theguardian.com/environment/blog/2014/jul/01/blast-fishing-borneo-bombs-coral-reefs>. See also Chris Greenwood, 'Tun Mustapha Park: The Creation of a Marine Protected Area: A Case Study on Malaysia' (2017).

[25] G Acciaoli, Helen Brunt and Julian Clifton, 'Foreigners Everywhere, Nationals Nowhere: Exclusion, Irregularity, and Invisibility of Stateless Bajau Laut in Eastern Sabah, Malaysia' (2017) 15 J Imm Refugee Stud 232, 238. See also Julian Clifton, 'Achieving Congruence between Conservation and Community: The Bajau Ethnic Group and Marine Management within the Wakatobi and South-East Asia' in Richard K F Unsworth, David J Smith and Julian Clifton (eds), *Marine Research and Conservation in the Coral Triangle: The Wakatobi National Park* (Nova 2010).

3

Nomadic Peoples and Civil Registration under International Law

3.1 Introduction

The Office of the United Nations High Commissioner for Refugees (UNHCR), UNICEF, and other international actors promote civil registration and legal identity as key tools to end statelessness.[1] Birth registration, however, is currently the only form of civil registration required under international law.[2] Chapter 3 interrogates the usefulness of birth registration in preventing nomadic statelessness. Chapter 3 will also look at other forms of registration that governments use to create a legal identity for nomadic peoples, which could be used to establish evidence of nationality, such as by establishing residency. It discusses how the international law framework may support access to other forms of civil registration that establish nationality or provide evidence of eligibility for nationality and the extent to which additional rights to registration may be necessary for nomadic peoples.

To inform this discussion, chapter 3 looks at the experiences with civil registration of the Bedouin, the Tuareg, the Fulani, and the Sama Dilaut in Kuwait, Mali, Côte d'Ivoire, and Malaysia.[3] In so doing, chapter 3 also discusses the long and frequently problematic relationship between nomadic communities and civil registration, including how a bias against nomadic peoples affected and intersected with nomadic registration. Much of the information discussed in chapter 3 will also be used to inform future

[1] See for example UNHCR, 'Handbook on the Protection of Stateless Persons under the 1954 Convention Relating to the Status of Stateless Persons' (Geneva 2014); United Nations Children's Fund (UNICEF), 'Ending Statelessness for a Bright Future for Every Child: The Right to a Nationality for Every Child' <https://www.unicef.org/thailand/livesuntold> accessed 27 May 2024; Human Rights Council, 'Birth Registration and the Right of Everyone to Recognition Everywhere as a Person before the Law: Report of the Office of the United Nations High Commissioner for Human Rights' Human Rights Council Twenty-seventh Session' A/HRC/27/22 (2014).

[2] Convention on the Rights of the Child, art 7; International Covenant on Civil and Political Rights, art 24.

[3] Much of the information in this chapter is drawn from the work of historians and anthropologists who study nomadic peoples. When there is a disagreement or lack of information, it will be noted.

The Nationality and Statelessness of Nomadic Peoples Under International Law. Heather Jean Alexander, Oxford University Press. © Oxford University Press 2025. DOI: 10.1093/9780197772362.003.0003

chapters on discrimination against nomadism in nationality law, nomadic peoples as indigenous peoples under international law, and the identification of nomadic peoples as stateless for the purposes of facilitated naturalization.

3.2 The Role of Civil Registration and Legal Identity in Ending Statelessness

Civil registration and legal identity are important tools to end statelessness because they (1) establish nationality in some countries, (2) provide evidence of nationality, and/or (3) provide evidence of a requirement to establish nationality (such as residence). Civil registration and ID are critical to many of the solutions for statelessness available under international law, such as by helping the individual to access facilitated naturalization.[4] It is important to recall, however, that lacking documents does not necessarily mean that an individual is stateless but can contribute to causing statelessness and placing someone at risk.[5] Civil registration also serves other functions besides establishing nationality and legal identity for individuals. Governments use it to track and quantify populations for the purposes of levying taxes, registering individuals for military service, gathering statistics, or other reasons.[6] It is also important to note that civil registration can serve as proof of statelessness or foreign status.[7] While the importance of documents and civil registration to the establishment of nationality is undisputed, it is important to analyze the intersection between civil registration, including birth registration, and human rights in the broader context of how states use such documents.

[4] Cristoph Sperfeldt, 'Digital Exclusions: Legal Identity, Identification, and the Sustainable Development Goals in Southeast Asia' (2023) 15 MOBILE Working Paper Series Copenhagen UP, 9.

[5] Amal De Chickera and Laura van Waas, 'Unpacking Statelessness' in Tendayi Bloom, K Tonkiss and P Cole (eds), *Understanding Statelessness* (Routledge 2017) 65. See also Paul Weis, *Nationality and Statelessness in International Law* (Brill 1979) 219–236. See also Patrick Weil, *Qu'est-ce qu'un français? Histoire de la nationalité française depuis la Révolution* (Grasset 2002) 402–405.

[6] Heather Alexander, 'Nomads and the Struggle for a Legal Identity' (2020) 2 Statelessness and Citizenship Rev 338.

[7] Laura van Waas, *Nationality Matters: Statelessness under International Law* (Intersentia 2008) 153. See also Gerard-Rene De Groot and Olliver Willem Vonk, *International Standards on Nationality Law: Texts, Cases and Materials* (Wolf Legal 2015) 21.

3.3 Civil Registration during Colonization

Many nomadic communities today suffer from low rates of civil registration dating back to the colonial period. This section explores the experiences of nomadic peoples with civil registration during colonialization, looking at Kuwait during the Protected State Period, French Soudan, and British North Borneo. It traces the encroachment of documents and registration into every aspect of nomadic life, including via licenses, tax registries, land registries, voter registration, and passports. "Colonial rule in West Africa initiated the incorporation of mobile people, particularly pastoralists, into Western territorial states."[8]

As this chapter will explore, however, colonial administrators and local authorities frequently used the registration of nomadic peoples as a tool to restrict nomadic movement and encourage, or even force, their settlement. Therefore, civil registration during the colonial period was not a pathway to rights and services but a form of coercive state control.

While coercive settlement policies and forced settlement were not unknown before European colonization, the Bedouin, the Tuareg, the Fulani, and the Sama Dilaut enjoyed a high degree of independence and political autonomy. Despite Moroccan political influence in the region, for example, the Tuareg nobility were politically independent for much of the period prior to French rule, particularly following the fall of the Songhay empire.[9] While urban-based sultans in the Sahel collected taxes from, or formed alliances with, the nomadic Tuareg nobility, they often had limited authority over them.[10] The Tuareg nobility enjoyed a considerable amount of political independence carved out in between the claims of competing empires. This would begin to change with the arrival of French bureaucracy.

[8] Mathew D Turner, 'Livestock Mobility and the Territorial State: South-Western Niger (1890–1920)' (2017) 87 Africa: J Intl Afr Inst 578, 605.

[9] Dida Badi, 'Genesis and Change in the Socio-political Structure of the Tuareg' in Anja Fisher and Ines Kohl (eds), *Tuareg Society within a Globalized World: Saharan Life in Transition* (I B Tauris 2010) 75. See also P Boilley, *Les Touaregs Kel Adagh. Dépendances et révoltes : du français au Mali contemporain* (Karthala 1999) 21–59; Mervyn Hiskett, *The Development of Islam in West Africa* (Longman 1984) 148–155 (on the independence of the Tuareg and Fulani after the fall of the Songhay empire); Ousmane Oumar Kane, *Beyond Timbuktu: An Intellectual History of Muslim West Africa* (Harvard UP 2016) 6 (on the decline of the Songhay empire and Moroccan invasion generally); J Spencer Trimingham, *Islam in West Africa* (Clarendon 1959) 185, 191.

[10] Djibo Hamani, *Au carrefour du Soudan et de la Berbérie : Le Sultanat Touareg de l'Ayar* (L'Harmattan 1989) 317–318 (on relations between nomadic Tuareg leaders and the sultans of Ayar and Agadez).

Some of the first experiences many nomadic peoples had with European documents came from treaties when many nomadic leaders signed treaties with European military commanders to establish their legitimacy and sovereignty. Invalidating treaties with nomadic peoples, however, also became a common way in the latter colonial period to deny the sovereignty of nomadic communities and favor European-educated, urban leaders, like Fily Dabo Sissoko, who represented the West African chiefs at the Brazzaville Conference.[11] The Berlin Act of 1880, for example, invalidated many early treaties with nomadic leaders, in part on the grounds that nomadic peoples could not fulfill their treaty obligations because they formed tribes, not states.[12] While many favored nomadic leaders, like Sobbo ag Fondogomo of the Tengeregif Tuareg confederacy managed to retain their independence during the early colonial period, many lost status as colonization wore on, as sedentary peoples became more important to French rule, and as the trans-Saharan caravan trade collapsed. However, the relationship between the French *commandants* and nomadic leaders is too complex to fully summarize here.[13] Over time, power centralized in the hand of the emirs and sultans of urban areas in many colonies, while nomadic leaders found themselves powerless to guide the development and enactment of many government policies, including future civil registration drives and the issuance of identity documents.

Colonial bureaucracy introduced a host of individual identity documents designed to register their conquered populations in places where paper registration documents had not previously been the norm.[14] The civil registration of nomadic peoples became an important tool to encourage and enforce nomadic settlement to eliminate nomadism and establish colonial sovereignty

[11] William J Foltz, *From French West Africa to the Mali Federation* (Yale UP 1965) 120. See also Jérémie Gilbert, *Nomadic Peoples and Human Rights* (Routledge 2014) 61; Bruce Hall, *A History of Race in Muslim West Africa, 1600-1960* (CUP 2011) 184–185.

[12] James Crawford, *The Creation of States in International Law* (2nd edn, OUP 2006) 269. See also Tendayi Bloom, 'Members of Colonized Groups, Statelessness and the Right to Have Rights' in Tendayi Bloom, K Tonkiss and P Cole (eds), *Understanding Statelessness* (Routledge 2017) 160–161 (on treaties generally).

[13] Hall (n 11) 184–195. See also Victor Azarya, 'Pastoralism and the state in Africa: Marginality or incorporation?' (1996) 38 Nomadic Peoples 11, 18–19 (on the Fulani).

[14] See for example the passports discussed in the memoir of John Harding, 'Matters Colonial, Consular and Curious' in Peter Hinchcliffe, John T Ducker and Maria Holt (eds), *Without Glory in Arabia: The British Retreat from Aden* (I B Tauris 2013) 282–283 (on the Adan Protected State). See also Crawford, *Creation of States in International Law* (n 12) 291–292; Laurie Fransman, *Fransman's British Nationality Law* (3rd edn, Bloomsbury Professional 2011) 266–272 (on British Protectorates); Gilbert (n 11) 90–102 (on protectorates in general); M Shaw, *International Law* (9th edn, CUP 2021) 197–198.

over the land. The use of registration and identity documents to achieve the settlement and assimilation of nomadic peoples would establish a lasting relationship between nomadic registration and nomadic assimilation. This relationship in the postcolonial period appeared to place civil registration in opposition to nomadism as a way of life, with devastating consequences for the future of nomadic nationality and inclusion. While much research is left to be done on the civil registration of nomadic peoples during colonization, this chapter draws out some of their experiences with both civil registration for the purposes of nationality and the use of documents as evidence of nationality during the colonial period.

Keeping records of nomadic populations did not begin with colonization. Societies in places like the Gulf, West Africa, and Borneo kept chronicles of events, dynasties, and more quotidian registries for things like the payment of taxes. In the Sahel, for example, the Sultan of Ayar kept chronicles of events,[15] and noble Tuareg families levied taxes on grain and other agricultural products from their vassals that were sometimes recorded.[16] Bedouin tribes and Fulani nobles would also collect taxes from vassals and pay them to urban rulers in exchange for protection, and it is likely that some of these relationships were recorded.[17] While according to anthropologists and historians, the Sama Dilaut did not have a formal system of written record keeping, they were mentioned in the records of others and arguably were recognized as a distinct group within broader Sulu/Borneo society by outsiders as far away as China.[18]

Colonization, however, would bring new, expanded, and individualized forms of civil registration and identity documents to these regions as part of the emerging colonial bureaucracy. Importantly, this bureaucracy did not emerge in a neutral setting for nomadic peoples but coincided with a colonial-era push to limit, or even end, nomadism in the interests of what

[15] For an example of the kinds of written records kept by rulers in nomadic regions in pre-colonial times, see the detailed description of the records of the Sultanate of Ayar at Hamani (n 10) 21–29.

[16] Boilley (n 9) 29, 54 (on the lwllemmedan confederation.) See also Hall (n 11) 250; Hamani (n 10) 313 (on the freeing of slaves as accompanied by writing); A Khazanov, 'Nomads in the History of the Sedentary World' in M Wink and A Khazanov A (eds), *Nomads in the Sedentary World* (Curzon 2001) 1; A Bourgeot, *Les sociétés touarègues : Nomadism, identité, résistances* (Karthala 1995) 25, 50.

[17] Claire Beaugrand, *Stateless in the Gulf: Migration, Nationality and Society in Kuwait* (I B Tauris 2018) 44, 63. See also David Commins, *The Gulf States: A Modern History* (I B Tauris 2012) 8–9 (on the payment of taxes by settled communities to Bedouin tribes).

[18] Barbara Watson Andaya and Leonard Y Andaya, *A History of Malaysia* (2nd edn, Palgrave Macmillan 2001) 15 (mentions of sea nomads in Chinese record), 80 (on Bajau sea peoples during the decline of Brunei). See also Virginia M Hooker, *A Short History of Malaysia: Linking East and West* (Allen and Unwin 2003) 72–77.

colonizing governments called security and development, as one of the many manifestations of a bias against nomadism in colonial policy. The next sections will examine how antinomadic bias impacted the colonial-era civil registration of nomadic peoples, particularly the ways in which colonial-era registration became linked to forced and coerced settlement policies, as the settlement of nomadic peoples emerged as a major goal of the colonial period in French West Africa, the Gulf region, and Borneo.

3.3.1 Settlement and Registration in the Kuwaiti Protected State

Settlement of Bedouin would be central to the policy and administrative goals of successive governments in Kuwait from the Ottoman period to the 1970s. During the Ottoman period, Kuwait Town was a center of regional trade and the pearl industry. It remained largely independent of Ottoman control, though the Empire had established an outpost at Basra. Beyond the walls of Kuwait Town, powerful Bedouin confederations controlled the desert, herding camels, sheep, and goats and trading in caravans between the Mediterranean and the various city-states along the Persian Gulf, including Kuwait Town.[19]

Bedouin leaders had a sometimes combative, sometimes collaborative relationship with the ruling Al-Sabah family in Kuwait Town, who relied on loyal Bedouin groups to protect the town from Saudi raids and to work in the pearl industry.[20] Connections with powerful Bedouin camel tribes gave the Al-Sabah family access to caravan routes.[21] Several of the tribes inhabiting what is now northern Kuwait also had extensive connections with urban rulers in what is now Saudi Arabia and Iraq.[22] Ottoman policy, however, framed nomadism as a "problem" to centralized rule, and Ottoman administrators officially promoted the settlement of the Bedouin as a

[19] Ben J Slot, *Mubarak Al-Sabah: Founder of Modern Kuwait: 1896-1915* (Arabian Publishing 2005) 8–11. See also Frederick F Anscombe, *The Ottoman Gulf, the Creation of Kuwait, Saudi Arabia and Qatar* (Columbia University Press 1997) 11; Robert Fletcher, '"Between the Devil of the Desert and the Deep Blue Sea": Reorienting Kuwait: 1900-1940' (2015) 50 J Hist Geo 51, 56; Beaugrand, *Stateless in the Gulf* (n 17) 11 (putting this history in the context of modern discourse on the *bidoon*).

[20] Peter Carmichael, *Nomads* (Collins and Brown 1991) 66–78.

[21] Anh Nga Longva, 'Citizenship in the Gulf States: Conceptualization and Practice' in Nils A Butenschon, Uri Davis and Manuel Hassassian (eds), *Citizenship and the State in the Middle East: Approaches and Applications* (Syracuse UP 2000) 181. See also Jacqueline S Ismael, *Kuwait: Dependency and Class in a Rentier State* (Florida UP 1993) 24–25. I am indebted to anthropologist Anthony Toth's comments on this topic.

[22] Beaugrand, *Stateless in the Gulf* (n 17) 50.

supposed solution to their nomadism.[23] The Ottoman Empire pursued settlement of the Bedouin as official policy even though agriculture was, and is, ill-suited to the desert environment.[24]

Beginning in 1899, a series of agreements between the Sheikh of Kuwait Town and the British government established Kuwait as a British Protected State.[25] Protected States technically enjoyed a form of indirect rule, with local leaders in charge of internal matters, while the British administration dealt with matters of foreign policy and provided military support.[26] Rather than seeing Bedouin tribes as authorities of equal sovereignty who needed their own Protectorate agreements, however, the British adopted the view that Kuwait City was at risk of being overrun by lawless Bedouin.

Under the Protected State system, British policy began vesting internationally recognized administrative and legal powers in the hands of the Al-Sabah family, including the collection of taxes, transforming the Al-Sabah family from a tribal leader into a "centralized power structure."[27] As the British consular officer in Aden, in the nearby protectorate of Mahra, put it, however, "'[s]tate' in this case was a misnomer, for Mahra . . . inhabited by fiercely independent tribes, was under the control of neither the British nor its titular ruler, [the] Sultan."[28]

In 1920, thousands of Bedouin fighters under Faisal al-Dawish, allied to Ibn Saud, leader of the Saudi State at Riyadh, attacked the oasis town of Jahra not far from Kuwait Town.[29] Families in Jahra worked nonstop for two months to build a wall around the town to repel the invasion, and the story

[23] Anthony Toth, 'Last Battles of the Bedouin and the Rise of Modern States in Northern Arabia: 1850-1950' in D. Chatty (ed), *Nomadic Societies in the Middle East and North Africa: Entering the 21st Century* (Brill 2006) 59–61. See also Briton Busch, *Britain and the Persian Gulf: 1894-1914* (California UP 1967) 31.

[24] I am indebted to Anthony Toth for his comments on Ottoman influence in Kuwait. Toth (n 23) 51, 59–62; Busch (n 23) 31.

[25] Abdulkarim Al-Dekhayel, *Kuwait: Oil, State and Political Legitimization* (Ithaca 2000) 2. See also Longva (n 21) 182; Slot (n 19) 111–113 (on the politics surrounding the agreement).

[26] Crawford, *The Creation of States in International Law* (n 12) 289–294. See also Jan Hendrik Willem Verzijl, *International Law in Historical Perspective. Vol 5: Nationality and Other Matters relating to Individuals* (Martinus Nijhoff 1998) 6–7, 13–14; Jacques Maury, 'Nationalité. Théorie générale du français' in A G De LaPradelle and J-H-P Niboyet (eds), *Répertoire de droit international* (Sirey 1931) 30–31; Weis (n 5) 17–22.

[27] Ismael (n 21) 55. See also Al-Dekhayel (n 25) 2–5; M Casey, *The History of Kuwait* (Greenwood 2007) 45, 49–50, 65 (on the evolution of the relationship between the Al-Sabah family and the British government); Slot (n 19) 117 (on the rights of Kuwait as a vassal state of the Ottoman Empire).

[28] J Harding, 'Matters Colonial, Consular and Curious' in P Hinchcliffe, J T Ducker and M Holt (eds), *Without Glory in Arabia: The British Retreat from Aden* (I B Tauris 2013) 282.

[29] Toth (n 23) 147–148. See also Casey (n 27) 54.

of the battle would take on an almost mythic significance in Kuwait's history and the concept of Kuwaiti nationality.[30]

Following the Battle of Jahra, the British High Commissioner and the British Agent in Kuwait met with Ibn Saud and the Iraqi Minister to establish a border that would divide the desert between Kuwait, Saudi Arabia, and Iraq, including a neutral zone that would allow some Bedouin migration to continue.[31] These negotiations resulted in the Uqair Protocol, which was in part based on previous treaties, like the Anglo-Ottoman agreement.[32] It reaffirmed the idea that everyone living in what was now the territorial state of Kuwait came, at least in theory, under the authority of the Sheikh. At the same time, Bedouin federations in the desert were left without a territorial state, divided by borders and at the mercy of aggressive settlement policies and border restrictions by the British, the French, the Al Sabah family, and other urban rulers in the region.[33] One purpose of the border was to securitize the desert, which, to the Sheikh and the British, meant restricting Bedouin movement. The desert likely appeared to all parties to be a reasonable place for the border due, in part, to antinomadic bias, which cast desert regions as remote, economically worthless, and ungovernable. However, more research is needed on the parties' views of the Bedouin in the setting of Kuwait's borders. As historian Ben Slot puts it, speaking of an earlier draft of Kuwait's borders circulated by the British as part of the negotiations, "[n]obody seems to have envisaged how this geometric circle might be applied to daily desert practice."[34]

During the protected state period, governments throughout the region tried similar policies through a combination of "carrot and stick" approaches to restrict the movement of the Bedouin, including financial rewards and penalties, intertribal marriages, formal recognition of smaller tribes, and forced emigration of problematic Bedouin leaders and groups.[35] As anthropologist and expert on nomadic and mobile peoples Dawn Chatty puts it, "[w]ith the consolidation of state power and authority in the 'nation-state' ... most of the nations of the Middle East turned to their pastoral populations

[30] Longva (n 21) 186–187.

[31] Beaugrand, *Stateless in the Gulf* (n 17) 81.

[32] Casey (n 27) 51. See also Ismael (n 21) 69–70 (listing the Uqair Conference participants and their concerns); Commins (n 17) 146; Slot (n 19) 384–387 (on the Anglo-Ottoman agreement).

[33] For an overview of the history of the drafting of the protocol, see generally E Lauterpacht and others, *The Kuwait Crisis: Basic Documents* (CUP 1991). See also Commins (n 17) 146 (discussing the Saudi blockade to enforce the border).

[34] Slot (n 19) 378.

[35] Beaugrand, *Stateless in the Gulf* (n 17) 68.

with a view to settling them in one place . . . (to) . . . assure control over them."[36]

Historian Anthony Toth describes this period as the "great historical transformation" that would culminate not only in the creation of modern states in the region but in the degradation of Bedouin political independence; "the long period of Bedouin hegemony in the desert and the steppe diminished, probably forever."[37]

In the 1960s, Kuwait's borders were still somewhat fluid, border posts few and far between, and Bedouin could continue their traditional way of life, albeit with increasing difficulty.[38] Following an influx of immigrants from the region to Kuwait between 1960 and 1987, the government tightened border restrictions. The government saw the settlement of the Bedouin as an imperative and began a massive housing construction program from the mid-1960s to 1980, razing informal shanty towns and seminomadic settlements and replacing them with low-cost, Western-style housing projects.[39] A result of these housing projects and movement restrictions on the Bedouin has been the mass settlement of former Bedouin and the eradication of nomadism from Kuwait.

The Protected State period didn't only continue the coerced settlement of the Bedouin; it centralized authority in the hands of the Al-Sabah family in Kuwait Town, a process of centralization that would accelerate after the end of the Protected State period.[40] The Protected State agreement invested the emir with the sole authority to sign an official decree on nationality in 1948 in what was now the territorial state of Kuwait,[41] but it would take time for the consolidation of legal and administrative powers in the hands of the Kuwaiti emir to result in the exclusion of many Bedouin from civil registration.

> Even years after the newly born states were established . . . Papers did not have the meaning they have now and consequently thousands of people fell through the net and remained undocumented. The indigenous stateless

[36] Dawn Chatty, *Mobile Pastoralists: Development Planning and Social Change in Oman* (Columbia UP 1996) 2.

[37] Toth (n 23) 145.

[38] Longva (n 21) 188.

[39] Al-Dekhayel (n 25) 145. See also Claire Beaugrand, 'Statelessness and Transnationalism in Northern Arabia: Biduns and State Building in Kuwait, 1959-2009' (thesis, London Sch of Econ 2010) 162; Beaugrand, *Stateless in the Gulf* (n 17) 99–100.

[40] Al-Dekhayel (n 25) 2–3.

[41] Kuwait Order n. 3, 23–30 (1948). See also Fransman (n 14) 496–498; Beaugrand, *Stateless in the Gulf* (n 17) 80–81 (stating that the royal family had essentially 'turned into the state itself.' ibid 81.

communities in the Gulf region, today called the "Bidoon," an Arabic word which means "without," are largely the victims of this process.[42]

Relying on both *jus sanguinis* and *jus soli* and combining aspects of Arabic and British nationality law,[43] the law adopted both traditional/ancestral and territorial-based approaches.[44] The latter required establishing a link of birth or residency to the arbitrary circle that was now the Kuwaiti state. "Original" (*asil*) Kuwaitis were defined as members of the ruling family, *residents* of Kuwait since 1899, the children of Kuwaiti fathers, or children born in Kuwait of an Arab or Muslim father.[45] Naturalization was granted in a separate decree for persons *residing* in Kuwait for at least ten years who could also speak Arabic and meet certain other requirements.[46] The decree also adopted tiers of nationality, cementing in Kuwaiti law a distinction between original Kuwaitis and naturalized persons. The reliance on residency as a key factor in establishing Kuwait's first body of nationals means that civil registration and identity documents that established a residence within Kuwait's recently created borders would become critical to accessing nationality. "Statelessness in the MENA (Middle East and North Africa) can be seen to have initially arisen following the creation of the modern states in the region."[47]

Despite the importance of civil registration, British policy at the time appeared to be primarily focused on maintaining Kuwait's pro-British stance rather than rolling out a robust system of civil registration.[48] Most Bedouin during this time, like most people in Kuwait, occupied a gray zone of undetermined nationality, without a legal identity establishing their residency

[42] Abbas Shiblak, 'The Lost Tribes of Arabia' (April 2009) 32 Forced Migration Rev 37.

[43] C Joppke, 'Citizenship in Immigration States' in A Shachar and others (eds), *The Oxford Handbook of Citizenship* (OUP 2017) 390. British Nationality and Status of Aliens Act, 1914, 4 & 5 Geo. V, c. 17, s. 10(1). See also Maury (n 26) 39–40;

V Stolcke, 'The "Nature" of Nationality' in V Bader (ed), *Citizenship and Exclusion* (Universiteit van Amsterdam 1997) 71.

[44] Longva (n 21) 185. See also Marie Lund-Johansen, *Fighting for Citizenship in Kuwait* (U of Oslo 2014) 24.

[45] Kuwait, Law no 2, 35–49 (1948) (my italics); Kuwait, Order No 3, 23–30 (1948). See also Fransman (n 14) 296–298; Gianluca Parolin, *Citizenship in the Arab World* (Amsterdam UP 2009) 89; Commins (n 17) 186.

[46] Kuwait Law no 2, 35–49 (1948). See also Kuwait, Order No 3, 23–30 (1948).

[47] Zahra al Barazi and Jason Tucker, 'Challenging the Disunity of Statelessness in the Middle East and North Africa' in Tendayi Bloom (ed), *Understanding Statelessness* (Routledge 2017) 87, 88.

[48] Andrew B Loewenstein, 'The Veiled Protectorate of Kowait': Liberalized Imperialism and British Efforts to Influence Kuwaiti Domestic Policy during the Reign of Sheikh Ahmad al-Jaber, 1938-50' (2000) 36 Middle E Stud 103, 103–123.

or other means of eligibility under the law. Kuwaiti historian Abdullah M. Alhajeri writes:

> Anyone who examines the historical development of this problem will find that a large part of it relates to the structure and mobility of the population in the Gulf region before the establishment of the state and the independence of the countries of the region. Before the issuance of the Citizenship Law, national ID cards (and passports) were given to Kuwaitis in the era of Sheikh Ahmad Al-Jaber (1921–50); Kuwaiti passports were issued in 1936, but it is not clear on what basis those passports were given, or according to what standards they were granted to individuals, especially since it was not clear who was Kuwaiti because of the lack of a citizenship law before 1959. Moreover, the Kuwaiti Citizenship Law number 2 was legislated in 1948, and it was unknown to many and therefore could not limit the number of Kuwaiti citizens at that time.[49]

Under the Protected State agreement, qualifying individuals in Kuwait were also technically entitled to British Protected Person (BPP) status, which came with its own passport and offered diplomatic and consular protection abroad.[50] Again, a lack of implementation meant that most of the people living in Kuwait, including most Bedouin, had no access to this document, though more research is needed on this crucial period of Bedouin history. After this period, however, access to civil registration for certain Bedouin tribes versus access for other communities, particularly settled communities, would sharply diverge, while registration would become linked to forced and coerced settlement for the Bedouin, which would, in turn, become a major goal of the Kuwaiti government.

3.3.2 Settlement and Registration in North Borneo

The Sama Dilaut also enjoyed some political independence in the Sulu Sultanate period, though they were constrained by their need for protective patronage relationships with land-based rulers.[51] They retained

49 Abdulluh A Alhajeri, 'The Bedoun': Kuwaitis without an Identity 51 Middle E Stud 17 (2015) 20.

50 See generally Fransman (n 14) 111.

51 Clifford Sather, 'Commodity, Trade, Gift Exchange, and the History of Maritime Nomadism in Southeastern Sabah' (2002) 6 Nom Peoples 20, 27–29. See also Clifford Sather, 'Sulu's Political Jurisdiction over the Bajau Laut' [1971] Borneo Res Bulletin 59; Hooker (n 18) 16–17; James Warren,

independence over their internal affairs, however, including the recognition of births, deaths, and marriages and their freedom of movement and to practice their way of life. Much of this independence would end during British colonialism and the Sama Dilaut are examples of the hostile position British administrators took toward nomadism as a way of life. The colonial period also began the marginalization of northern Borneo as the British instead focused mainly on their colonies in the Malay Peninsula, contributing to a future imbalance of power between North Borneo (Sabah) and the rest of Malaysia.[52]

In the Sulu Sea, there seems to have never been any effort by any colonial authority to recognize the political independence of the Sama Dilaut, either by signing treaties with them or recognizing their territories, though more research is needed into this critical period in Sama Dilaut history. Instead, the Spanish first signed a series of treaties with the Sultan of Sulu in the mid-1600s and early 1700s, and in 1877, the Sultan of Sulu signed a new treaty with the British North Borneo Chartered Company (BNBC), a quasi-sovereign, private entity.[53] North Borneo officially became a Protected State in 1888 but remained under the administration of the BNBC.[54] It would briefly become a Crown Colony following World War II.

North Borneo suffered from shifting and unclear borders, sandwiched between Dutch-controlled territories and the Spanish-controlled Philippines. Over a period from 1891 to 1915, however, the Dutch and British officially established the border between their colonies bisecting the Sulu Sea, the domain of the Sama Dilaut, which became the modern-day border between Malaysia and Indonesia. In 1930, the British and the United States, which succeeded the Spanish in the Southern Philippines, fixed the boundary between north Borneo and the Philippines.[55] One result of this period was

The Sulu Zone: 1768-1898 (Singapore UP 1981) 67–69 (where he states that the Sama Dilaut were 'dependent' on land-based groups for security, but nevertheless enjoyed independence over their internal affairs); Clifford Sather, *The Bajau Laut: Adaptation, History, and Fate in a Maritime Fishing Society of South-eastern Sabah* (OUP 1997) 60–63.

[52] Andaya and Andaya (n 18) 125–129. See also Hooker (n 18) 135.

[53] Andaya and Andaya (n 18) 190. See also N M Saleeby, 'Studies in Moro History, Law and Religion' (Project Gutenberg Ebook 2013, originally published by the Philippines Dept of the Int 1905) 164.

[54] Andaya and Andaya (n 18) 188–189. See also Kevin Young, Willem C F Bussink and Parvez Hasan, *Malaysia: Growth and Equity in a Multiracial Society* (Johns Hopkins UP 1980) 12–13; Hooker (n 18) 131; J Warren, *The North Borneo Chartered Company's Administration of the Bajau, 1878-1909: The Pacification of a Maritime, Nomadic People* (Ohio UP 1971) 2–3, 33–35.

[55] *Case Concerning Sovereignty over Pulau Ligitan and Pulau Sipadan (Indonesia v. Malaysia)* (Merits) [2002] ICJ Rep 625. See also Treaty of Peace between the United States and Spain (signed 10

the division of the Sulu Sultanate and Sama Dilaut territories into separate colonies, with borders dividing the Sulu Sea, including Sama Dilaut fishing zones. The Sulu Sea likely appeared to be a rational place to place the border, due to antinomadic bias that saw nomadic areas like oceans as remote and/or ungovernable.

There is no evidence the colonial powers in the region took previous migration patterns and trade routes into account when setting these borders, nor were the Sama Dilaut consulted in any way, though more research is needed. These treaties set aside centuries of trade and political unity.[56] They would lay the foundation for the modern maritime borders in the region and the breakup of the region into discrete, territorial units, with borders dividing Sama Dilaut areas.

The BNBC saw the settlement of the Sama Dilaut as the solution to the "problem" of their uncontrolled mobility. As historian James Warren states, "Essential to the establishment of thorough control in the region (Borneo) would be a reorientation of the Bajau (Sama Dilaut and related groups) toward a surplus productivity involving them in a cash economy and in more sedentary habits."[57]

The BNBC cast the Sama Dilaut as pirates and as a threat to British sovereignty and took aggressive steps to curtail their movement, similar to measures being taken by other colonial powers in the region.[58] By the 1840s, the colonial powers that had come to dominate the Sulu Sea had reduced noncolonial trade, often conflated with piracy, with disastrous results for the local economy.[59] This led to a sharp decline in the Sulu Sultanate and a breakdown of the patronage system that had sustained the Sama Dilaut for centuries.

December 1898, entered into force 11 April 1899) US Congress, 55th Cong, 3d Sess, Senate Doc No 62, Part 1 (US Government Printing Office 1899) 5–11, Part III; Hooker (n 18) 132; Warren, *North Borneo Chartered Company's Administration* (n 54) 48–51; Convention between the United States of America and Great Britain Delimiting the Boundary between the Philippine Archipelago and the State of North Borneo (2 January 1930) UST No 856.

[56] Andaya and Andaya (n 18) 125–128.

[57] Warren, *North Borneo Chartered Company's Administration* (n 54) 77–78.

[58] J Warren, 'Looking Back on "The Sulu Zone": State Formation, Slave Raiding and Ethnic Diversity in Southeast Asia' (1996) 69 J Malaysian Branch Royal Asiatic Soc 21, 30. See also Warren, *North Borneo Chartered Company's Administration* (n 54) 4, 14, 91–99 (for an overview of colonial efforts to settle and pacify the Sama Dilaut).

[59] Stefan Eklöf, *Pirates in Paradise, A Modern History of Southeast Asia's Maritime Marauders* (Nus Press 2006) 11. See also Warren, 'Looking Back on "The Sulu Zone"' (n 58) 28 (on piracy and raiding in the Sulu Sea).

The BNBC also encouraged settlement through more indirect means. The British granted pardons to Bajau and Sama pirates, which meant traders and fishermen who attacked their ships in exchange for their settlement. The introduction of a cash economy and wage labor also played a role, as did the growth of Semporna Town and its market.[60] Such indirect means of promoting settlement were part of Britain's so-called development programs in the region, many of which had ending boat nomadism as an explicit goal. As one Company official put it, "[U]nder British rule, the Bajau is proving himself a good workman, and is building up a permanent home, in place of leading the roving piratical life he was formerly accustomed to."[61]

Starting in 1909, the BNBC began relocating Sama/Bajau villages to more central locations near big towns to bring them under centralized control. This brought many nomadic Sama Dilaut groups into contact with the British administration for the first time. The Sama Dilaut, however, developed the practice of moving to Jolo, outside the reach of BNBC tax collectors, which cut off one of the main ways the colony sought to make money. To end this practice, the BNBC forced the Sama Dilaut and other nomadic groups to settle and take up agriculture, even though agriculture was ill-suited to the jungle interiors and the Sama Dilaut had no experience with it.[62]

It involved massive manpower and policing to round up scattered villages and flotillas of Bajau peoples, both nomadic and seminomadic, and relocate them to coconut farms in the interior. Expert Carol Warren calls the efforts by the British to settle the Sama Dilaut as "strenuous."[63] Eventually, the settlement of nomadic peoples became its own justification, and when the United States took over the Philippines from the weak Spanish administration in 1898, and the Sama Dilaut could no longer easily relocate to the southern Philippines to escape, Sama Dilaut settlement accelerated.

Anthropologists like Clifford Sather and James Warren, who were researching the Sama Dilaut in Sabah at that time, noted a decline in boat nomadism.[64] The postcolonial government continued to push for the settlement of the Sama Dilaut, including by creating infrastructure around water

[60] Sather, 'Commodity, Trade, Gift Exchange' (n 51) 38–39.

[61] L Lovegrove, employee of the BNBC, quoted in Warren, *North Borneo Chartered Company's Administration* (n 54) 86, n 226.

[62] Sather, *The Bajau Laut* (n 51) 49.

[63] C Warren, 'Consciousness in Social Transformation: The Sama Dilaut of East Malaysia' (1980) 5 Dialectical Anthro 227, 228.

[64] Sather, *The Bajau Laut* (n 51) 332; see also Warren, *North Borneo Chartered Company's Administration* (n 54) ix.

villages to encourage settlement, and by 1969, the sedentary population of settlements near Semporna Town had doubled.

To raise money and restrict Bajau Laut movement, the BNBC introduced a system of boat licenses,[65] which forced Sama Dilaut fishermen to pay to register their boats in a specific location, but which also may have served as a form of ID. These licenses, as the previous section discussed, were actively used as a tool in the BNBC policy to end "boat nomadism" and did, in fact, contribute to the end of Sama Dilaut's long-distance migration to the southern Philippines and Indonesia. Experts on the period claim that many Bajau communities viewed these licenses as an impermissible attempt to restrict their freedom of movement.[66]

British agents traveled the islands issuing and checking licenses and, as expert Clifford Sather explains, for most of the first decade of the twentieth century, the BNBC was very occupied with enforcing boat registration as a means to collect revenue, restrict mobility, and get the local communities to provide "acknowledgment of Company sovereignty."[67] A similar system of boat registration was introduced by the United States in the Philippines, but the systems were not integrated, meaning that boats registered in Borneo could not easily travel to what was now the Philippines. While boat licenses may, therefore, be seen as an early form of ID for the Sama Dilaut, they were forever linked to coercive settlement policies and the end of nomadism.

Boat registration was not relaxed until after independence, but by that point, many Sama Dilaut families had settled in "water villages" near urban centers like Semporna. Government registration of the Sama Dilaut came to be linked to forced and coerced settlement and the lack of recognition of Sama Dilaut political independence. Meanwhile, the BNBC did not roll out a formal civil registration system, and the British only began issuing identity cards on the nearby Malaya peninsula in 1948.

3.3.3 Settlement and Registration in French West Africa

The French government had secured European recognition for their sovereignty over West Africa at the Conference of Berlin in 1884–1885, but French

[65] Andaya and Andaya (n 18) 135–136.
[66] Sather, *The Bajau Laut* (n 51) 47–48; Warren, *North Borneo Chartered Company's Administration* (n 54) 79–82.
[67] Sather, *The Bajau Laut* (n 51) 47.

presence on the ground was for many years limited to a few military outposts and had only a small effect on the lives of pastoral populations. This would drastically change by the end of the colonial period. "It may well turn out that Europe's most enduring legacy to Africa is the nation-state."[68]

In the early decades of French colonialism, the French *commandants* struggled to have much impact in the vast Sahel, which was mainly important to the French government during the early colonial period for strategic reasons to prevent land grabs by other powers.[69] The French government needed to occupy the desert and sign treaties with local rulers to establish French sovereignty over the territory needed to connect France's colonies in North Africa with those in West Africa. Many French politicians and administrators saw exporting French law and bureaucracy as a means to unify France's African colonies under the policy of assimilation.[70]

One outcome of the colonial period was the setting of borders that were, at best, arbitrary and, at worst, harmful from the point of view of local communities.[71] The border between Algeria and French West Africa, for example, was set where two French military rivals and explorers met near the wells of Timiaouine.[72] The Sahara was a likely place for colonial borders partly because the French government viewed the desert as remote, ungovernable, and economically worthless. Until the twentieth century, however, borders were essentially meaningless to pastoral peoples, but this would begin to change as French bureaucracy expanded into all aspects of Sahel life.

In the early 1900s, the fluid borders between the various colonies of the French West and North Africa slowly solidified, bringing increased movement restrictions and ID requirements. The French government created internal borders as well in the form of administrative regions, or *cercles*, around their military outposts, which were located near towns, cutting through pastoral regions.[73] This administrative system served the goal of pacifying the

[68] Ali Mazrui, 'Francophone Nations and English-Speaking States: Imperial Ethnicity and African Political Formations' in Donald Rothchild and Victor A Olorunsola (eds), *State Versus Ethnic Claims: African Policy Dilemmas* (Routledge 1983) 25.

[69] Boilley (n 9) 203.

[70] John Chipman, *French Power in Africa* (Basil Blackwell 1989) 53–56. It should be noted that many colonial administrators preferred a hands-off approach to administration, following a policy of association between French government agents and local rulers. ibid 57.

[71] Thomas Benetti, 'Entwicklung des Verhältnisses zwischen Tuareg und staatlichen Strukturen in Mali' (U of Vienna 2008) 43.

[72] Foltz (n 11) 119.

[73] Hall (n 11) 137–139, 305. See also C Gremont, 'Villages and Crossroads: Changing Territorialities among the Tuareg of Northern Mali' in James McDougall and Judith Scheele (eds), *Saharan Frontiers: Space and Mobility in Northwest Africa* (Indiana UP 2012) 185.

nomadic population, which included their sedentarization.[74] For the Tuareg and Fulani, the introduction of ID as a requirement to traverse borders and administrative zones would mark the beginning of restrictions on pastoralism, the decline of Saharan trade, and their conversion to a more sedentary life.

While many French military leaders held the nomadic Tuareg nobility in high esteem, the French *commandants* also held racial attitudes about the Tuareg as being tribal.[75] To tamp down on what they saw as the tribal nature of the Tuareg, they appointed friendly Tuareg leaders who would impose French policies rather than following Tuareg succession law. The French *commandants* in the Sahel also began an aggressive, explicit campaign to settle the Tuareg noble class to keep them within the newly created administrative limits to reduce nomadism and to protect agricultural communities.[76] Their response to Tuareg resistance was to forcibly return nomadic communities to their assigned territories.[77] There appears to have been a lack of willingness on the part of many French officials to see the point of view of nomadic leaders who relied on mobility as a way of life but were suddenly confronted by borders. Controller-General Barba, a French administrator, stated that nomadic leaders on the border between Niger and Algeria seemed "not to understand" the reasons for the difference in administration and taxation between the two colonies.[78]

French administration also had an indirect tendency to encourage or coerce settlement. The French government introduced taxation based on administrative regions and divided it between taxes on the sedentary population and taxes on nomadic peoples, with the two groups often paying different rates. Jean-Marie Payen, head of French administration in Niger, admitted that the Tuareg got little in return for their taxes, as the services

[74] Benetti (n 71) 43. See also Bourgeot, *Les sociétés touarègues* (n 16) 276–279, 460–462.

[75] See for example the opinions of French explorer and priest Charles de Foucauld in A Bourgeot, 'Sahara: espace géostratégique et enjeux politiques (Niger)' (2014) 31 NAQD: Revue d'Etudes et de Critique Sociale 153, 168–171. For an overview of the topic of race in the Sahel, see also the work of Bruce Hall.

[76] Jacques Frémeaux, 'La mise en place d'une administration aux marges sahariennes de l'A.O.F. (1891-1930)' in E Bernus and others (eds), *Nomades et commandants : administration et sociétés nomades dans l'ancienne AOF* (Karthala 1993) 24; Sara Randall and Alessandra Giuffrida, 'Forced Migration, Sedentarization and Social Change: Malian Kel Tamasheq' in Dawn Chatty (ed), *Nomadic Societies in the Middle East and North Africa: Entering the 21st Century* (Brill 2006) 434–435.

[77] Benetti (n 71) 49.

[78] Jean-François Barba, 'L'administration en zone frontalière algero-soudanaise' in E Bernus and others (eds), *Nomades et commandants : administration et sociétés nomades dans l'ancienne AOF* (Karthala 1993) 38–39.

provided by the French were located in towns and oriented toward the settled population. *Commandants* signed agreements with Tuareg leaders to limit their movements. Payen framed Tuareg registration not in terms of rights or the provision of services but rather as a way to reduce Tuareg mobility and liberty, a form of "administrative confinement" for the Tuareg.[79]

This began the separate administration and registration of nomadic peoples as distinct from settled and urban populations under what the former French *Commandant* in Timbuktu called a "double administration."[80] Over time, as French administrators began to consolidate administrative functions in urban areas, the French *commandants* kept the Tuareg in northern French Soudan under military rule. While this system of double administration appeared to preserve Tuareg autonomy, in reality, Tuareg independence was now an illusion. The Tuareg began to be isolated and separated from the administrative functions of French colonialism, with serious consequences for their future registration.

The *commandants* also tried to educate the Tuareg nobility in French schools to equip them to participate in the French bureaucracy, a process that required the abandonment of many nomadic practices and which many in the Tuareg nobility actively resisted. French administrators like Commander Betrix of the Gao region encouraged, or sometimes forced, the Tuareg to settle and send their children to European-style schools.[81] Schools and health centers for the Tuareg were usually in cities like Timbuktu and Gao, far from Tuareg areas. Children were required to be separated from their nomadic parents, preventing them from learning nomadic skills.[82] According to Ibrahim Ag Litny, former student of a nomadic school in Kidal, French schools for the Tuareg were mostly a failure.[83] Tuareg resistance to French

[79] J-M Payen, 'Le recensement et l'impôt' in E Bernus and others (eds), *Nomades et commandants : administration et sociétés nomades dans l'ancienne AOF* (Karthala 1993) 121–125 (on the payment of taxes by nomadic and sedentary communities). See also Boilley (n 9) 246; Barba (n 78) 36. For information on the Fulani under British taxation, see generally Derrick J Stenning, 'Transhumance, Migratory Drift, Migration; Patterns of Pastoral Fulani Nomadism' (1957) 87 J Royal Anthropological Inst Great Britain Ireland 57.

[80] Phillip Loiseau, 'L'administration et les rapports nomades/sédentaires' in E Bernus and others (eds), *Nomades et commandants : administration et sociétés nomades dans l'ancienne AOF* (Karthala 1993) 160–161. See also Gremont (n 73) 136.

[81] Rissatan ag Alfarouk, 'La politique coloniale d'affaiblissement de la confédération Kel Denneg de 1900 à 1949' in E Bernus and others (eds), *Nomades et commandants: administration et sociétés nomades dans l'ancienne AOF* (Kathala 1993) 90–91.

[82] Boilley (n 9) 197, 207–232.

[83] Ibrahim Ag Litny, 'La première école de l'Adagh' in E Bernus and others (eds), *Nomades et commandants : Administration et sociétés nomades dans l'ancienne AOF* (Karthala 1993) 153–154.

schooling placed them at a disadvantage at decolonization, however, when French-style schooling became a requirement for many government posts.

The French government aggressively promoted agriculture in the Sahel, primarily to encourage nomadic settlement, including by signing conventions on nomadism with Tuareg leaders. As Michel de Geyer d'Orth, the former French administrator of the Agadez region, put it, to many members of the French colonial government, nomadism presented an "insurmountable handicap" to development, while to others, nomadism was an inevitable response to the dry environment but would nevertheless need to be phased out more gradually.[84] French policy attempted to apply a land tenure system, already used by the agricultural Songhai communities, to the Tuareg.[85] French administrators also settled some Tuareg vassal families, assigned them land, and developed infrastructure to encourage agriculture, introducing European-style irrigation and building roads.[86] The abolishment of slavery weakened the power of the Tuareg nobility and empowered agricultural groups.

The promotion of agriculture led to conflict between the Tuareg and the Songhai, as well as between Songhai clans, as unoccupied agricultural land became scarce and the Tuareg nobles who remained nomadic lost their dominance and, therefore, the ability to enforce their grazing rights.[87] Agriculture in the Sahel was often not well suited to the desert environment in many areas where the French military pushed for nomadic settlement, causing land overuse and drought. Nevertheless, practices to promote agriculture would later be aggressively adopted by postcolonial governments.[88] The experience of the Tuareg under French colonialism demonstrates the direct and indirect ways in which colonial administration facilitated nomadic settlement, using the tools of colonial administration, including registration and ID. The Tuareg, however, opposed this emerging system of centralized, French-administered bureaucracy.[89]

[84] Michel de Geyer d'Orth, 'Les actions de développement' in E Bernus and others (eds), *Nomades et commandants : Administration et sociétés nomades dans l'ancienne AOF* (Karthala 1993) 127.

[85] Boilley (n 9) 196.

[86] ibid 204.

[87] Hall (n 11) 264–271.

[88] ibid 285.

[89] ibid 138. See also E Bernus, P Boilley, J Clauzel and J-T Triaud, 'Dates, Dromedaries, and Drought: Diversification in Tuareg Pastoral Systems' in John G Galaty and Douglas L Johnson (eds), *The World of Pastoralism: Herding Systems in Contemporary Perspective* (Guilford P 1990), 161; B Lecocq, *Disputed Desert: Decolonisation, Competing Nationalisms and Tuareg Rebellions in Northern Mali* (Brill 2010) 14 (on the separate French administration of the Tuareg and sedentary communities); Foltz (n 11) 13, 119 (discussing the fact that French administrators were less inclined to meddle in Tuareg political structures than in those of sedentary communities).

At the end of the colonial period, the French administration began to rethink their antinomadism policies. They considered the idea of mobile schools that would travel with the Tuareg families and incorporate more traditional skills, but independence came before this idea could be implemented, and the French administration left a legacy of mistrust of centralized government administration on the part of many Tuareg.[90]

Those Fulani who remained pastoralists during the colonial period also found themselves politically marginalized by the emerging colonial bureaucracy in West Africa. As sociologist Victor Azarya, an expert on the colonial period and its effects on pastoralists in Africa like the Fulani, puts it,

> Some of them (pastoralists) were considered violent (by colonial governments) and all of them were considered difficult to control as long as they continued to pursue their nomadic life. They were pushed away from their grazing areas, some of which reverted to agriculture, to mixed farming and to new settlement of both Africans and Europeans. They (the pastoralists) were either relocated in closed reserves or had to move away to more arid and less accessible areas, unless they already lived in the desert or in its fringes.[91]

The French administration often collaborated with the urban Fulani elite, relying on their local expertise to help set up the emerging bureaucracy, incorporating preexisting state structures and leveraging the patronage relationship many Fulani nobles had with pastoral groups to encourage settlement. For nomadic Fulani, also subject to the emerging borders and movement restrictions of French West Africa, the abolition of slavery impacted their nomadic way of life and contributed to their decision to move to northern Côte d'Ivoire.[92] Some Fulani also moved north, into Tuareg areas.

The later colonial period completed the separation of West Africa into separate states, bringing further movement restrictions to both the Fulani and Tuareg. Léopold Senghor lamented what he called the "balkanization" of Africa,[93] as Africans, including nomadic peoples, who were accustomed to moving easily between colonies, now found themselves facing international

[90] Henri Combelles, 'La scolarisation et les écoles nomades au Mali' in E Bernus and others (eds), *Nomades et commandants : Administration et sociétés nomades dans l'ancienne AOF* (Karthala 1993) 137–138.

[91] Azarya, 20 (my paratheses).

[92] T J Bassett, 'Fulani Herd Movements' (1986) 76 Geo Rev 233, 237.

[93] Leopold S Senghor, 'Balkanisation ou Fédération?' (1956) 2 Afrique Nouvelle 180.

borders. Perhaps no groups would be more affected by the so-called balkanization of Africa than nomadic peoples like the Fulani and the Tuareg, who now found themselves unable to adjust their pastoral routes to respond to climate change and conflict.[94] Governments in the Sahel began branding nomadic movement, which necessitated crossing borders, as inherently illegal.

In this climate of antinomadic policies, taxation, forced schooling, and movement restrictions, the French government introduced civil registration. Prior to 1945, civil registration in West Africa was not compulsory for the African population, and only those few individuals holding French citizenship were required to register.[95] Certain events, such as traditional marriages, were seen as outside the scope of French administration. By 1944, the French government had made only about 100,000 entries in the *état civil* for indigenous persons in French West Africa, mostly for births. When registration did occur, it was usually among the urban population.

As political participation expanded in West Africa, the French government recognized the need for expanded access to civil registration. After 1945, the new Constitution extended suffrage throughout the French empire, with large numbers of Africans eligible to vote for the first time, and local administrators faced the monumental task of registering millions of people. As expert Ruth Dickens describes it, "[r]egistration of births, marriages, and deaths on the *état civil* was so routine in France that metropolitan officials thought it a perfectly reasonable expectation for the colonies."[96]

As a report summarizing civil registration in Mali put it,

> [t]he civil status registration was introduced in Mali by the French colonial administration in the late 19th century and beginning 20th century. During that period, the registration and documentation system was generally poor and access was limited to large cities. There was a lack of means and of verification/control by the civil registry officers as well.[97]

[94] Boilley (n 9) 247.

[95] For a history of civil registration in West Africa during the French colonial period, see Frederick Cooper, *Citizenship between Empire and Nation: Remaking France and French Africa 1945-1960* (Princeton UP 2014) 152–174.

[96] Ruth Dickens, *Defining French Citizenship Policy in West Africa: 1895-1956* (Emory UP 2001) 255.

[97] International Criminal Court, 'Public Registry's Report on Proof of Identity Documents Available in Mali and Transmission of Proposed Application Forms for Rule 85(b) RPE Victims and Groups of Victims' Annex I, No ICC-01/12-01/18.

The realities of registering rural and nomadic populations in vast areas with little French presence presented an enormous challenge to French administrators on the ground. From the beginning, French administrators saw civil registration as better suited to the sedentary and agricultural populations of the Sahel, than to nomadic peoples. According to the governor of French Soudan, for example, "such tasks (civil registration) . . . could be accomplished only for the sedentary part of his population, step by step, and at high cost."[98]

While nomadic peoples suffered from many of the same cultural barriers which also impeded registration of rural peoples in general across French West Africa, the territorial organization of French West Africa also meant that it was far easier for sedentary farmers to register, as they were organized in cantons and districts headed by a *chef de canton* or district chief.[99] Attempts in French Soudan and Upper Volta (today, Burkina Faso) to establish electoral lists and issue family cards were limited to the sedentary population and French administrators made few efforts to bring voting to the nomadic population until the very end of the colonial period.[100]

In recognition of the need for an *état civil*, French administrators relaxed coercive settlement policies toward the end of the colonial period, but it was often too little, too late. For example, they began allowing nomadic peoples to apply for special permits to leave their areas to find better pasturage, and to apply for such permits, families had to register with the French authorities and obtain identity documents, such as family cards.

These reforms appeared to have had little effect on the overall trend of nomadic society toward coerced settlement and low participation in administrative functions like civil registration and voting. It is unclear the extent to which nomadic Fulani were voting.[101] Many Fulani pastoralists, facing both drought and antinomadic policies in both Mali and Burkina Faso, would shift their grazing southward into northern Côte d'Ivoire.

There is more information on nomadic Tuareg voting patterns from the work of expert Pierre Boilley. Voter registration in French Soudan increased rapidly from approximately one million to two million people between 1958 and 1959, but voter turnout among the Tuareg remained low, and the

98 Cooper (n 95) 154, citing the governor.
99 ibid 270–273 (on registration during the *loi cadre* period).
100 A Gaudio, *Le Mali* (2nd edn, Karthala 1988) 88, citing French administrator from 1930–1940 Francis Nicolas.
101 See generally Nicolas Guy, 'Communautés islamiques et collectivité nationale dans trois États d'Afrique occidentale' (1981) 250 Revue française d'histoire d'outre-mer 156.

rate of participation in elections by the nomadic population, Tuareg and Arab, decreased as time went on.[102] In 1958, a critical year for Malian independence, more than 90 percent of the nomadic population in Adagh did not vote.

Toward the end of the colonial period, the chief of the Kounta Tuareg traveled across northern French Soudan to educate the Tuareg about the importance of registering with the French before independence so that they could vote, but he subsequently reported that many Tuareg did not want to participate.[103] Nevertheless, even though political participation by the Tuareg remained low and many resisted the census and other forms of French administration, some Tuareg were registering and voting. Toward the end of the colonial period, the French began appointing Tuareg to key posts in the military, police, and administration as part of their policy of Africanization. According to Lecocq, this cooperation between French *commandants* and Tuareg nobles in northern Mali created distrust among southern politicians fearful of separatism and Tuareg connections to neighboring French colonies.[104]

Independence from France meant that many pastoralists were now divided by international borders between often hostile neighboring states. Many Tuareg did not feel a sense of common purpose with the rest of the Soudan.[105] Some Tuareg leaders entered the decolonization process intent on Tuareg independence, which aligned with the goals of some members of the French government in uniting Tuareg regions into a single, postcolonial state, the *Sahara Français*.[106] Yet, African governments and the international community supported existing borders under the doctrine of *uti possidetis*.[107] Though prominent southern politicians visited the north throughout the late 1950s and early 1960s to campaign against partition and in favor of Malian unity, many Tuareg leaders pushed for independence.[108] According to Lecocq, for many Tuareg, colonization continued with the sublimation of Tuareg independence under the rule of southerners, about whom many

[102] Boilley (n 9) 272–280. See also Benetti (n 71) 53–54; C O Diarrah, *Vers La IIIe République Du Mali* (L'Harmattan 1991) 31–34 (on voting in Mali generally during this period).

[103] G Féral, 'Administrations comparées en pays nomade' in E Bernus and others (eds), *Nomades et commandants : Administration et sociétés nomades dans l'ancienne AOF* (Karthala 1993) 110–111.

[104] Lecocq, *Disputed Desert* (n 89) 170–171.

[105] Boilley (n 9) 277–278. See also Lecocq, *Disputed Desert* (n 89) 43–47.

[106] Bourgeot, 'Sahara' (n 75) 170. See also Gremont (n 73) 137.

[107] Malcolm Shaw, 'Peoples, Territorialism and Boundaries' (1997) 3 Eur J Intl Law 478, 491–495. See also Organization of African Unity, Resolution 16(1) (1964).

[108] Boilley (n 9) 305.

Tuareg nobles held racist beliefs.[109] An independent Tuareg state, which presumably would have had its own system of nationality laws and civil registration, would not come to pass, however, and French Soudan would become independent as a single territorial unit, Mali, with both the Tuareg and the Fulani now divided by international borders. At independence, hostility between the Malian government and the Tuareg would break out into armed conflict, greatly influencing Tuareg civil registration. At the same time, many Fulani would move south into Côte d'Ivoire to escape antipastoral policies and to preserve access to cattle markets.

3.4 Civil Registration at Decolonization

The next sections will summarize some of the problems the Bedouin, the Fulani, the Tuareg, and the Sama Dilaut faced during and after decolonization to register as nationals with their governments and to obtain vital documents in Kuwait, Côte d'Ivoire, Mali, and Malaysia.

3.4.1 Civil Registration in Kuwait and Bedouin Exclusion

While there is a lack of information on Bedouin civil registration during the Protected State period, their problems with civil registration in Kuwait today are well documented. The majority of the *bidoon jinsiya*, or those without status, can trace their family history back to a Bedouin grandparent or great-grandparent who remained unregistered during the crucial postcolonial period when Kuwait established its first body of nationals. Claire Beaugrand, an expert on the *bidoon* in Kuwait, calls the subsequent registration as stateless of many members of this population a form of "administrative violence."[110] Testimony from affected members of the *bidoon* community demonstrates both the connection between Bedouin ancestry and *bidoon* status and the devastating impact of Bedouin exclusion at decolonization on their descendants' status today.

[109] Lecocq, *Disputed Desert* (n 89) 104–105.
[110] Claire Beaugrand, 'Statelessness and Administrative Violence: Biduns' Survival Strategies in Kuwait' (2011) 101 The Muslim World 228, 229.

> The appellant... and his family are bidoons meaning "without nationality". His grandparents, he believes, and their forebears were desert-dwelling Bedouins . . . He understands from his father that his grandparents had a permanent house—the location of which he is uncertain—though they would move with their sheep during springtime, living in their tents. They sold their sheep in Kuwait City. His parents, from the time of their marriage, have lived a settled life in the city though his father has always traded in sheep.[111]

Kuwait and Britain terminated their Protected State agreement in 1961[112] with civil registration largely incomplete for the Bedouin, as far as this book could determine. Most Bedouin likely held no identity documents of any kind, though more research is needed on this critical moment in Kuwait's history of nationality.

Importantly, no international mechanism was put in place during decolonization to require adjacent states like Kuwait and Saudi Arabia to negotiate to find a solution for the nationality of cross-border populations, nor, as indicated in previous sections, does it appear that the British government took any responsibility for the lack of civil registration that left so many Bedouin without a legal identity. In an example of the extent and pervasiveness of the bias against nomadic peoples in international policy, decolonization appears to have taken little account of the requirements of nomadic populations to be able to traverse borders to maintain their way of life.

In some former British colonies, BPP status provided at least a minimum legal identity for certain communities whose nationality was in doubt. The passage of state-level nationality laws throughout the former British Protected States and Protectorates essentially brought about the automatic termination of BPP status for those who gained a new nationality,[113] but those who were ineligible for nationality in any postcolonial state were, in theory, eligible to retain BPP status. While some scholars now argue that postcolonial BPP was, itself, a type of statelessness,[114] the passports could have provided a legal identity to Bedouin families, including proof of residence and place of birth.

[111] See for example the applicant in Refugee Appeal No 74467 (2004) New Zealand: Refugee Status Appeals Authority.

[112] Crawford, *The Creation of States in International Law* (n 12) 319. Crawford notes that the Protected State arrangement's termination happened over time, culminating in 1961.

[113] Fransman (n 14) 111. See also Alexander and Simon, 2016, 315–316.

[114] See generally Augusta Waldie, *Contesting an Elastic Constitution: British Nationality and Protection in the Mandates*, vol 16 (Edinburah UP 2023).

As stated in the last section, this book was unable to find any information on the use of BPP status by members of the Bedouin community, meaning that many Bedouin families likely entered the post-Protected State period without any legal identity or documents of any kind to prove their place of birth or residence, facts that would become crucial to establishing their eligibility for Kuwaiti nationality.

Despite a widespread lack of civil registration for the Bedouin, Kuwait's government, made up of the Al-Sabah family and powerful, urban merchant families, and with the help of international experts, arranged to draft Kuwait's first post-Protected State nationality law in 1959. Like many postcolonial nationality laws, it relied in part on both *settlement* and *residence* to establish nationality as well as favoring persons of Arab origin.[115] Documents establishing residency would now be crucial to qualify for Kuwaiti nationality under the law, which read,

> [o]riginal Kuwaiti nationals are those persons who were *settled* in Kuwait prior to 1920 and who maintained their *normal residence* there until the date of the publication of this Law. *Ancestral residence* shall be deemed complementary to the period of residence of descendants. A person is deemed to have maintained his *normal residence* in Kuwait even if he resides in a foreign country if he has the intention of returning to Kuwait.[116]

The concepts of ancestral or customary residence were not defined, but 1920 was the date of the Battle of Jahra when the inhabitants of Kuwait Town defended it from Bedouin attack.[117] More will be said in future chapters about the significance of this event to Kuwaiti nationality law, but it is important to note that the battle invokes the idea of settlement in town as central to the concept of nationality in Kuwait, and nomadism as a hostile, foreign way of life.[118]

The British tendency to vest urban rulers with vast authority over nomadic populations would significantly impact the civil registration process

[115] Amiri Decree No 15, 5 Dec 1959, cited in Ismael (n 21) 118–119. See also Fransman (n 14) 185. The law was amended in 1960, 1965, and 1966.

[116] Kuwait: Ministerial Decree No 15 of 1959 promulgating the Nationality Law, *Last amended by: Law No. 33 of 2004 (effective 27 June 2004)* (1959), art 1 (UNHCR translation, my italics).

[117] Marie Lund-Johansen, 'Fighting for Citizenship in Kuwait' (masters thesis, Oslo U 2014) 24. See also G Parolin, *Citizenship in the Arab World* (Amsterdam UP 2009) 90.

[118] Farah al-Nakib, 'Revisiting Hadar and Badū in Kuwait: Citizenship, Housing, and the Construction of a Dichotomy' (2014) 46 Intl J Middle E Stud 11, 11–12.

in Kuwait following the passage of this law. Kuwaiti registration committees were usually based in towns and run by officials drawn from urban areas. They had enormous discretion to determine who should qualify.[119] Beaugrand notes the lack of experience of many committee members with Bedouin society.[120] The focus of the law on residence and settlement as the crucial factors in determining eligibility left the status of many Bedouin, with a history of migration throughout the region, a lack of documents, and ties to what were now Iraq and Saudi Arabia, vague and open to interpretation.

Even Bedouin families that produced evidence of owning property in Kuwait Town had trouble registering if they came from tribes with historical ties to other countries or owned land in what was now other countries.[121] Many Bedouin did not have any documentation to prove their ties to Kuwait. As Beaugrand notes, the committees often had access to "almost no documentary records to prove settlement before 1920" and did not always appear to understand Bedouin culture and norms of tribal membership.[122] There was a systemic lack of documents, or insufficient documents, and a bias against, or incomprehension of, nomadic ways to establish belonging. In place of applying the law, it appears that committees may have used alliances with the Kuwaiti royal family, rather than residence, to determine Bedouin eligibility, though more information is needed on this crucial period of Kuwait's history.

Many Bedouin may have refused to participate in registration, perhaps given negative experiences with previous attempts at controlling their movements through registration and taxation, though more research is needed on the perspectives of Bedouin families trying to navigate the registration process.[123] Others may not have had enough information on the process or did not understand its significance. As one descendant explained,

> [t]he appellant believes his paternal grandfather would have applied for citizenship under the 1959 Citizenship Law. However, as there was a limited period in which to do so and the grandfather was an illiterate nomad, possibly with little appreciation of the significance of such legal requirements, he cannot be certain of the actual situation.[124]

[119] Beaugrand, *Stateless in the Gulf* (n 17) 82–83.
[120] Beaugrand, *Statelessness and Transnationalism in Northern Arabia* (n 39) 83, 124–125.
[121] Lund-Johansen (n 117) 25.
[122] Beaugrand, *Stateless in the Gulf* (n 17) 83–84.
[123] Gilbert (n 11) 161.
[124] Refugee Appeal No 74467 New Zealand: Refugee Status Appeals Authority (1 September 2004).

The government later issued many former Bedouin with the official status of *bidoon jinsiyya* under a special administrative process.[125] Bedouin children were issued birth certificates certifying their birth in Kuwait and, if applicable, their *bidoon* status.[126] Many *bidoon* only had birth certificates but no other documentation. In 1965, the process of registering as an "original Kuwaiti" was closed.[127] The government also made issuance of a birth certificate compulsory, meaning that it became almost impossible to avoid the *bidoon* designation.[128] In 1969, the committee in charge of registrations was dismantled, and registration would now occur on an ad-hoc basis.

During the 1960s, the government also began a parallel program to naturalize a certain number of Bedouin from certain tribes considered allies of the Al-Sabah family. Naturalization was done on an ad hoc basis, making it a type of extralegal process with no appeals or judicial review.[129] The selected Bedouin received naturalization (*bi-l-tajannus*) by decree, as opposed to the status of Kuwaitis at birth (*bi-l-asl*) under the nationality law.[130] There was no question that naturalization was inferior to being an "original" Kuwaiti. Naturalized citizens could not vote for fifteen years, they could not pass on their nationality to their children, and the government could revoke naturalization at any time. For the government, selecting which Bedouin to naturalize was a political decision based on clan alliances and will be discussed in greater detail in chapter 4.[131]

Over time, the rules for naturalization became more and more restrictive, and the government imposed new document requirements. The naturalization program came to an end in 1980. Also in the 1980s, the Kuwaiti government became increasingly concerned that the *bidoon* population was being infiltrated by what they called outside agitators, particularly agents from Iraq, fears that appeared to be borne out during the Iraq invasion.[132] In

125 Longva (n 21) 188. See also Beaugrand, 'Statelessness and Transnationalism in Northern Arabia (n 39) 23; Beaugrand, *Stateless in the Gulf* (n 17) 86–89; P Carmichael, *Nomads* (Collins and Brown 1991) 122; Neil Partrick, 'Nationalism in the Gulf States' in David Held and Kristian Ulrichsen (eds), *The Transformation of the Gulf* (Routledge 2011) 56–57.

126 Sixty-fourth session Committee on the Rights of the Child, 'Item 4 of the provisional agenda: Consideration of reports of States parties: List of issues in relation to the second periodic report of Kuwait' (16 September–October 2013)

127 Lund-Johansen (n 117) 26.

128 The way Beaugrand describes the use of birth certifciates to establish nationality is to call them a type of "third-degree" nationality. Beaugrand, *Stateless in the Gulf* (n 17) 88, citing Fawzia and Al-Fahed. See also Beaugrand, 'Statelessness and Transnationalism in Northern Arabia (n 39) 129.

129 Beaugrand, *Stateless in the Gulf* (n 17) 86–87.

130 Ismael (n 21) 118–119. See also Longva (n 21) 188.

131 ibid 185–188.

132 Beaugrand, 'Statelessness and Transnationalism in Northern Arabia (n 39) 150. See also Longva (n 21) 188.

the decades since, the government has adopted several proposed solutions for the *bidoon* problem, including one-off registration drives, but in general, access to nationality and rights for the *bidoon* has only become more and more limited.[133] The government has set up a central body to resolve the status of the *bidoon*, the Central System to Resolve Illegal Residents' Status, but as of yet, little progress has been made, and the system is now being used to roll out various forms of biometric identification for stateless persons. Meanwhile, naturalized Kuwaitis continue to enjoy fewer rights than "original" Kuwaitis. The example of the descendants of Bedouin in Kuwait, therefore, demonstrates how a lack of registration during the colonial period and at decolonization laid the groundwork for statelessness. It also showed how subsequent civil registration entrenched, rather than resolved, nomadic statelessness and second-class nationality.

3.4.2 Civil Registration in Mali and Tuareg Exclusion

Lack of civil registration is common in Africa, particularly among rural populations, and is not a problem specific to nomadic peoples. According to UNICEF, Mali has a 50 percent birth registration rate, fairly average for African countries.[134] A lack of civil registration and documents does not mean that most Africans are stateless, though it does place them at risk. As Odinkalu, an expert on Nigerian nationality, puts it, "The African political, educated and urban elite emerged (from colonization) as a new class ripe with economic and social mobility, while uneducated, rural peoples remained locked in extended postcolonial exclusion."[135]

Many rural Africans, however, are afforded a presumption of nationality when interacting with state offices and officials, and many have gained

[133] Shiblak (n 42) 39. See also Beaugrand, 'Statelessness and Transnationalism in Northern Arabia (n 39) 149; Jill Crystal, 'Public Order and Authority: Policing Kuwait' in Paul Dresch and James Piscatori (eds), *Monarchies and Nations: Globalisation and Identity in the Arab States of the Gulf* (I B Tauris 2005) 178; Lund-Johansen (n 117) 45–46.

[134] UNICEF, 'Strengthening Birth Registration in Africa: Opportunities and Partnerships Technical Paper: Opportunities and Partnerships Technical Paper' (2012) 3, 7. See also African Commission on Human and Peoples' Rights, 'The Right to Nationality in Africa' (May 2014) paras 4, 186.

[135] Chidi A Odinkalu, 'Natives, Subjects, and Wannabes: Internal Citizenship Problems in Postcolonial Nigeria' in Rhoda E. Howard-Hassmann and Margaret Walton-Roberts (eds), *The Human Right to Citizenship: A Slippery Concept* (Pennsylvania UP 2015), 113. See also Derek Heater, *Citizenship: The Civic Ideal in World History, Politics and Education* (3rd edn, Manchester UP 2004), 133.

documents over the decades as African states slowly update their civil registration systems. This has emphatically not been true for many minorities, however, as Bronwen Manby, an expert on African nationality, noted in her survey of African nationality law.[136] As Manby puts it, "an undocumented person who is a member of the dominant ethnic or religious group and comes from a settled community and stable family is far less likely to be refused when applying for a nationality document."[137]

As Laura Smith, an expert on nationality in Ethiopia, puts it, "Although formal legal nationality had been assured in most countries of sub-Saharan Africa at independence, meaningful nationality has remained elusive for individuals who are members of particular groups."[138]

While more research is needed, experts have noted that pastoralists have fared particularly poorly in postcolonial African states. "It is striking to see how little difference independence made with respect to the central government's attitude towards nomadic pastoralists."[139]

As the African Committee of Experts on the Rights and Welfare of the Child notes, "[t]he Committee wishes to particularly stress the risk of becoming stateless for unregistered children of nomadic indigenous parents who frequently move across the borders of different countries."[140]

The Malian government also faces real and systemic challenges in registering nomadic peoples under colonial-influenced, administrative systems designed to encourage nomadic settlement. Poverty, illiteracy, and weak government structures all play a role in the lack of civil registration among the Tuareg. Also, cultural aspects of life in rural Africa may make registration difficult under the French legal system not designed for African contexts,[141] while fraud and fake Malian documents continue to be a problem across Mali.[142]

[136] Bronwen Manby, *Citizenship in Africa: The Law of Belonging* (Hart 2018) 330.

[137] Bronwen Manby, 'Who Belongs? Statelessness and Nationality in West Africa' (Migration Policy Inst 2016) 1.

[138] Laura Smith, *Making Citizens in Africa: Ethnicity, Gender and National Identity in Ethiopia* (CUP 2013) 21.

[139] Azarya (n 13), 26.

[140] Human Rights Committee, 'General Comment on Article 6 of the African Charter on the Rights and Welfare of the Child' (2014) 6, 29–30.

[141] Alexandre Zatzépine, *Le Droit de la Nationalité des Républiques Francophones d'Afrique et de Madagascar* (Librairie générale de droit et de jurisprudence 1967) 7–8.

[142] Michel Offermann, 'Les risques d'apatridie au Mali et pour les Maliens vivant à l'étranger en application des législations et pratiques relatives à la nationalité, au Mali et dans les pays d'accueil de Maliens' (UNHCR 2020), 32.

Unlike many other rural and unregistered Malians, however, the nationality status of the Tuareg is a highly controversial topic, such that their widespread lack of civil registration[143] must be understood in the context of the political question of their potential separatism, as well as the insecurity engendered by a state of almost constant conflict in Tuareg areas since political independence. This combination of factors places future generations of Tuareg at risk of statelessness in a part of the world now suffering from a vacuum of statehood.[144]

Since colonial independence, several major Tuareg uprisings have occurred in the three northern provinces of Gao, Kidal, and Timbuktu. The first was in the early 1960s, the second in the early 1990s, the third in 2006, and most recently in 2012, leading to a regional conflict and the current vacuum of Malian state authority in northern Mali. Civil war, and now regional war, has meant the Tuareg would continue to be subject to military rule and displacement, both within Mali and abroad, impeding civil registration of any kind, while continuing the violent debate over the very question of Tuareg inclusion in the Malian state.[145] Conflict is often a serious barrier to civil registration, particularly when it intersects with pastoralism and border disputes. As Bronwen Manby puts it, "In Africa, those most affected by statelessness include the descendants of colonial-era migrants, nomadic pastoralists, populations divided by arbitrary colonial borders or affected by more recent transfers of sovereignty, and those displaced by conflict."[146]

The roots of the present conflict lie in the failure to settle the question of Tuareg political autonomy at colonial independence. In 1960, French Soudan, renamed Mali, became independent from France under the socialist government of Modibo Keïta, whose attempts to abruptly liberate Mali from French economic and political domination would lead to a financial and political crisis.[147] The capital of Mali remained in the south of the country, at Bamako, and the government was dominated by urban and southern elites

[143] According to an interview with noted Mali specialist Arsène Brice Bado of the Centre de Recherche et d'Action pour la Paix (CERAP) in Abidjan, Cote d'Ivoire in Fall 2018.

[144] UNHCR, 'Global Report 2013, Mauritania' (2013) 2, on the risk of statelessness for the Tuareg in the region.

[145] According to an interview with noted Mali specialist Arsène Brice Bado of the Centre de Recherche et d'Action pour la Paix (CERAP) in Abidjan, Cote d'Ivoire in Fall 2018.

[146] Manby, *Citizenship in Africa* (n 136) 1–2, 18, 330.

[147] Loi no 60-14 du 20 juin 1960 'proclamant solennellement l'indépendance nationale de la fédération du Mali,' JOFM 383 (22 juin 1960). See also P Decheix, 'Le Code de la Nationalité Malienne' (1963) 697 Penant 300, 302; Diarrah (n 102) 37–64; Gaudio (n 100) 107. Note that Mali was briefly federated with what is now Senegal.

educated under the French system. As Lecocq notes, even "the name of the new republic reflected the dominance of its core populations: the Mande and Bambara."[148] Post-independence, Malian land use policy in the north continued colonial policy, with the promotion of agriculture the central focus, though mining and oil exploration would become increasingly important over the decades, as will be discussed in greater detail in chapter 5.

The Malian government placed the northern Kidal province back under military rule following the Tuareg separatist conflict that broke out in 1963, with widespread oppression against Tuareg leaders. The region to the south near the Niger River, where the Tuareg and Fulani were heavily mixed with settled Songhai and other groups, saw the aggressive introduction of programs to promote agriculture at the expense of pastoralism and the nationalization of land and key sectors of the economy.[149] All these policies had disastrous effects on pastoralists' ability to pursue pastoralism just at the time when the introduction of the Malian Franc led to an economic crisis throughout the country, during which pastoralists were not eligible for government subsidies like other communities.[150] Throughout the period following independence, settlement of pastoralists accelerated, accompanied by, as Bourgeot describes it, a breakdown of Tuareg society and relations between the Tuareg and the new government.[151]

The Tuareg are, therefore, experiencing a particular set of circumstances that greatly increase their chances of statelessness. The present-day lack of Tuareg civil registration stems in large part from the civil war over Tuareg independence,[152] which not only impedes registration but presents the registration of the Tuareg as a potential security risk to the Malian state rather than a technical problem to be solved with the proper resources. The problem of Tuareg civil registration has, therefore, been subsumed into a larger conflict over the question of Tuareg separatism.

Even if armed conflict had never occurred, however, it's possible that many Tuareg would still have faced serious barriers to registration. It's worth examining these potential barriers because they demonstrate that merely

[148] Lecocq, *Disputed Desert* (n 89) 73.
[149] ibid 78–81. See also Diarrah (n 102) 42 (on agriculture being identified as the "pillar" of the Malian economy); Gaudio (n 100) 245–248.
[150] Diarrah (n 102) 43, 46–64 (on the Malian franc). See also Boilley (n 9) 316 (on Malian economic policy toward the Tuareg during the period of the Malian franc).
[151] Bourgeot, *Les sociétés touarègues* (n 16) 268–269.
[152] Interview with Mali specialist Arsène Brice Bado of the Centre de Recherche et d'Action pour la Paix (CERAP) in Abidjan, Cote d'Ivoire in Fall 2018.

ending the armed conflict in northern Mali will not automatically solve the problem of Tuareg registration. When the *Loi Lamine Guèye* of 1946 granted French nationality to the inhabitants of the overseas territories, it employed the term *ressortissants*,[153] usually translated as "nationals," but also meaning anyone who was under colonial protection.[154] Weis notes that French courts had sometimes "given the term a wider meaning than 'national' to include . . . protégés, protected persons."[155] Verwilghen notes that the term included not only nationals but "privileged foreigners."[156] The term *ressortissant* would be repeated in the 1946 Constitution, which would, in turn, be used as the basis for the nationality laws of many of the newly independent colonial states.

> All "*ressortissants*" (nationals/protected persons) of the overseas territories have the quality of a citizen on the same basis as French citizens of the metropole or of the overseas territories. Specific laws will establish the conditions under which they will exercise their rights as citizens.[157]

Tuareg confederations living across French colonies in Africa would likely have qualified as *ressortissants* of France, but this vast area was now bisected by borders, many of which went through Tuareg areas. One of the first tasks of the Malian government was to replace French colonial nationality with Malian nationality by creating a concrete category of persons who would qualify as Mali's "first body of nationals" and excluding those who would now be the nationals of foreign states, including adjacent former French colonies like Niger and Algeria.

Nationality was first established by a transitional Ordinance in 1960,[158] followed by a permanent nationality code in 1962.[159] The Ordinance adopted

[153] Tendant à proclamer citoyens tous les ressortissants des territoires d'outre-mer, Loi no 46-940, 30 JORF 3888 (7 mai 1946).

[154] Marc Verwilghen, *Conflits de nationalités, Plurinationalité et apatridie* (Brill 1999) 86–88. See also Weis (n 5) 8; Crawford, *The Creation of States in International Law* (n 12) 317.

[155] Weis (n 5) 9.

[156] Verwilghen (n 154) 86 (my translation).

[157] Constitution of 27 October 1946, *Republic of France* (27 October 1946) art 80 (my translation). See also Décret no 53-161 du 24 février 1953 déterminant les modalités d'application du code de la nationalité française dans les territoires d'outre-mer, 50 JORF 1984 (27 février 1953); Paul Lagarde, *La Nationalité Française* (4th edn, Dalloz 1989) 307–321.

[158] Ordonnance no 55 du 24 novembre 1960 'relative à l'attribution de la nationalité malienne à tous les ressortissants de la République du Mali' JORM (24 novembre 1960) 986. Provisions in French law for retaining French nationality may be found in Loi no 60-752 du 28 juillet 1960 'portant modification de certaines dispositions du code de la nationalité,' JORF *du 30 juillet 1960* (28 juillet 1960). See also Heather Alexander, 'Report on Citizenship Law: Mali' (GlobalCit 2020); Decheix (n 147) 302.

[159] Loi no 62-18 AN-RM du 3 février 1962 portant Code de la nationalité malienne telle que modifié par la Loi no 95-70 du 25 août 1995(25 août 1995). The code was updated in 1995 and replaced by the *Code des Personnes et de la Famille* in 2011.

a territorial approach and was heavily influenced by French nationality law, with its focus on *jus sanguinis* and double birth. Article 1 of the transitional Ordinance stated that all "*ressortissants*" of Mali were now Malian nationals, except French citizens and those with French civil status, and their spouses and descendants.[160] This clause was unclear and vague given that it was never established to what extent specific Tuareg confederations were under Malian, as opposed to Nigerian or Algerian, protection. Article 68 of the subsequent 1962 Malian Nationality Code adopted the concept of residence to establish eligibility, with a strong presumption of nationality for those living in Mali.

> All persons *resident* in Mali at the time of the enactment of the nationality code are presumed nationals of Mali unless proven otherwise. Nationality certificates should not be issued unless residence can be proven or local public officials such as the *chef d'arrondissement* attest that the individual has the *de facto* status of being Malian.[161]

Lawyer and former chef of administration for the French *Outre-mer*, Alexandre Zatzépine, in his analysis of the law, argued that "residence" meant habitual residence.[162] The fact that the Tuareg were nomadic and split across multiple states left their place of habitual residency somewhat vague. While colonial-era documents could have been used as evidence of Tuareg residency, the lack of a robust, colonial-era *état-civil* would have left many Tuareg in a gray zone of eligibility, even if the government had attempted a thorough registration drive among pastoral populations.

As was common in Francophone West Africa, Malian law provided a solution on paper to this problem by granting a presumption of nationality for those who had always behaved as nationals and been accepted as nationals by the authorities.[163] While this presumption was very helpful to many rural and unregistered Malian villagers, for many Tuareg, the *chef d'arrondissement* was a middle-level functionary who was often not Tuareg, due to the French custom of giving jobs in the colonial administration to sedentary communities and the fact that southerners ran the new government.

[160] Loi n. 60-752 du 28 juillet 1960 portant modification de certaines dispositions du code de la nationalité (28 juillet 1960). See also Decheix, 302.

[161] Code de la Nationalité Malienne Loi No 6218 of 3 February 1962 as modified by the Loi No 9570 of 25 August 1995 and replaced by the Loi 2011-087 of 30 December 2011 (my translation).

[162] Zatzépine (n 141) 20–21. My italics and translation.

[163] ibid 20–21, citing to Malian *Circulaire d'application no 331*. See also Bronwen Manby, 'Trends in Citizenship Law and Politics in Africa Since the Colonial Era' in E. Isin and P. Nyers (ed), *Routledge Handbook of Global Citizenship Studies* (Routledge 2014) 174.

It was, in fact, very common in postcolonial Mali for this tradition to continue, with southerners sent to northern Mali to serve as administrators. These problems demonstrate that even had the war never happened, Tuareg civil registration would likely have been a fraught exercise.

Even if a lasting peace is declared in northern Mali and the government enacts a robust and transparent registration drive in northern Mali, including granting the Tuareg the presumption of Malian nationality, the French-influenced system of civil registration arguably creates extra barriers to Tuareg registration due to its complexity. The Certificate of Nationality, the cornerstone of nationality documentation under French-influenced systems, became the primary document establishing Malian nationality.[164] As a matter of daily use, the identity card, the *Carte Nationale d'Identité* (CNI), issued pursuant to a decree in 1988,[165] is usually sufficient to establish nationality in most cases today, and it, or a *carte consulaire* if abroad, is now obligatory.[166] Mali is moving to a system of biometric registration. In 2006, Mali rolled out a new law providing a universal ID number, called the "NINA card,"[167] which is obligatory for all Malian citizens, residents, and others on Malian territory and under its legal jurisdiction.[168] Other forms of ID in Mali that are relevant to proving nationality include the birth certificate, the *Jugement supplétif d'acte de naissance,* and the Family Book, issued to the head of household. The number of different types of documents and the complex procedures sometimes used to obtain them would likely complicate any effort to register Tuareg populations in northern Mali.

The Malian government made some changes in 2006 and 2011 to help nomadic peoples register, which may help to resolve some of the legal and technical problems described in this section. Article 1 of the 2006 law on civil registration expressly provided for mobile clinics to register nomadic peoples.[169] A 2011 law allows for the creation of special birth registration centers

[164] Zatzépine (n 162) 101. Title V regulates the issuance of nationality documents. See also Decheix (n 147) 309.

[165] Décret no 014/PG- RM du 09 janvier 1988 portant institution et règlementation de la délivrance de la carte d'identité et de la carte consulaire, Décret no 014/PG- RM (09 janvier 1988).

[166] Mali Décret no 55-014/PG-RM du 9 janvier 1988, no 55-014/PG-RM (9 janvier 1988).

[167] 'NINA card, including date and circumstances of its introduction; method used to collect data on future cardholders, including data collection period; opportunity to correct or update card information, such as place of residence and occupation; procedure to correct or update card information' (26 August 2016 Canada: Immigration and Refugee Board of Canada).

[168] Loi no 06-040 du 11 août 2006 portant institution du numéro d'identification nationale des personnes physiques et morales (Mali).

[169] Loi no 06-024 du 28 juin 2006 régissant l'État civil (2006); Offermann (n 142) 14, 33.

in nomadic areas.[170] Mali also created a commission to study the issue of statelessness, including nomadic statelessness, in 2014,[171] and attempted a mass registration exercise in 2015 targeting returning refugees and internally displaced persons (IDPs), including many Tuareg.[172] At the regional level, the ECOWAS (Economic Community of West African States) Protocol on Transhumance (1998) mandates that pastoralists have identity documents, but it does not provide a mechanism by which herders can prove their eligibility, and it has not led to better registration policies for nomadic peoples in Mali.[173]

Between 2013 and 2016, bilateral treaties were signed between Mali and Niger, on the one hand, and Mauritania and Burkina Faso, on the other, including provisions for the return of Malian refugees to Mali, with the Office of the UN High Commissioner of Refugees (UNHCR) issuing travel documents for them.[174] The situation in northern Mali was so unstable, however, that many were not ready to return.[175] According to interviews conducted as part of a 2019 study by UNHCR, most registration centers in Tuareg regions in northern Mali are not functioning.[176] Many Tuareg are also stateless in Libya.[177]

The question of Tuareg registration and documents continues to be closely linked to the issue of elections, just as the question of Tuareg inclusion influenced voting in the colonial period. In 2013, UNHCR attempted to arrange for out-of-country voting for Malian refugees, including Tuareg, but the program was not implemented by the Malian government and the rate of voting among the displaced and refugee population remains low.

[170] Loi no 11-080 portant code des personnes et de la famille, JORM Spécial (31 January 2012) art 84.

[171] Décision no 2014-0191/MJDH-SG Mali, Création d'un comité interministériel sur l'apatridie (17 November 2014).

[172] Reliefweb, 'Thousands to receive birth certificates in Mali' (18 February 2015) <https://reliefweb.int/report/mali/thousands-receive-birth-certificates-mali> accessed 19 April 2024.

[173] Relating to the regulations on Transhumance between ECOWAS Member States Twenty-first conference of heads of states, Abuja., Decision A/DEC.5/10/98 (31 October 1998) art 12.

[174] Offermann (n 142) 58.

[175] UN High Commissioner for Refugees, 'Mali Situation: UNHCR Regional Update, December 2015–February 2016' <https://reliefweb.int/report/mali/mali-situation-unhcr-regional-update-december-2015-february-2016> accessed 29 April 2024. See also Refugees Deeply, 'In Limbo: Malian Refugees in Burkina Faso' (20 April 2016) <https://deeply.thenewhumanitarian.org/refugees/community/2016/04/20/in-limbo-malian-refugees-in-burkina-faso> accessed 27 May 2024.

[176] Offermann (n 142) 28–29.

[177] US Department of State, 'US Country Reports on Human Rights Practices for 2013, Libya (2013). See also Intl Deplacement Monitoring Centre, '2016 Africa Report on Internal Displacement' (December 2016).

Meanwhile, the lack of civil registration and identity documents has a very real and negative effect on the ability of many Tuareg to continue pastoralism and maintain family and social connections across borders, as this excerpt from a story by Al Jazeera demonstrates: "Some of those who have registered told Al Jazeera that their real motive is to acquire Malian national ID cards that would hopefully facilitate their movement across the border and within Mali and help them revisit their families back home."[178]

These legal and technical solutions, however, have been ineffective in the face of continuing conflict, which now includes combatants from throughout the region, Islamic terrorist groups that recruit from both the Tuareg and, increasingly, Fulani populations, and Russian mercenaries hired by Mali's new president, who came to power in a coup in 2021.

3.4.3 Civil Registration in Malaysia and Sama Dilaut Exclusion

The Sama Dilaut suffer from ongoing and systemic exclusion from civil registration that is directly linked to their cross-border nomadism. Irregular cross-border migrants in Malaysia generally suffer from statelessness.[179] Disputes over the linked questions of nationality and contested borders have only gained prominence in Southeast Asia over the decades, as evidenced by what Alice Nah calls "the remarkable steadfastness of ASEAN states in holding onto a Westphalian notion of state sovereignty, in particular, when constructing immigration control regimes."[180]

Accurate statistics on documentation among the Sama Dilaut community are unavailable, but civil society groups have noted that the Sama Dilaut generally suffer from low levels of documentation even when compared to other indigenous groups in Sabah.[181] Rural registration rates are low across Southeast Asia, but whereas the government treats lack of registration and

[178] M. Vall, 'Anger in Refugee Camp ahead of Mali Vote: Refugees on Mauritanian Border with Mali Are Angry as they Have Yet to Get IDs ahead of Crucial Elections' *Al Jazeera*. See also Office of the Commissioner General for Refugees and Stateless Persons, *Libya: Nationality, Registration and Documents*, December 2014) 11.

[179] Rodziana M. Razali, Rohaida Nordin and Tamara J. Duraisingam, 'Migration and Statelessness: Turning the Spotlight on Malaysia' (2015) 23 Pertanika J Soc Sci Human 19, 22–23, 28–29.

[180] Alice Nah, 'Globalisation, Sovereignty and Immigration Control: The Hierarchy of Rights for Migrant Workers in Malaysia' (2012) 40 Asian J Soc Sci 486, 487.

[181] Right 2 Identity Newsletter, June 2015 (no longer available online). See also the work of Helen Blunt.

documents among the rural poor in Sabah as a technical problem that is the responsibility of the government to solve,[182] it views the Sama Dilaut's lack of registration as a security issue and evidence of their nonnational status and criminality. The hardening of colonial-era borders has caused governments in the region to reframe the question of Sama Dilaut registration not as a technical issue to be solved by a registration drive but as one of national security.

In 1963, following the results of a survey by the Cobbold Commission indicating that the majority of the population of Borneo favored joining Malaysia, the Malaysia Act amended the constitution to join Sabah (North Borneo) and neighboring Sarawak with peninsula Malaysia.[183] The extent to which the Commission considered the needs or opinions of nomadic populations is unclear. Sabahans had ten years within which to register as Malaysian nationals.[184] The constitution also provided for the creation of a national registration department (NRD).[185] Vague language around residence in Sabah left a great deal of room for interpretation in applying the law to nomadic and border populations.

The laws creating the first body of nationals in Sabah and Sarawak were different than those of Peninsular Malaysia. Under the 1957 Constitution, persons "ordinarily resident" in Sabah and Sarawak for seven years prior to Malaysia Day were nationals of Malaysia if they were either born, registered, or naturalized in the Borneo territories and satisfied certain other requirements, including knowledge of Malay, English, or "any native language currently in use in Sarawak."[186] The provision was clearly intended to ease registration in the Borneo territories, a region with less of a history with formal registration in comparison to the Peninsular states. The law, however, adopted a territorial approach based on "ordinary residence," a potentially vague term when it came to a nomadic, ocean-going population like the Sama Dilaut.

[182] Winnie Kasmir, '70,000 Late Registration Cases in Sabah' Borneo Post accessed 21 April 2024.

[183] North Borneo and Sarawak The Commission of Enquiry, 1961-1962, 'Report of the Commission of Enquiry, North Borneo and Sarawak, 1962 (Cobbold Commission)' (21 June 1962). The Constitution was later amended to remove reference to Singapore.

[184] See also Visu Sinnadurai, 'Nationality and International Law in the Perspective of the Federation of Malaysia' in Ko Swan Sik (ed), *Nationality and International Law in Asian Perspective* (Martinus Nijhoff 1990) 325, 331.

[185] Malaysian Federal Const (1957, rev 2007), Second Schedule pts I–III.

[186] Malaysian Const, art 16(a) and Second Schedule pts I–III (1957).

According to Clifford Sather, anthropologist and expert on the Sama Dilaut, many Sama Dilaut could not prove they qualified for nationality under the law.[187] Sather's work provides what might be the clearest picture of Sama Dilaut registration, where he describes the divide that appeared between more land-based populations, which were registered, and Sama Dilaut, who were themselves divided between those who could establish residency and those who could not, or did not, because they did not see the purpose of Malaysian documents. Lack of civil registration created a "major division" at independence in Semporna between those from the Bajau/Sama community who were now nationals of Malaysia and those who were not. According to Sather, the registration of Sama Dilaut was quickly complicated by the arrival of many refugees from the southern Philippines, who were themselves of Sama/Bajau ethnicity.

The Sabah government began a sponsorship program for noncitizens in Sabah, whereby temporary workers must obtain a Malaysian national as a sponsor in order to remain. When the program began, it classified many Sama Dilaut not as nationals but as aliens, though more research is needed on this critical moment in Sama Dilaut history. As a result, many Sama Dilaut were required to find a guarantor from among the settled population, often Bajau peoples themselves, and pay their guarantor a tax. Carol Warren compared this work permit system, descended from the traditional patronage arrangements dating from the precolonial period, to a type of indentured labor.[188] It could also be said to mark the beginning of formal statelessness for many Sama Dilaut families because it was the beginning of their classification as aliens (or refugees) rather than nationals, beginning an association between Sama Dilaut and refugees that would continue over subsequent decades.[189] The impact of this framing on the indigenous status of the Sama Dilaut will be discussed further in chapter 5.

Also relevant is the fact that during NRD rural registration drives,[190] Sama Dilaut nomadic peoples were not afforded the same presumption of nationality as settled and unregistered rural communities.[191] According to testimony given during a Royal Commission of Inquiry into immigration and ID in Sabah, a registration exercise for the Sama Dilaut was last conducted in

[187] Sather, *The Bajau Laut* (n 51) 87–88.
[188] Warren (n 63), 228.
[189] Sather, *The Bajau Laut* (n 51) 332 (discussing nomadic Sama Dilaut as refugees).
[190] 'Mobile Court Brings Citizenship to Villagers' *Daily Express* (20 May 2015), accessed 21 April 2024.
[191] Sather, *The Bajau Laut* (n 51) 87 (where he states that up to 40 percent of Bajau Laut were considered to be *pelarian*, or refugees).

the 1960s,[192] but it required a recognized village headman (a title conferred by the government), something most Sama Dilaut communities did not have.[193] Over subsequent decades, the Malaysian government tightened registration procedures as the issue of immigration to Sabah became highly politicized. Many who did not register in the decade following independence were locked out of the system, leading to intergenerational statelessness.[194]

Beginning in 1990, under the National Registration Regulation, applicants had to produce both a birth certificate and their parents' identity cards. This made it virtually impossible for the children of undocumented persons to register. In 2002, ID cards were replaced with the MyKad smart card containing a chip with biometric data, including race, thumbprints, ID cards, voting status, banking info, health information, criminal record, and more.[195] This card is an example of how digital and biometric IDs worldwide have raised the stakes for unregistered populations like many nomadic peoples. The lack of identity documents has serious repercussions for the Sama Dilaut (as it does for other stateless people in Sabah). For example, Sama Dilaut children cannot attend Malaysian government schools, Sama Dilaut are regularly detained, and the Malaysian government sometimes deports Sama Dilaut to the Philippines.[196] According to media reports, the Malaysian government has also begun issuing identity documents to undocumented communities in Sabah that officially register them as noncitizens.[197]

As the issue of statelessness in Sabah has been taken up as a human rights issue by civil society and the media, the government has promised to address it.[198]

[192] Testimony of a Sama Dilaut village leader in Tan Sri Datuk Amar Steve Shim Lip Kiong (Chairman) and Commissioners, 'Report of the Commission of Enquiry on Immigrants in Sabah' (Royal Commission of Enquiry 2012) 219. See also F Holst, *Ethnicization and Identity Construction in Malaysia* (Routledge 2012) 135.

[193] Sather, *The Bajau Laut* (n 51) 203–204.

[194] Helen Brunt, 'Stateless Stakeholders: Seen but Not Heard? The Case of the Sama Dilaut in Sabah, Malaysia' (masters thesis, U Sussex 2013) 291. See also 'Thousands Register for Green MyKad' *Malaysia Today* <http://www.malaysia-today.net/thousands-register-for-green-mykad/>.

[195] See generally Thomas Mathews, 'Is Malaysia's Mykad the 'One Card to Rule Them All'? The Urgent Need to Develop a Proper Legal Framework for the Protection of Personal Information in Malaysia' (2004) 28 Melbourne U L Rev 474. See also the Malaysian NRD website <http://www.jpn.gov.my/en/perkhidmatan/kanak-kanak-bawah-12-tahun/> accessed 22 October 2024.

[196] Chan Tau Chou and L Gooch, 'Malaysia's Invisible Children' (2015) *Al Jazeera* <https://www.aljazeera.com/features/2016/7/5/malaysias-invisible-children> accessed 23 October 2024. I am indebted to Helen Brunt for her comments on this point.

[197] See for example Muguntan Vanar, 'Sabah Set to Issue Foreigner Cards for Refugees, Stateless People' *The Star* (2022) <https://www.thestar.com.my/news/nation/2022/06/02/sabah-set-to-issue-foreigner-cards-for-refugees-stateless-people> accessed 23 October 2024.

[198] See for example 'Sabah Must Emulate Sarawak, Help Stateless Children: Warisan Rep: Sri Tanjong's Justin Wong Laments Slowness to Act to Solve Issue' *Philippine Daily Inquirer* (27 March 2023) accessed 21 April 2024.

Malaysia has joined other regional governments and the United Nations Economic and Social Commission for Asia and the Pacific to "Get Everyone in the Picture" by improving civil registration, including birth registration.[199] In neighboring Philippines, Bajau communities have benefited from birth registration drives.[200] Malaysia has also signed a tripartite agreement on statelessness with the Philippines and Indonesia and a Memorandum of Understanding with Indonesia,[201] but these initiatives have not resolved the status of many Sama Dilaut.

Even as the region pushes for greater cooperation and trade, and as freedom of movement has increased for certain segments of society, such as foreign workers who qualify under the "smart card" program between Singapore and Indonesia, there has been a corresponding increase in restrictions and reduction on mobility for "sea nomads," irregular migrants, and other so-called undesirable groups.[202] The issue of statelessness in Sabah has arguably been subsumed into a larger conversation over illegal immigration to Sabah and border security.[203] The framing of Sama Dilaut mobility as a problem for border security mirrors colonial-era concerns with piracy,[204] even though the Sama Dilaut are often the victims of piracy rather than the perpetrators.[205] In order to work in Malaysia and avoid punishment, imprisonment, and deportation, irregular migrants allegedly purchase fake documents.[206] The issue has been widely reported in the media and elsewhere and also linked to voter fraud.[207] As a result, even as the region's governments

[199] See the webpage of UNESCAP, 'Get Everyone in the Picture' <https://www.getinthepicture.org/> accessed 7 October 2024.

[200] See for example 'Badjaos Recognized through Pilot Birth Registration' (17 December 2019) accessed July 2020. See also R Lacuata, 'Unlisted No More: Sama Bajaus in Zamboanga City Get Birth Certificates' ABS-CBN News (10 December 2019) accessed July 2020.

[201] See for example 'Malaysia, Indonesia to Tackle Sabah Stateless Issue' *The Star* (24 April 2019) accessed 21 April 2024. See also 'Stateless: Three-Nation Pact Soon' *Daily Express* (25 July 2018) accessed 21 April 2024.

[202] Cynthia Chou, *The Orang Suku Laut of Riau, Indonesia: The Inalienable Gift of Territory* (Routledge 2010) 118–119, 127 (on the Orang Suku Laut, a sea nomadic group, border restrictions, and the Growth Triangle between Indonesia, Malaysia, and Singapore).

[203] Andrew Carruthers, 'Sabah ICs for Sabahans: Will it Help?' (2016) Yusof Ishak Inst 1.

[204] Eklöf (n 59) 157.

[205] ibid 41–43.

[206] Tan Sri Datuk Amar Steve Shim Lip Kiong (Chairman) and Commissioners, 'Report of the Commission of Enquiry on Immigrants in Sabah' (Royal Commission of Enquiry 2012) 305–308. See also Fausto Barlocco, *Identity and the State in Malaysia* (Routledge 2014) 77–79 (on public perceptions of immigration in Sabah).

[207] Kamal Sadiq, 'When States Prefer Non-Citizens over Citizens: Conflict over Illegal Immigration into Malaysia' (2005) 49 Intl Stud Q 102. See also 'RCI Report: Who Are the Illegals?' *The Star* (accessed 4 December 2014; 22 April 2024); Romzi Ationg, 'Citizenship-for-Votes Scandal in Sabah' New Mandala (28 April 2013, accessed 22 April 2024).

pursue greater freedom of movement to boost the economy, there has been a corresponding increase in restrictions and a reduction on mobility for nomadic groups and irregular migrants. Perhaps unsurprisingly, after years of struggle for recognition and hostile treatment by successive governments dating to the colonial period, Helen Brunt, who has interviewed the Sama Dilaut, reports that they have a great deal of mistrust and confusion around registration and that they are often the victims of document scams, which is then used as further evidence of their supposed criminality.[208]

3.4.4 Civil Registration in Côte d'Ivoire and Fulani Exclusion

Many nomadic Fulani are not stateless because they hold documents from countries in the region that practice *jus soli*, including Mali and Burkina Faso. In Côte d'Ivoire, it is children born in the sedentary Fulani community who are at risk of statelessness due to restrictive nationality laws and a lack of civil registration. Nomadic Fulani, however, rely on an increasingly stateless sedentary community to access pastorage and liaise with landowners and the police in Côte d'Ivoire. Their lack of Ivorian identity documents also impacts their ability to cross the border, facts which call into question solutions for nomadic statelessness at the individual state level that do not protect nomadism as a way of life at the community and regional level.

Statelessness among the sedentary Fulani community is part of a much larger problem of statelessness in Côte d'Ivoire, which became independent from France in 1960 under the presidency of Félix Houphouët-Boigny. Neighboring Burkina Faso also gained independence as Upper Volta the same year, fixing in place the border imposed in 1919 by the French government between the two colonies with enormous consequences for the Fulani. In the 1960s and 1970s, however, there were few border restrictions between Mali and Côte d'Ivoire, and Fulani began moving to Côte d'Ivoire in response to desertification in the Sahel, problems with Mali's new, antipastoral government, and access the growing market for beef in Côte d'Ivoire's expanding cities. The Ivorian government also encouraged this migration in the 1970s, when the SODREPA project, funded in part by the German

[208] I am indebted to Helen Brunt for her comments on this issue.

government, supported transhumance and pastoralism, including free vaccination programs for cattle.[209]

Meanwhile, political conflict, desertification, and other factors led Fulani from Burkina Faso to relocate to Côte d'Ivoire, often passing via Mali due to increased border restrictions between Burkina Faso and Côte d'Ivoire. Immediately following independence, some Fulani became sedentary and established a village in northern Côte d'Ivoire. Other Fulani migrated to Côte d'Ivoire in the 1990s for wage employment and to participate in sedentary forms of herding under a system of *tutorat*, herding cattle on behalf of wealthy landowners. Meanwhile, in recent decades, desertification and conflict have made northern Côte d'Ivoire a crucial part of pastoral routes in the region. However, the tse tse fly makes pastoralism in southern Côte d'Ivoire impossible. According to Diallo, many nomadic communities were circulating between northern Côte d'Ivoire and Burkina Faso as recently as the 1990s,[210] and interviews in 2019 confirm that nomadic communities continue to cross the border to northern Côte d'Ivoire before the border closings of the 2020 global pandemic.

Fulani integration in northern Côte d'Ivoire, however, has been very difficult since the 1990s, as Côte d'Ivoire's role in the region as an immigration destination from its poorer neighbors to the north, coupled with its restrictive nationality laws and complex system of civil registration, has produced anti-immigrant policies and one of the highest rates of statelessness in West Africa. The children of urban and settled Fulani who were born in Côte d'Ivoire form part of this stateless group. The identity documents held by nomadic Fulani from neighboring countries do not secure them any rights within Côte d'Ivoire, including, most importantly, the right to access grazing land.

The statelessness of sedentary Fulani has an impact on nomadic Fulani, as the two communities are closely linked. Sedentary Fulani men play an important mediation role between nomadic Fulani and farmers. Sedentary Fulani mediators are needed for nomadic Fulani to camp on farmland.[211] Nationality in Côte d'Ivoire is also required to own land, which means that most sedentary Fulani cannot own land in Côte d'Ivoire, either under

209 Diallo (2008), 189–204.
210 ibid 194.
211 ibid 197–198.

formal or customary law.[212] This leaves pastoral Fulani at the mercy of local landowners who are not Fulani and have little incentive to support the nomadic way of life. Recently, a surge in refugees crossing the border from Sahel countries has caused relations between Fulani pastoralists, local government officials, and local landowners to worsen, further putting pastoralism in northern Côte d'Ivoire at risk. The Ivoirian government has branded Fulani migration to northern Côte d'Ivoire as a security risk, conflating Fulani migrations with infiltration by terrorist groups, even as terrorist attacks and violence have driven many civilians across the border, including many Fulani.

Even before this period of violence, it was difficult for settled Fulani born in Côte d'Ivoire to obtain ID. Like Mali, Côte d'Ivoire has established a complex documentation regime based on the French system that creates problems for immigrant and minority groups even in the absence of conflict.[213] A complex birth registration system requires families to register their children's births during the first four months of life or go through an expensive and time-consuming judicial process to obtain a *judgement supplétif* from the courts. While the law was updated in 2018 to expand access to civil registration and cut down on fraud, and a special law was introduced the same year to assist unregistered persons in obtaining birth certificates,[214] it remains very difficult for many rural people to obtain a birth certificate, and birth registration is crucial to proving descent from an Ivoirian national under the law. In the 1990s, the government of Henri Konan Bédié introduced new documentation restrictions on foreigners, requiring them to carry a residency card *(carte de séjour)*. While there is a procedure for naturalization in Cote d'Ivoire requiring two years of residence, in practice, few people achieve Ivorian nationality this way due to the difficulty and expense of the process, corruption, lack of knowledge of the procedures by local authorities, and the inability to provide the proper documentation, including birth certificates.[215]

[212] Norwegian Refugee Council, 'Land Conflict and Food Security in the Liberian-Ivoirian Border Region' (December 2012) 12.

[213] World Bank, 'ID4D: Country Diagnostic: Côte d'Ivoire' (World Bank Group 2016).

[214] De rétablissement d'identité et de transcription d'acte de naissance, 101 JOR Côte d'Ivoire 17 Decembre 2018 1277. Loi no 2018-862 relative à l'etat civil; Loi no 2018-863 du 19 Novembre 2018 instituant une procédure spéciale de déclaration de naissance, JOR Côte d'Ivoire (17 Decembre 2018).

[215] Mirna Adjami, 'Statelessness and Nationality in Côte d'Ivoire—A Study for UNHCR' (December 2016) 24.

Like many other African countries, the government is rolling out a biometric ID system in partnership with the privately run Semlex company.[216] Neighboring Burkina Faso[217] and Mali[218] are also putting biometric ID systems into place, as is ECOWAS.[219] Because Côte d'Ivoire is home to many stateless and undocumented persons,[220] it is not clear how the rollout of a biometric ID card might impact human rights relating to the practice of nomadism. There is a risk that vulnerable populations and minorities, including Fulani, will be unregistered, further pushing them into the shadows, or that they will officially be registered as noncitizens.[221]

An internal study for UNHCR identified five main weaknesses in the civil registration system in Côte d'Ivoire: (1) the destruction of civil registries because of the Ivoirian civil war, (2) the centralization in Abidjan of the registration and production of birth certificates for persons born to foreign parents, (3) the distance from nomadic camps and remote villages to civil registration offices, (4) how registration agents are recruited and their lack of training and resources, and (5) the existence of a large trade in fake documents, which has created mistrust between the Malian and Burkinabè communities, on one side, and the Ivorian government on the other.[222] Many Burkinabè and Malians, including Fulani, use other people's documents to get by in a country where, as in many other parts of the world, documents are now required for many social services and to access jobs.

Interviews with sedentary and nomadic Fulani men in northern Côte d'Ivoire in 2019 provide a snapshot of their views on civil registration and

[216] Semlex, 'Semlex in Côte d'Ivoire' <https://www.semlex.com/2021/10/12/semlex-cote-divoire-2/> accessed 22 April 2024.

[217] World Bank, 'Country Diagnostic, Burkina Faso' <https://documents.worldbank.org/pt/publication/documents-reports/documentdetail/653431522763079651/id4d-country-diagnostic-burkina-faso> accessed 22 April 2024.

[218] Canada: Imm and Ref Board of Canada, 'Mali: NINA card, including date and circumstances of its introduction; method used to collect data on future cardholders, including data collection period; opportunity to correct or update card information, such as place of residence and occupation; procedure to correct or update card information (2009-September 2016)' (2016).

[219] Ayang Macdonald, 'ECOWAS Agrees to Accelerate Implementation of ENBIC Regional ID Card for Stronger Integration' (2024) Biometric Update <https://www.biometricupdate.com/202410/ecowas-agrees-to-accelerate-implementation-of-enbic-regional-id-card-for-stronger-integration> accessed 22 October 2024

[220] Adjami (n 215). See also Manby, *Citizenship in Africa* (n 136) 48–50.

[221] See the discussion in Richard Banegas and Armando Cutolo, *ID Wars in Côte d'Ivoire: A Political Ethnography of Identification and Citizenship* (OUP 2024), ch 5. For more on the issue of statelessness in Côte d'Ivoire, see Heather Alexander, 'The Ethics of Counting Statelessness' in Tendayi Bloom and Lindsey N Kingston, 'Statelessness, Governance, and the Problem of Citizenship' (Manchester UP 2021).

[222] Unpublished 2019 UNHCR internal report, 4–6.

the challenges they face. Only Fulani whose families had settled in Cote d'Ivoire prior to colonial independence had Ivorian nationality documents, though interest in Ivoirian nationality among young Fulani men born in Côte d'Ivoire who are members of the settled community is high. By contrast, many nomadic people have identity documents from neighboring countries, and interest in Ivorian nationality is low. Nomadic Fulani men associate registration with the payment of taxes, and identity documents are mostly seen as a way to avoid arrest and fines as they move through Côte d'Ivoire on their seasonal migrations. Many of the Fulani men interviewed in seasonal, nomadic camps were unfamiliar with the process of Ivoirian birth registration. Most Fulani births happen at home, while the birth registry offices are in town. The fact that nomadic Fulani men travel on their migrations makes it difficult to register births, as the male head of household typically does the registration.

The primary form of identification held by foreign-born Fulani men, and the document that is the most used and relied upon by the nomadic Fulani community as a whole, is the *carte consulaire,* which is an ID card given by the Burkinabè and Malian consulates exclusively for use abroad. Most foreign-born Fulani men report that a *carte consulaire* from their home countries and a cattle vaccination card are now the two primary documents they need to cross the border. The *carte consulaire*, however, cannot be used to obtain Malian or Burkinabè documents for children born abroad.

Several other forms of ID were mentioned as particularly important to the nomadic community. The first is the vaccination card, and the second is the biometric ECOWAS ID card. Nomadic Fulani use these cards to ease passage through the border and avoid fines by the police. Yet while the ECOWAS card is intended to promote freedom of movement, in reality, nomadic Fulani reported difficulties crossing the border, harassment by police, and a discriminatory legal system that prioritized the needs and rights of farmers over the urgent need of pastoralists to locate pastures for their animals and pastoral corridors to access cattle markets.

The problem of nomadic and settled Fulani documentation and nationality is occurring in a context where beef consumption in Côte d'Ivoire continues to rise while space for nomadism continues to shrink as more open land is converted to farms. Many nomadic Fulani have been forced to move their cattle along the grassy verges of the highway, as these provide some of the few remaining public spaces in Côte d'Ivoire. Armed conflict, drought, and climate change[223] pushed more pastoral Fulani southward, while the pandemic of 2020 brought increased border closures and restrictions. Reports from 2024 indicate that the government has concerns over an influx of Fulani refugees from Burkina Faso and Mali, with growing fears of conflict and terrorism spreading to Côte d'Ivoire and the possible radicalization of the Fulani community.[224]

3.4.5 Nomadic Peoples and Civil Registration

While the examples cited in this chapter do not necessarily represent all nomadic peoples, they demonstrate some of the problems nomadic peoples have obtaining identity documents and establishing their legal identity. The examples show how different forms of colonial registration and ID affected nomadic peoples, including licenses, voter cards, school registries, tax registries, colonial passports, and title registries. Nomadic peoples faced several serious problems with colonial-era registration, largely due to the colonial context of widespread policies to end nomadism as a way of life. Many of the nomadic peoples discussed in this chapter received no record of their births during colonization, and they have struggled to access this important document in the decades since to avoid the risk of statelessness.

In French Soudan, Kuwait, and North Borneo, antinomadic bias in colonial policy marginalized nomadic leaders during the colonial period, a fact with enormous repercussions for the decolonization process, including the passage of nationality laws and the rollout of civil registration. When colonial powers began creating a bureaucracy in their colonies, they often located such functions in towns, and it was often urban rulers who were vested with the authority to issue or validate documents, not nomadic leaders. Even for favored communities like the Tuareg, colonial policy frequently divided their lands by borders, coerced and forced their settlement, and failed to successfully recruit them into the emerging civil service, with serious consequences for their status during the decolonization process.

[223] Tor A Benjaminsen and Boubacar Ba, 'Fulani-Dogon Killings in Mali: Farmer-Herder Conflicts as Insurgency and Counterinsurgency' (2021) 14 Afr Sec 4, 6.

[224] International Organization for Migration, 'Northern Côte d'Ivoire Crisis Response Plan' (2024) <https://crisisresponse.iom.int/response/northern-cote-divoire-crisis-response-plan-2024> (accessed 4 September 2024).

In some regions, nomadic communities and settled communities were administrated separately, with urban and settled persons more likely to be registered than rural and nomadic peoples. However, more research on this division during colonization is needed. Also, hostility to antinomad policies and a lack of shared identity with the colony as a territorial unit led some nomadic peoples, like the Tuareg, to reject registration as a form of outsider control, instead advocating for their independence and the right to govern themselves. While the problems with the civil registration of nomadic peoples would only worsen in the postcolonial period, some nomadic peoples entered decolonization with colonial identity documents. Many of those, however, would also settle, abandoning nomadism as a way of life.

Those communities that remained nomadic appeared to have entered the postcolonial period with some of the lowest rates of civil registration in their regions. However, more research is needed on this critical period of nomadic history. This situation had serious implications for their inclusion in what this book called "the first body of nationals" of postcolonial states. In the postcolonial period, the four examples cited in this chapter highlighted how problems with civil registration for nomadic peoples are occurring in tandem with increased violence, movement restrictions, border restrictions, and fears of separatism, border disputes, and terrorism. The burden of securitization of borders has fallen heavily on nomadic communities and, for them, "[t]he achievement of independence did not automatically bring birth citizenship."[225]

Nomadic peoples faced deep structural and conceptual barriers to civil registration that stemmed from the conflict between the requirements of a nomadic lifestyle and the realities of hard borders, particularly in an age of climate change and conflict. Discrimination against nomadic peoples in the distribution of identity documents has been widespread, though more information is needed on this critical period in nomadic history, as registration committees also faced serious barriers to registering nomadic peoples under systems designed for sedentary and urban communities. During decolonization, the nomadic peoples cited as examples found themselves divided by borders, impeding cross-border nomadism and permanently dividing many nomadic communities, sometimes across multiple countries.

The power to issue documents had vested during the colonial period with settled and urban rulers, meaning that many nomadic peoples could not

[225] Heater (n 135) 132.

issue their own documents or control the civil registration process, setting the stage for discrimination. Some nomadic peoples, like the Tuareg, had nationality documents from the colonial period, but these documents appear to have yet to be used to obtain new documents in postcolonial Mali. Postcolonial states also faced very real barriers to registering mobile, nomadic peoples under systems inherited from the colonial era that were very much designed for the urban and agricultural populations. As Conklin puts it, regarding but one of many barriers, "members of nomadic and travelling groups generally lack fixed addresses, which are needed to qualify for nationality documentation."[226]

Treaties and transitional laws during decolonization often contained provisions to establish the postcolonial state's first body of nationals, employing residence and birth in the territory of the state.[227] One key issue that emerged for nomadic peoples during the postcolonial period was the problem of using documents and registries to establish their residency. Both the international community and postcolonial governments largely supported existing borders during decolonization, meaning that nomadic peoples with ties to multiple states due to international borders would now need to overcome doubts about their eligibility by providing a high level of proof. In some cases, no number of documents was likely sufficient. International law at decolonization could have offered states more guidance in enacting universal registration policies.[228]

The concept of residence in nationality law, including related concepts like habitual resident and domicile, was hard to apply in border zones and to cross-border populations like nomadic peoples. Nomadic peoples often lack the sorts of documents, like land deeds, that might prove residency, and documents that nomadic peoples may have used to establish residency under the law in postcolonial states appear not to have been used in this capacity. In the case of the Fulani, access to documents in one country has not helped resolve their access to grazing land in other countries. At the same time, the statelessness of sedentary Fulani impacts the rights of nomadic Fulani in complex ways, showing the need for regional and holistic solutions that operate both at the individual and the community level. Meanwhile, the

[226] William Conklin, *Statelessness: The Enigma of an International Community* (OUP 2014) 124.

[227] Ruth Donner, *The Regulation of Nationality in International Law* (2nd edn, Brill 1994) 278–282 (discussing Britain and France). See also R Brubaker, 'Citizenship Struggles in Soviet Successor States' (1992) 26 Intl Migration Rev 278 (on succession and nationality in former Soviet states); Weis (n 5) 152–153 (discussing partial succession).

[228] Weis (n 5) 201–202 (discussing evidence of nationality before international tribunals).

securitization of borders and the reframing of nomadic communities as terrorist or security threats have further impeded solutions, framing nomadic movement and lack of documents as security threats rather than technical problems for the governments to resolve through registration drives. The next section will explore the extent to which international law addresses the problems faced by nomadic peoples in obtaining ID. Future chapters, however, will draw on the information contained in chapter 3 to interrogate the extent to which other areas of international law can resolve some of the deeper problems exposed in this chapter, including discrimination against nomadic peoples, the desire of some nomadic peoples to have their own states, and the labeling by governments of nomadic peoples as foreign, security threats.

3.5 Civil Registration under International Law

As the examples showed, civil registration alone cannot solve the bigger and deeper problems facing nomadic communities, including violence, separatism, and the disconnect between nomadism as a way of life and the rigid border controls many states implement. To the limited extent that civil registration can contribute to a solution, however, it's worth interrogating to what extent international law is facilitating the ability of nomadic peoples to obtain documents in ways that do not violate their rights. The rest of chapter 3 will explore this question and propose reforms to international law to improve the effectiveness of civil registration to prevent and resolve statelessness. Future chapters will explore other solutions under international law that might address some of the additional and more serious problems highlighted in this chapter.

There is no debate that civil registration and a legal identity are crucial to resolving statelessness under an international system dominated by laws requiring paper documents and evidence of nationality. Birth registration is the only form of civil registration required by international law, though treaties exist at the regional level regulating other forms of civil registration, for example, certificates of nationality.[229] Birth registration is key to

[229] See for example Convention on the Issue of a Certificate of Nationality (adopted 25 September 1999, entered into force 1 May 2004) ICCS Convention No 28. See also the Hague Convention relating to Civil Procedure (adopted 1 March 1954, entered into force 12 June 1957) 286 UNTS 265.

preventing statelessness by establishing legal identity, place of birth, and family connections. Discrimination in registering births is prohibited under international law, specifically under Article 24 of the International Covenant on Civil and Political Rights. Nevertheless, as the examples demonstrated, even if every nomadic child were registered at birth, this may not resolve nomadic statelessness without other reforms, some of which are simply beyond the power of international law to achieve.

One huge problem with birth registration as a solution to nomadic statelessness is the fact that it is often used to establish statelessness or lesser forms of nationality, such as is the case with the *bidoon* in Kuwait. In a world rapidly moving toward forms of biometric registration, it is worth pausing to consider the impact of this for persons registered as stateless, and whether the requirement that every child be registered at birth also requires that every child's birth certificate grant them a nationality. This book stops short of recommending this reform, as it would require sweeping changes to nationality laws worldwide, but it is worth further debate and discussion.

Other forms of civil registration besides birth registration may provide evidence of other important requirements of nationality beyond the place of birth and parentage, including residence, raising the question of whether international law should require different forms of civil registration. This book does not recommend that other forms of documentation and registration besides birth registration be required under international law, however, because states have often used various forms of documentation abusively against nomadic peoples in the past, to force or coerce their settlement and secure their assimilation. As well, the example of the Fulani shows that civil registration at the nation-state level is often insufficient to protect the rights of cross-border, nomadic populations, which require a regional solution. Given that civil registration is a fact of the modern nation-state system, however, it is worthwhile considering what reforms might help nomadic peoples gain a nationality while preserving nomadism.

Proposed reforms to international law that may be more helpful than blanket mandates requiring documents include reforms specific to nomadic peoples mandating, for example, that states simplify civil registration procedures, particularly under *jus sanguinis* systems. International law could mandate bilateral, tripartite, or regional registration agreements for nomadic peoples to register them as cross-border populations and grant them a regional passport. Another reform, as recommended by the Committee on the Rights of the Child, would be to mandate mobile registration units that would bring registration facilities to nomadic communities.[230]

Any reforms to the international laws of civil registration that are specifically tailored to nomadic peoples, however, also risks placing them in a special category of persons who are treated differently from others, raising the specter of discrimination, which will be discussed at length in chapter 4. Such specialized solutions would require extensive community consultations, and even with the best of intentions, the historical connection between civil registration and coerced and forced settlement remains so overwhelming that it is not clear it can ever be fully overcome.

As the examples demonstrated, the concept of habitual residence is often crucial both to qualifying for nationality in many countries and to obtaining documents. One additional reform that international law could make to improve access to civil registration for nomadic peoples without specifically targeting them as a discrete population would be to better define the concept of residency, or habitual residency, in a way that is more friendly to mobility and nomadism. The next sections will discuss this potential reform in more detail.

3.5.1 Habitual Residence as a Concept under International Law

Habitual residence, as the examples showed, was widely used at decolonization and in the decades since to determine eligibility for nationality, but it may be problematic for nomadic peoples. As international law expert Ian Brownlie explains in his discussion of *Nottebohm,* habitual residence may create a presumption of nationality under international law.[231] Despite the importance of the concept of habitual residence for civil registration, there is no accepted definition under international law, creating a gap that governments have arguably exploited, as the examples showed, to exclude nomadic peoples. The language on habitual residency that currently exists under international law is often circular, conclusory, and/or conceptually vague, particularly regarding mobile populations. One proposed reform to international law would, therefore, be a definition of nomadic residence for

[230] Committee on the Rights of the Child, Algeria, para 36, quoted in Gilbert (n 11) 161.

[231] James Crawford, *Brownlie's Principles of Public International Law* (9th edn, OUP 2019) 495, 511.

the purposes of civil registration that would be conceptually clear but also both nomadic-friendly and flexible.

This section will look at treaty law, soft law, case law, and the opinions of international experts to survey current definitions of habitual residency and to examine what a nomadic-friendly definition might look like. The European Committee of Ministers, in a report on parental rights, defined habitual residence as "the place where the person had established, on a fixed basis, his permanent or habitual centre of interests, with all the relevant facts being taken into account for the purpose of determining such residence."[232]

The 1951 Refugee Convention also provides a definition of residence in article 10, implying that residence is a single location.[233] The Protocol to the African Charter on Human and Peoples Rights on the Specific Aspects of the Right to a Nationality and the Eradication of Statelessness in Africa defines habitual residence as "stable factual residence, or the place where a person has established his or her permanent or habitual centre of interests."[234]

The Council of Europe in 1983 recommended that,

> [f]or the establishment of (nationality), one or more of the following criteria could in particular be taken into consideration: a. the state concerned is the state of birth or origin of the nomadic or the state of origin of his immediate family; b. habitual residence or frequent periods of residence of the nomadic in the state concerned provided that the residence in question is not unlawful; c. the presence in the state concerned of members of the nomadic's immediate family lawfully staying in that state or possessing its nationality.[235]

The usefulness of this list of criteria for establishing nomadic residence is doubtful. "Frequent periods of residence" is not defined, nor does this list

[232] Explanatory Report to EU Council of Ministers Regulation (EC) No 2201/2003 concerning jurisdiction and the recognition and enforcement of judgments in matrimonial matters and the matters of parental responsibility (known as Brussels II) prepared by Dr Alegría Borrás, para 32) as quoted in the Protocol to the African Charter on Human and Peoples' Rights on the Specific Aspects of the Right to a Nationality and the Eradication of Statelessness in Africa (adopted 3 February 2024): Explanatory Memorandum.

[233] Convention Relating to the Status of Refugees (adopted 28 July 1951, entered into force 22 April 1954) 189 UNTS 137.

[234] Protocol to the African Charter on Human and Peoples' Rights on the Specific Aspects of the Right to a Nationality and the Eradication of Statelessness in Africa, para 32.

[235] Council of Europe, 'Recommendation No. R (83) 1 of the Committee of Ministers to Member States on Statelessness Nomadic peoples and Nomadic peoples of Undetermined Nationality' (Committee of Ministers 22 February 1983).

enumerate the types of evidence used to establish frequency. The focus on "lawful" residence may also be problematic for stateless nomadic peoples, creating a self-reinforcing cycle of exclusion.

Turning to the opinions of experts, Paul Weis, a noted expert on statelessness and international law, said, for example, that for residence to be established for the purposes of civil registration in the establishment of a country's nationals during a transfer of territory, "physical presence at the material time is essential," but that residence should exclude "persons who happen to be in the territory accidentally or temporarily."[236] He notes the importance of some sort of intent on the part of the individual to establish residence but provides no clear guidance on how such intent is to be established or how to define "temporarily." For persons outside the territory of the state at the time nationality is being determined, Weis recommends that "return or travel to the transferred territory with the intention of establishing residence there may be regarded as implicit acceptance (of nationality)."[237] Such a definition would create problems for cross-border, nomadic, and mobile groups.

Conklin, in his book on statelessness, points out the conceptual vagueness in definitions of residency under international law, asking,

> [h]ow long does it take for residence to become habitual? How do we account for the exclusion of nomadic and traveller groups or the continued risk of the withdrawal of nationality? What if there is not a perfect fit between a state's border and the habitual residents of its territory? What if a person is unable to return to her/his state of habitual residence?[238]

The next section will propose a better definition for residency, one that is easier to apply to nomadic and mobile peoples.

3.5.2 Defining Residency for Nomadic Peoples

A definition of habitual residency under international law should not rely on establishing a single, fixed place of abode because a narrow focus on a single point of residency ignores the realities of nomadic life, where nomadic

[236] Weis (n 5) 151.
[237] ibid 155.
[238] Conklin (n 226) 224.

peoples may not have a single, fixed address, and historically have had difficulty proving land ownership and other links to the territory of the state that rely on documents and registries.[239] "What of those who . . . fail to acquire nationality in the place where they have permanently resided because they are deemed to have links elsewhere?"[240]

As well, an international definition of residency should expand how residency can be established beyond a reliance on paper documents. Article 8 of the Protocol to the African Charter adopts a nomadic-friendly set of criteria, including oral testimony, water points, seasonal grazing zones, and the burial sites of ancestors, taking into account the realities of nomadism as a way of life.

UNHCR has also defined residence somewhat more flexibly, allowing for dual or multiple residencies to identify stateless children under the 1961 Convention: "It follows from the factual character of "habitual residence" that in cases where it is difficult to determine whether an individual is habitually resident in one or another State, for example *due to a nomadic way of life*, such persons are to be considered as habitual residents in both States."[241]

Dual residency for nomadic peoples is discussed at more length in chapter 6.

International law could also do more to require governments to accept nondocumentary forms of proof of residency, including oral testimony, family records, and the historical or present-day use of wells and moorage points. Such alternative proofs might also include the recognition of precolonial land arrangements, trade agreements, payment under traditional tax systems, and genealogies. Jérémie Gilbert and Ben Begbie-Clench discuss how the "mapping" of nomadic lands may be used by courts to establish their ownership,[242] an approach that could also be used to prove residency. The intersection between nomadic land ownership and establishing indigenous status for the purposes of nationality will be explored in more detail in chapter 5.

[239] Hannah Arendt, *The Origins of Totalitarianism* (Houghton Mifflin Harcourt 1973) 289.

[240] Carol Batchelor, 'Statelessness and the Problem of Resolving Nationality Status' (1998) 10 Intl J Refugee L 156, 177.

[241] UNHCR, 'Guidelines on Statelessness No. 4: Ensuring Every Child's Right to Acquire a Nationality through Articles 1-4 of the 1961 Convention on the Reduction of Statelessness' (December 2012), 10 (my italics).

[242] Jérémie Gilbert and Ben Clench, 'Mapping for Rights: Indigenous Peoples, Litigation and Legal Empowerment' (2018) 11 Erasmus L Rev 6, 3–4, 9–11, 20 citing a case over land ownership brought by the Batwa in Uganda.

Another way international norms could assist nomadic peoples in establishing residency would be to shift the burden of proof of residency from individuals to the government, in part by giving nomadic peoples present in the country on their seasonable migrations a presumption of residency that the government must expressly disprove.

There is some support in regional law for shifting the burden of establishing residence specifically for nomadic peoples to the government, particularly in Europe and Africa. The Council of Europe Recommendation 83(1) requires states to "facilitate" the establishment of residence for nomadic peoples.[243] In *Anudo Ochieng Anudo v. Tanzania,* the African Court on Human and Peoples' Rights mandated that in the African context, the burden is on the state to disprove nationality for persons who have documents to prove nationality, and therefore prior residency, in the predecessor state.[244] Shifting the burden of proving residency to states, for example, could be helpful for nomadic peoples who retain colonial-era documents in their families, and, to prevent the singling out of nomadic peoples under the law, could be made universal under international law.

Another solution for nomadic peoples might be to apply a presumption of nationality to all members of a nomadic community with a precolonial presence in a specific region as a group or community, and who are recognized as members by that community, through whatever internal process that community has or creates, and subject to a due, transparent, and deliberative process. Inspiration could be taken from the French principle of *possession d'état de national.* This solution, however, would be difficult to fashion into a universal principle and, therefore, may cause more problems than solutions for nomadic communities.

3.6 Conclusion and Recommendations

This chapter provided a snapshot of the fraught relationship between some nomadic communities and governments regarding legal identity and civil

[243] European Committee of Ministers, 'Recommendation No. R (83) 1 of the Committee of Ministers to Member States on Statelessness Nomadic Peoples and Nomadic Peoples of Undetermined Nationality' (22 February 1983) Principle 2.

[244] *Anudo Ochieng Anudo v Tanzania* (Merits) App No 012/2015 (ACHPR, 22 March 2018). See also Bromwen Manby, 'Case Note: Anudo Ochieng Anudo v. Tanzania (Judgement) (African Court on Human and Peoples Rights, APP No. 012/2015, 22 March 2018)' (2019) 1 Statelessness and Citizenship Rev 170.

registration, including birth registration. While the right to be registered at birth remains an important tool to end statelessness, this chapter has exposed some difficulties in relying on birth registration to protect nomadic peoples against statelessness. This book does not advocate, however, that international law should require other forms of civil registration besides birth registration due, in part, to the ways in which states have used civil registration to coerce nomadic statelessness and the dangers that more rigid and universal registration requirements will only accelerate nomadic settlement and the end of nomadism as a way of life. International law could do more to acknowledge the fact that while civil registration is a useful tool for ending statelessness, it has often also been a very useful tool for ending nomadism.

Many of the problems highlighted in this chapter cannot be resolved through changes to the international laws regarding civil registration. Still, there are nevertheless reforms to international law that will improve the usefulness of civil registration in preventing nomadic statelessness. The case of the *bidoon* in Kuwait demonstrated the dangers of civil registration in creating statelessness and the need for more express and forceful prohibitions on this abusive use of registration. The case of the Fulani showed how modern documentation regimes are ill-suited to the needs of many nomadic communities, particularly how limiting civil registration to individual nation-states obscures the need for regional passports and documents to permit regional nomadism. This chapter also discussed habitual residency as a predicate for obtaining documents in many states, exploring the possibility of establishing a clearer and more nomadic-friendly definition under international law for this vital concept.

Finally, it's important to reiterate that changes to the international laws of civil registration cannot solve many of the serious problems raised in this chapter. Some of these problems, however, will be addressed in future chapters. For example, some of the laws that have been discussed in the examples in this chapter might amount to prohibited discrimination under international law, a solution that will be explored in chapter 4.

4

Prohibiting Discrimination in Nationality Law against Nomadic Peoples

4.1 Introduction

The UN Office of the High Commissioner of UNHCR and many experts agree that discriminatory nationality laws cause statelessness.[1] Chapter 3 discussed the prohibitions under international law of discrimination in the registration of births, but chapter 4 will focus on the prohibitions under international law of discrimination in the granting of nationality under the law.

As chapter 3 discussed, the settlement of nomadic peoples was a major goal at various points in the history of Kuwait, Mali, Côte d'Ivoire, and Malaysia, which raises the question if nationality laws in those four countries discriminate against nomadism or nomadic peoples. If so, chapter 4 concludes with an analysis of the international prohibitions against discrimination in nationality law and the extent to which these prohibitions, if properly implemented by states, would effectively prevent discrimination against nomadic peoples in nationality law. This chapter looks at the fullest extent of international antidiscrimination law to see if it would be effective in addressing the specific types of discrimination against nomadic peoples discussed in this chapter, in the hypothetical case of full state adoption and taking a progressive approach.

4.2 Discrimination against Nomadic Peoples in Colonial-Era Nationality Laws

Nationality laws enacted in Kuwait during the British colonial period did not discriminate against nomadic peoples on their face, but a closer look

[1] See for example UNHCR Ibelong Campaign, 'This Is Our Home: Stateless Minorities and Their Search for Citizenship' (UNHCR 2017). See also Amal De Chickera and J Whiteman, 'Addressing Statelessness through the Right to Equality and Non-Discrimination' in Laura van Waas and Melenie Khanna (eds), *Solving Statelessness* (Wolf 2017) 99, 102.

The Nationality and Statelessness of Nomadic Peoples Under International Law. Heather Jean Alexander, Oxford University Press. © Oxford University Press 2025. DOI: 10.1093/9780197772362.003.0004

reveals hidden forms of bias. Following the advice of international experts, as described in chapter 3, the government of Kuwait combined British norms of nationality, international norms, and principles from Islamic law to enact the 1948 decree establishing Kuwaiti nationality. This decree didn't mention the Bedouin,[2] but, as chapter 3 discussed, the law divided Kuwaiti society into "original" Kuwaitis who were settled in towns, naturalized Bedouin, and stateless Bedouin, creating an unequal dichotomy in Kuwait between so-called real citizens and those who were naturalized or stateless, with the Bedouin making up most of the latter two categories. As a result, the law produced a discriminatory effect.

Similarly, Malaysian nationality law does not mention nomadic peoples but also contains subtler forms of bias that might amount to discrimination. As well, Malaysian nationality law has a long history of producing stateless populations in Malaysia. In 1946, the British proposed a nationality law for the Federation of Malaya, which did not include the Borneo states and was based on *jus soli* and fifteen years of residence.[3] The sultans rejected this law because it would have granted nationality to peninsular Malaysia's ethnic-Chinese population.[4] Instead, under the 1948 Federation of Malaya Agreement, most non-Malays had to apply to be naturalized. In this way, Malaya adopted tiers of nationality. The 1952 Federation of Malaya Agreement opened up the possibility of federal citizenship for non-Malays. The law, however, was complicated and poorly implemented, and by the end of 1953, almost two million non-Malays were still without nationality in the new Federation, including many Chinese.[5] In this way, statelessness became an entrenched fact of life for many minorities in peninsular Malaysia.

Meanwhile, nationality law in North Borneo developed separately from than in Peninsular Malaysia. In 1931, the British government passed the North Borneo Ordinance No. 1. Adopting the norms of British nationality

[2] Kuwait, Law no 2, 35-49 (1948). See also Kuwait, Order No 3, 23–30 (1948).

[3] V. Sinnadurai, 'Nationality and International Law in the Perspective of the Federation of Malaysia' in Ko Swan Sik (ed), *Nationality and International Law in Asian Perspective* (Martinus Nijhoff 1990) 313. The Federation of Malaya came into existence in 1948.

[4] Marshall Clark and Juliet Pietsch, *Indonesia-Malaysia Relations: Cultural Heritage, Politics and Labour Migration* (Routledge 2014) 161.

[5] Federation of Malaya Agreement (signed 21 January 1948, entered into force 1 February 1948) 11 UNTS 30. See also Sinnadurai (n 3) 314; K Young, W C F Bussink and P Hasan, *Malaysia: Growth and Equity in a Multiracial Society* (Johns Hopkins UP 1980) 16; Helen Ting, 'Malaysian History Textbooks and the Discourse of Ketuanan Melayu' in D Goh and others (eds), *Race and Multiculturalism in Malaysia and Singapore* (Routledge 2009) 42–43.

law, as well as a uniform approach that rejected a system of tiers, nationality at birth was granted to,

> [a]ny person born within the State of North Borneo unless and until he proves that at the time of his birth he possessed under the law of some other State the nationality of such State, and . . . Any person born out of the State of North Borneo whose father was a citizen of the State at the time of that person's birth and either was born within the State or was a person to whom a certificate of naturalization had been granted under the provisions of this Ordinance, and . . . Any person born on board a ship registered in the State of North Borneo unless and until he proves at the time of his birth he possessed under the law of some other State the nationality of such State.[6]

When North Borneo became a Crown Colony in July 1946 following four years of Japanese occupation, nationality was automatically converted to British Subject status, at least on paper. Chapter 3 has already discussed, however, the almost complete lack of civil registration in North Borneo at the time. Nevertheless, according to the North Borneo Cession in Council of 1946, "all persons who on the fifteenth day of July, 1946, are citizens of the State of North Borneo by virtue of the provisions of the North Borneo Naturalisation Ordinance, 1931, shall, on that day become British subjects."[7]

Before civil registration could be completed in North Borneo under this law, however, North Borneo was incorporated into the Federation of Malaysia.[8] The inclusion of non-Malays, historical migrants, and immigrant groups in Malaysia would dominate discussions around access to Malaysian nationality, as Malaysia emerged as an economic powerhouse in the region.

Most of the inhabitants of French West Africa, by contrast, would receive a nationality under French law by the end of the colonial period, and many would be issued with documents establishing their nationality, as chapter 3 discussed. French law based nationality on both residency and *jus sanguinis*, as well as the principle of double birth.[9]

[6] Cited in Laurie Fransman, *Fransman's British Nationality Law* (3rd edn, Bloomsbury Professional 2011) 534.

[7] North Borneo Succession Order in Council 1946, SI 1946/121.

[8] V M Hooker, *A Short History of Malaysia: Linking East and West* (Allen and Unwin 2003) 209. See also Barbara Watson Andaya and Leonard Y Andaya, *A History of Malaysia* (2nd edn, Palgrave Macmillan 2001) 265, 283.

[9] P Lagarde, *La Nationalité Française* (2nd edn, Dalloz 1989)

138. See also Jacques Maury, 'Nationalité. Théorie générale du français' in A G De LaPradelle and J-H-P Niboyet (eds), *Répertoire de droit international* (Sirey 1931) 30, 86–87; P Weil, *Qu'est-ce qu'un*

Despite the supposed universality of *citoyenneté,* however, French law in the colonies at first created a system of tiered nationality based on race and religion, distinguishing between the holders of so-called active and passive nationality.[10] For much of the colonial period, the French Civil Code did not apply to most Tuareg and Fulani, as they were classified as *les indigènes*, and were French subjects, not nationals. Their personal status was regulated by special laws and decrees, including the *Code de l'Indigénat*, which subjected Africans to forced labor and arbitrary punishment by special courts. While the term *indigène* was never defined, it was applied to most Africans, who were banned from politics, and under the jurisdiction of a French administrator.[11] The number of Africans with French nationality remained extremely small and concentrated in urban and coastal areas.[12]

By the postwar period, however, the French government began a process to incorporate the colonies into a type of "greater France" with a single nationality. The process of enfranchisement came in stages: in the period before 1945, the vast majority of Africans were French subjects but not nationals; 1946–1955 created the French Union with limited voting rights for many Africans; 1956 saw both the implementation of the *Loi Cadre* granting universal suffrage, though not equal representation, and the creation of the French Community, and 1958–1962 was the transition to full independence.[13]

While the nationality laws of French West Africa, Kuwait, and North Borneo therefore appeared neutral on their face and complied with the norms

français? Histoire de la nationalité française depuis la Révolution (Grasset 2002) 83; Fabienne Jault-Seseke, Ségolène Barbou des Places and Sabine Corneloup, *Droit de la nationalité et des étrangers* (Presses universitaires de France 2015) 95.

[10] Décret no 53-161 du 24 février 1953 déterminant les modalités d'application du code de la nationalité française dans les territoires d'outre-mer, 50 *JORF* 1984 (27 février 1953). See also F Cooper, *Nationality between Empire and Nation, Remaking France and French Africa 1945-1960* (Princeton UP 2014) 14.

[11] Fixant Décret du 5 novembre 1928, sauf en ce qui concerne les indigènes, les conditions de jouissance des droits civils d'acquisition, de perte, et de recouvrement de la qualité de français dans les colonies autres que la Guadeloupe, la Martinique et la Réunion, *JORF* du 15 novembre 1928 (1928). See also Catherine Coquery-Vidrovitch, 'Nationalité et Citoyenneté en Afrique Occidentale Français: Originaires et Citoyens dans le Sénégal Colonial' (2001) 42 J Afr Hist 285, 289–290.

[12] Coquery-Vidrovitch, 'Nationalité et Citoyenneté en Afrique Occidentale Français (n 11) 300. See also J. Chipman, *French Power in Africa* (Basil Blackwell 1989) 57 (on French nationality in Algeria); Cooper (n 10) 43, 133; Maury (n 9) 90.

[13] Loi no 56-619 du 23 juin 1956 autorisant le gouvernement à mettre en œuvre les réformes et à prendre les mesures propres à assurer l'évolution des territoires relevant du, Arrêté de promulgation no 1059 APA du 10 août 1957 (1956) du 28 septembre 1958 Constitution de la Ve République, promulguée par le président de la République le 4 octobre 1958.

of European nationality law that were common at the time, as the examples showed, these laws could be discriminatory against nomadic peoples when considered in context. First, the concept of tiers of nationality, common under colonial-era nationality laws, was a form of discrimination, though not necessarily one that was directed at nomadic peoples. Nevertheless, the very idea of tiers of nationality arguably normalized the concept of discrimination in postcolonial states. Second, it was very common for colonial-era nationality laws to adopt birth, residence, and descent as the three ways to establish eligibility for nationality, in compliance with both European and local norms of nationality and belonging. All three of these ways of establishing nationality rely on a territorial conception of the state that is sometimes difficult to square with nomadic lifestyles or appear difficult for nomadic peoples to comply with, particularly when nomadic communities are divided by borders, as was standard across all four examples cited in this book. The next section will look at the nationality laws passed at decolonization and examine the extent to which these laws contained structural or hidden examples of bias or discrimination against nomadic peoples.

4.3 Nationality Law at Decolonization

4.3.1 The Bedouin under Kuwait's Nationality Law

In 1959, as mentioned in chapter 3, Kuwait adopted a nationality law[14] that, like many postcolonial nationality laws, relied on both *settlement* and *residence* as the key determents of nationality.[15] These terms, "settlement" and "residence," appear neutral but may have a discriminatory effect when applied to nomadic peoples. While the law did not mention Bedouin by name, nor did it refer to individual tribes, it required that individuals prove that they settled in Kuwait at the time of the 1920 Battle of Jahra, continuing to place this event at the heart of Kuwaiti nationality.[16] The centering of this

[14] Kuwait Nationality Law (1959), art. 1 (translation on Refworld). See also Claire Beaugrand, *Stateless in the Gulf: Migration, Nationality and Society in Kuwait* (I. B. Tauris 2018) 2; Marie Lund-Johansen, 'Fighting for Citizenship in Kuwait' (thesis, Oslo U 2014) 24; J S Ismael, *Kuwait: Dependency and Class in a Rentier State* (UP of Florida 1993) 118.

[15] Fransman (n 6) 496–498.

[16] Farah Al-Nakib, 'Revisiting Hadar and Badū in Kuwait: Citizenship, Housing, and the Construction of a Dichotomy' (2014) 46 Int J Middle E Stud 5, 11–12. See also Lund-Johansen (n 14) 24.

event was arguably indirectly discriminatory against the Bedouin because the Battle of Jahra was often presented as evidence in Kuwaiti society that the Bedouin were unreliable allies, even though certain Bedouin tribes helped to defend the town. As Beaugrand puts it, "This idea of the desert as a hostile environment subject to foreign influence and manipulation was deeply anchored in the minds of the Kuwaiti townspeople by the time of the definition of nationality."[17]

The law also applied tiers of nationality, a form of discrimination and discriminated in favour of persons of Arab ethnicity.[18] With many Bedouin serving in the Kuwaiti military,[19] and to balance the newly created parliament by bringing in new voters with supposedly traditional values, the Al-Sabah family naturalized one hundred thousand of their closest Bedouin allies.[20] As chapter 3 explained, naturalization was clearly inferior to being an original Kuwaiti. Many Hathar, or urban Kuwaitis, saw the newly naturalized Bedouin as having pledged allegiance to the Al-Sabah family in exchange for handouts from the state. By the 1990s, naturalized former Bedouin made up 60 percent of Kuwaiti nationals.[21] Meanwhile, many other Bedouin remained stateless *bidoon,* including many of those serving in the military.

"[I]t is only through the aid of tribalism that people can earn their 'citizenship', residency, and jobs. Currently a sizable number of Bedouins have been denied the right to citizenship. Without citizenship, they do not have free access to such basic services as education, medical care and housing. It is only through the mediation of tribal sheiks that citizenship can be earned."[22]

[17] Beaugrand, Stateless in the Gulf (n 14) 67. See also Commins, 159–160 (on tribalism and borders in the region); Al-Nakib (n 16) 9–12 (noting that some Bedouin took refuge within the wall during the 1920 attack).

[18] Ismael (n 14) 118–119.

[19] A N Longva, 'Citizenship in the Gulf States: Conceptualization and Practice' in N A Butenschon, U Davis and M Hassassian (eds), *Citizenship and the State in the Middle East: Approaches and Applications* (Syracuse UP 2000) 188. See also J Crystal, 'Public Order and Authority: Policing Kuwait' in P Dresch and J Piscatori (eds), *Monarchies and Nations: Globalisation and Identity in the Arab States of the Gulf* (I B Tauris 2005) 171–176.

[20] Claire Beaugrand, 'Statelessness and Transnationalism in Northern Arabia: Biduns and State Building in Kuwait, 1959-2009' (PhD thesis, London Sch of Econ 2010). 207. See also Greg Power, 'The Difficult Development of Parliamentary Politics in the Gulf' in D Held and K Ulrichsen (eds), *The Transformation of the Gulf: Politics, Economics and the Global Order* (Routledge 2012) 32–33.

[21] Al-Nakib (n 16) 14. I am indebted to Professor Mohammad Al-Wuhaib for his comments on this point.

[22] .

Experts argue that the majority of the *bidoon* population comes from what are sometimes referred to as the northern tribes. As Claire Beaugrand, a noted expert on the *bidoon* in Kuwait, puts it,

> Biduns claim their entitlement to first degree Kuwaiti nationality on the basis of a pre-state understanding of sovereignty and territoriality, when political power was associated with the control of inland tribes, together with the trade routes they commanded and far-flung military resources they could mobilize so that their immemorial roaming patterns and seasonal *musabila* (Bedouin's seasonal visits to the town markets for the sale and purchase of goods) is as good a proof of their presence in the North Arabian region.[23]

Beaugrand goes on to state that many Bedouin who later came to settle in what is now Kuwait had what she calls "transnational" ties to the region,[24] including Saudi Arabia.[25] It should be noted, however, that the origins and affiliations of various Bedouin tribes is now contested history. The intent of this section is not to determine the origins of Kuwait's Bedouin tribes, but rather to explain how the concept of residency in one territorial state versus another was weaponized against a mobile, cross-border population like the Bedouin. Over time, the identity of stateless Bedouin tribes settled in Kuwait became subsumed into the identity of *bidoon.*

Future generations of *bidoon,* which now included the descendants of more recent immigrants from both inside and outside the region, would be locked out of Kuwaiti nationality by *jus sanguinis.* It is important to note the discriminatory use of *jus sanguinis*, also a seemingly neutral concept, in a context of recent and arbitrary borders in a region with a history of nomadism and caravan trade. Finally, Kuwaiti nationality law prevents women from passing their nationality to their children, which is clearly discriminatory and further cuts down on options for the *bidoon* to regularize their status.

[23] Beaugrand, 'Statelessness and Transnationalism in Northern Arabia' (n 20) 29. See generally Claire Beaugrand, 'Framing Nationality in the Migratory Context: The Elusive Category of Biduns in Kuwait' (2014) 6 Middle East Law and Governance 173. See also Keo Salih, 'Kuwait Primary (Tribal) Elections 1975-2008: An Evaluative Study' (2011) 38 Brit J Middle E Stud 141, 144.

[24] Beaugrand, 'Stateless in the Gulf' (n 14) 62.

[25] ibid 86, citing R Maktabi, 'The Gulf Crisis (1990-91) and the Kuwaiti Regime—Legitimacy and Stability in a Rentier State' (U of Oslo P 1992).

Chapter 5 will discuss in more detail the reframing of former Bedouin as foreigners and naturally stateless people, but for the purposes of this chapter, the use of *jus sanguinis* to lock the *bidoon* out of a nationality, a population who are made up of mostly former Bedouin nomadic peoples, along with the territorial conception of Kuwait as a state, produced a discriminatory effect. Most former Bedouin are either stateless or have received the lesser status of naturalization, based on their former existence as Bedouin nomadic peoples and their tribal affiliations, in a historical context of antinomadic bias. The statelessness of many former Bedouin has now become a form of circular logic, where statelessness justifies future statelessness, under the otherwise neutral seeming principle of *jus sanguinis.* "There is a misconception in Kuwaiti discourse today that the stateless or *bidun* are people who came from somewhere else (Syria, Jordan, Iraq) and destroyed their original nationality papers."[26]

4.3.2 The Sama Dilaut under the Nationality Laws of Sabah, Malaysia

As historian Cheah Boon Kheng explains, Tunku Abdul Rahman, Malaysia's first prime minister, saw universal nationality laws as the key to accomplishing the difficult task of forging a common national identity in a country where 50 percent of the population was non-Malay, while simultaneously preserving the centrality of Malay identity.[27] Despite the need for social inclusion, however, sizable numbers of persons of Chinese and Indian descent, as well as minorities like the Sama Dilaut, would end up stateless in Malaysia, and statelessness in Malaysia persists despite protections written into the law.[28] "[I]n Malaysia, statelessness as an issue is always embroiled in wider moral and political arguments . . . in many contexts, statelessness is not just an issue of legal identification but is embroiled in contentious politics of national and regional belonging."[29]

[26] Al-Nakib (n 16) 13. See also Crystal (n 19) 174–175. But see, contra, Longva, 188 (where she argues that some *bidoon* do come from other countries, including Iraq).

[27] Cheah Boon Kheng, *Malaysia: The Making of a Nation* (Institute of Southeast Asian Studies 2002) 76–77.

[28] UNHCR, 'Ending Statelessness in Malaysia' (2024) <https://www.unhcr.org/my/ending-statelessness-malaysia> accessed 29 April 2024.

[29] Catherine Allerton, 'Contested Statelessness in Sabah, Malaysia: Irregularity and the Politics of Recognition' (2017) 15 J Immig and Refugee Stud 250, 251.

Following federation, the government of Malaysia needed to draft a nationality law that would unify the patchwork of laws from the colonial period, as previously discussed in chapter 3, incorporating principles from both Islamic law and European norms.[30] In 1957, the new Federal Constitution created a federal nationality at birth, removing the requirement that federal citizenship be derived from state nationality. Following a period of transition to establish the Peninsula's first body of nationals, nationality thereafter passed via *jus sanguinis,* but, unlike in Kuwait, with protections against statelessness. Malaysia would grant nationality to every person born on Malaysian territory who "is not born a citizen of any other country."[31]

In 1963, when the Malaysia Act amended the Constitution to include Sabah and Sarawak, transitional laws were written to establish nationality in the newly added states. To preserve their semiautonomy and prevent immigration from Peninsular Malaysia, Sabah and Sarawak were given independent control over immigration from other states. The inclusion of the Borneo territories in Malaysia in 1963 resulted from political negotiations very much tied to Malay concerns over ethnic balance.[32] Like many postcolonial states, the governments of Malaysia and Sabah have struggled to unite disparate groups under a single nationality.[33] With a huge increase in immigration in recent decades, including to Sabah, Malaysia's nationality laws have become a tool to exclude foreign and immigrant groups. As economists Young and colleagues put it, "the Malay nationalist project came to rely on the idea of the Malay bangsa, or 'race-nation', as a foundation of its political and territorial claims."[34]

Since independence, irregular migrants searching for employment have come to Sabah by boat, traversing clandestinely the maritime border

[30] Constitution of Malaysia, art 14, Second Schedule (1957). See also Sinnadurai (n 3) 312–318.

[31] Constitution of Malaysia, art 14, Second Schedule, pt II (1957). See also R Razali, 'Addressing Statelessness in Malaysia: New Hopes and Remaining Challenges' (2017) Statelessness Working Paper Series No 2017/9.

[32] Charles Hirschman, 'The Meaning and Measurement of Ethnicity in Malaysia' (1987) 46 J Asian Stud 555, 559 (on the history of the census in Malaysia). See also Sinnadurai (n 3) 311 (on nationality, ethnicity, and religion in Malaysia). Singapore would depart the Federation in 1965.

[33] Helen. Brunt, 'Stateless Stakeholders: Seen but Not Heard? The Case of the Sama Dilaut in Sabah, Malaysia' (masters thesis, U Sussex 2013), 38. See also the Malaysia Asia Pacific Refugee Rights Network, 'The Vulnerability of Sama Dilaut (Bajau Laut) Children in Sabah' (2015) 4; UN High Commissioner for Refugees (UNHCR), 'Submission by the United Nations High Commissioner for Refugees for the Office of the High Commissioner for Human Rights' Compilation Report—Universal Periodic Review: Malaysia' (March 2013).

[34] K Young, 'Malay Social Imaginaries: Nationalist and Other Collective Identities in Indonesia' in W Mee and J Kahn (eds), *Questioning Modernity in Indonesia and Malaysia* (NUS Press 2012) 61.

between Sabah and the Philippines.[35] As a result, the lines between clandestine border crossings, boat migration, Sama Dilaut migrations, and irregular migration to Sabah from the Philippines have become blurred, exacerbating the climate of tension between the two countries and confusing the identity of the Sama Dilaut as an immigrant or indigenous group, as chapter 5 will discuss in more detail.

Though these nationality laws are neutral on their face when it came to nomadic peoples, the swift imposition of *jus sanguinis* meant that unregistered border populations like the Sama Dilaut, populations that were already being rebranded as immigrants, now risked being locked out of nationality unless, ironically, they could establish that they were stateless, rather than foreign. It is worth recalling from chapters 2 and 3 the historical tendency for successive governments in Sabah to brand the Sama Dilaut as pirates and as people whose animist beliefs set them apart from the majority culture and religion in the region. The swift imposition of *jus sanguinis* was therefore arguably discriminatory in a context of a recently constituted state with fuzzy borders and mobile, cross-border, and nomadic populations that have traditionally suffered from biased opinions as to their culture, religion, and origins, in a context where the only solution under the law is to be officially recognized as stateless.

4.3.3 The Tuareg and Fulani under the Nationality Laws of Mali and Côte d'Ivoire

In Mali, Burkina Faso, and many other Sahel countries, liberal nationality laws would remove the tiers of nationality based on race and religion that had typified French nationality law for much of the colonial period, bringing universal nationality, at least on paper, while in Côte d'Ivoire, liberal nationality laws would be sharply restricted in the 1970s by strict *jus sanguinis,* locking immigrant groups out of Ivorian nationality, and leading to one of the largest stateless populations in Africa. None of these laws, however, mentioned nomadic peoples, though they did contain subtler forms of bias.

[35] Azizah Kassim and Zin Ragayah Haji Mat, 'Policy on Irregular Migrants in Malaysia: An Analysis of its Implementation and Effectiveness' (Philippine Institute for Development Studies (PIDS 2011) 53. See also R M Razali, R Nordin and T J Duraisingam, (2015) 23 Pertanika J Soc Sci Human 19, 27.

In part in response to the aggressive settlement policies of the new government, as chapter 3 discussed, many Tuareg leaders entered the decolonization process intent on uniting Tuareg regions into a single, postcolonial state. This attempt at self-determination would fail, meaning that all Tuareg in Mali would need to qualify for nationality under Malian law, the laws of another country, or risk statelessness.

Though Ivoirian President Houphouët-Boigny and other leaders supported the idea of regional nationality, former French colonies in West Africa adopted individual nationality laws.[36] African nationality law expert Bronwen Manby explains that, "[a]mong the most difficult challenges of nation-building tasked to the newly independent African States of the 1960s was the determination of who could claim membership of these polities: the definition of who was a citizen."[37]

In Mali, as chapter 3 discussed, however, it was not clear who qualified under the nationality code[38] in a country that had only begun to exist months before and had been originally conceived of as being in a federation with Senegal, given that many persons under colonial protection did not have documents.[39] Despite the so-called Balkanization of Africa, however, Pan-Africanism remained a powerful political force in the region in the 1960s and 1970s. Until 1980, for example, foreigners "of African origin" could participate in Côte d'Ivoire's elections.[40] Persons "of African origin" also received favorable access to Malian citizenship until this clause was removed in 2011. Governments did not always extend the idea of Pan-Africanism, however, to nomadic peoples like the Fulani and Tuareg. For example, Malian officials have sometimes labeled the Tuareg "white" and the Tuareg also sometimes presented themselves this way.[41] As the concept of African origin was never defined, it remained vague and open to political interpretation. In addition to discriminating based on gender, the use of the term "of African origin" was

[36] Adjami, citing Alfred Babo, 'La Politique Publique de l'Etranger et la Crise Sociopolitique en Côte d'Ivoire,' in *Côte d'Ivoire : La Réinvention de Soi Dans la Violence* (CODESRIA, 24 September 2011) 39–62.

[37] B Manby, 'Trends in Citizenship Law and Politics in Africa Since the Colonial Era' in E Isin and P Nyers (eds), *Routledge Handbook of Global Citizenship Studies* (Routledge 2014), 172.

[38] Loi no 62-18 of 3 February 1962 as modified by the Loi no 9570 of 25 August 1995 and replaced by the Loi 2011-087 of 30 December 2011 (my translation). See also P Decheix, 'Le Code de la Nationalité Malienne' (1963) 697 Penant 300, 309

[39] Decheix (n 38) 303.

[40] Ousmane Dembele, 'Migration, Emploi, Pression Foncière et Cohésion Sociale en Côte d'Ivoire' (IOM 2009).

[41] For a general exploration of race in northern Mali, see the work of Bruce Hall, *A History of Race in Muslim West Africa, 1600-1960* (CUP 2011)

clearly racially discriminatory, and while there is no evidence of nomadic peoples being excluded from Malian nationality, it is an example of the ways in which nationality laws may contain coded bias against nomadic peoples.

Adopting the French principle of double birth afforded extra protections against statelessness in Mali. According to Decheix, an expert on Mali's early nationality laws, the provision on double birth was retained in the 1962 law over objections in part to resolve the question of nationality in border zones.[42] Besides the use of double birth to protect from statelessness, the Malian government could grant nationality to individuals who had been residents in Mali for two years,[43] provided automatic nationality to children born to unknown parents (foundlings),[44] and allowed children born to foreigners to naturalize after five years under certain conditions.[45] Also, persons born in Mali who had their habitual residence in Mali could opt for Malian nationality.[46] Decheix concluded at the time that the 1962 law was, "modern . . . conforming to the principles of international human rights law inspired by the profound sentiments of the African and informed by the political concerns of the hour to realize the union of the continent."[47]

Following amendments in 1995, the Malian government passed a new nationality code in 2011, the *Code des personnes et de la famille*.[48] Among other changes, the Code replaced the provision granting Malian nationality to children born to a parent "of African origin" with a provision granting Malian nationality to children born to a parent with nationality in another African country. This removed racial discrimination from Malian law.

Article 43(bis) of the Malian nationality code contained a further article that could be discriminatory against nomadic peoples in certain contexts, though it appears neutral. This article provided for the denationalization by decree of "any Malian national serving in or helping a foreign army or

[42] Decheix (n 38) 305.

[43] The Code de la Nationalité Malienne Loi no 6218 of 3 February 1962 as modified by the Loi no 9570 of 25 August 1995 and replaced by the Loi 2011-087 of 30 December 2011. Also relevant are the Ordonnance No 02-062/P.RM of 7 June 2002 of the Code of the Protection of the Child, and the Loi no 06-024 of 28 June 2006 on Civil Registration.

[44] Alexandre Zatzépine, *Le Droit de la Nationalité des Républiques Francophones d'Afrique et de Madagascar* (LGDJ 1963), 54.

[45] The Code de la Nationalité Malienne Loi no 6218 of 3 February 1962 as modified by the Loi no 9570 of 25 August 1995 and replaced by the Loi 2011-087 of 30 December 2011, art 27.

[46] Zatzépine (n 44) 56.

[47] Decheix, (n 38) 304, 314. The Malian nationality code was drafted by judges, government officials, union leaders, and an adviser from Europe.

[48] Loi no 95-098, Portant modification code de la nationalité (1995); Loi no 11-080 portant code des personnes et de la famille, *Journal Officiel de la République du Mali (JORM)* Spécial (31 January 2012) Titres IV, V (2011 Code).

foreign public service provided the host country is, with his help, engaged in hostilities against Mali."[49]

It is not clear, however, if this provision in the law was ever applied, but, as development expert Manuela Leonhardt put it,

> [t]he involvement of some pastoralists in armed conflicts such as in northern Mali has led to an emerging narrative of pastoralism as a security issue (World Bank, 2014) or even the unhelpful perception that pastoralists are terrorists (Global Terrorism Index, 2015). Such discourse feeds into the existing stigmatization of pastoralists as the dangerous "Other" and obstructs efforts at establishing peaceful and productive relationships between pastoralists and other groups.[50]

Many Fulani in Mali and Burkina Faso obtained a nationality in the decades following decolonization due to the relatively liberal nationality laws of those countries, as most of the former colonies of French West Africa opted for laws based on *jus soli* and rejected the tiers of nationality that had typified much of the French colonial period. The situation of Fulani, who settled in Côte d'Ivoire, is very different. The country's first nationality law was adopted in 1961, when it also adopted a liberal approach to nationality in the period immediately following independence. Amendments in 1972, however, made in the wake of large-scale immigration from Sahal countries, including by Fulani herders, prompted the government to introduce a strict system of *jus sanguinis,* or nationality based on descent.[51]

Today, Côte d'Ivoire has some of the most restrictive nationality laws in the region, and the children of sedentary Fulani families who moved to Côte d'Ivoire after 1972, when the country adopted strict *jus sanguinis*, are now stateless. As discussed in chapter 3, this has had an indirect effect on the rights of nomadic Fulani in Côte d'Ivoire, who form one community, as climate change and conflict in Mali and Burkina Faso drive more and more

[49] Loi no 95-098, Portant modification code de la nationalité (1995); Loi no 11-080 portant code des personnes et de la famille, JORM Spécial (31 January 2012) Titres IV, V (2011 Code). My translation.

[50] Manuela Leonhardt, 'Regional Policies and Response to Manage Pastoral Movements within the ECOWAS Region Study on behalf of the International Organization for Migration (IOM), within the framework of the Support to Free Movement of Persons and Migration in West Africa' (FMM West Africa Project 2019) 9.

[51] Official Journal Loi no 61-415 du 14 décembre 1961 portant Code de la nationalité ivoirienne, 20 December 1961 et Décret no 61-425 du 29 décembre 1961 portant application du Code de la nationalité ivoirienne, Official Journal of the Republic of Côte d'Ivoire, 18 January 1962.

pastoralists southward. While pastoralists typically adjust seasonal migration routes to accommodate environmental and social change, the creation of borders and separate documentation and nationality regimes has made these adjustments very difficult.

4.3.4 Discrimination against Nomadic Peoples in the Granting of Nationality

Few of the laws discussed above are discriminatory on their face against nomadic peoples, though reference to "African origin" in Mali's laws might hypothetically be considered discriminatory in a context where the government labels the Tuareg "white." Also, tiers of nationality and second-class nationality are clearly discriminatory under international law, as are laws discriminating on the basis of gender. This section, however, also explored discrimination in nationality law that is evidenced through an examination of the context in which certain terms and concepts, like "residency" and *jus sanguinis,* are applied to nomadic peoples.

The recent imposition of borders in regions occupied by nomadic and cross-border communities arguably made the sudden imposition of *jus sanguinis* in countries like Malaysia and Côte d'Ivoire discriminatory in a context of antinomadic bias and a widespread lack of civil registration, particularly among nomadic peoples. Use of the terms "residence" or "habitual residence" may be discriminatory for nomadic peoples in a context where nomadic residence is made impossible to establish, or nomadic peoples are assumed to be incapable of residency. An oblique reference to the conflict between nomadic peoples and the state, like the Battle of Jahra or Tuareg separatism, may render otherwise neutral laws discriminatory. In the case of nomadic Fulani who have a nationality in neighboring countries but who need to migrate to Côte d'Ivoire to practice pastoralism, strict *jus sanguinis* may be discriminatory in a region where pastoralists need to travel long distances and adjust their routes to respond to climate change and conflict. It is worth therefore asking if the division of nomadic communities by international borders and the lack of bilateral or regional nationalities may, itself, be a form of discrimination. The next section will examine how international law addresses these more subtle and indirect forms of discrimination in nationality law against nomadic peoples.

4.4 The International Laws Prohibiting Discrimination in the Granting of Nationality

None of the nationality laws of Kuwait, Mali, Côte d'Ivoire, or Malaysia explicitly mention nomadic peoples or nomadism, but section 4.3 highlighted various forms of indirect discrimination against nomadic peoples in the nationality laws of Kuwait, Mali, Côte d'Ivoire, and Malaysia. As statelessness experts De Chickera and Whiteman point out, "[r]ules which appear to apply equally . . . may, on closer examination, disadvantage stateless children and so amount to indirect discrimination."[52]

While nationality laws may be discriminatory on their face by, for example, excluding certain religious or ethnic groups, sometimes it is necessary to understand the political and social context in which laws were drafted to uncover the discrimination behind otherwise neutral-sounding terms.[53] Some discrimination is indirect, yet still explicit, like racial provisions for persons of African origin, while some is so deeply embedded in the structure of nationality law itself, like *jus sanguinis* in postcolonial contexts, that it appears neutral even under international norms.

Laws that do not mention nomadic peoples by name may nevertheless discriminate against them because of the meaning of certain terms and phrases when the political and social context surrounding them are considered. Nomadic groups may be racial, ethnic, religious, or linguistic minorities, protected from discrimination under international law, even if that discrimination is indirect. Terms and phrases in nationality laws may also produce a discriminatory effect against nomadic peoples by, for example, creating requirements that appear neutral but are, in fact, more onerous for nomadic peoples to fill. This chapter has therefore undertaken both a textual analysis of the laws of Kuwait, Mali, Malaysia, and Côte d'Ivoire while also providing historical and cultural context to provide a deeper understanding of how neutral-seeming terms may be discriminatory when the political and social context is considered.

Chapter 4 looked at three main areas of indirect discrimination against nomadic peoples: (1) the adoption of tiers of nationality granting different

[52] De Chickera and Whiteman (n 1) 100.

[53] See for example the case of Urdu speakers in Bangladesh, described in Kelly Staples, 'Recognition, nationality, and statelessness: State-based challenges for UNHCR's plan to end statelessness' in Tedayi Bloom, Katherine Tonkiss and Philip Cole (eds), *Understanding Statelessness* (Routledge 2017) 173, 174–175.

rights to different groups; (2) the adoption of nationality based on residency in a certain territory or region on or before a certain date, such as Kuwait before the battle of Jahra, or Côte d'Ivoire before decolonization, in a context where the concept of residency is difficult to establish for nomadic peoples; (3) the rapid adoption of *jus sanguinis* in some postcolonial states in a context of colonial-era, disputed borders, historical migration, and/or mobility and nomadism as a way of life; and (4) the common requirement that international obligations are met when a single nationality has been granted to a cross-border, mobile, and nomadic group. It should be recalled that all these postcolonial laws were drafted with the input of international experts and largely conformed to the norms of nationality of the day. It is worth asking, therefore, if the forms of implicit discrimination against nomadic peoples that were uncovered in the examples is prohibited by international law today.

> I do not think that the issue of statelessness can be addressed simply by throwing money at it, because it is self-inflicted, because it is man-made, because of deep-seated stereotyping, because of discrimination, because of deep-seated pigeon-holing of those individuals who belong and those who do not belong.[54]

The question addressed by this chapter is whether international law, even at its most progressive and in the hypothetical case of full state adoption, provides solutions to nomadic statelessness by prohibiting the kinds of implicit discrimination contained in many postcolonial nationality laws, in a climate where many states were struggling to unify their populations and exclude so-called problematic groups like nomadic peoples.

Even though "it is generally accepted today that nationality is an inherent right of all human beings,"[55] and nondiscrimination has long been a founding principle of human rights law, nationality law remains, by its very nature, discriminatory, in that it creates an in-group and an out-group.[56] The

[54] An interview with Benyam Dawit Mezmur, chairperson of the United Nations Committee on the Rights of the Child, in Institute on Statelessness and Inclusion, 'The Worlds Stateless Children' 137.

[55] *Case of the Girls Yean and Bosico,* para 138, quoting Proposed Amendments to the Naturalization Provision of the Constitution of Costa Rica (Advisory Opinion OC-4/84 of January 19, 1984), Series A no 4, para 35.

[56] Laura van Waas, *Nationality Matters: Statelessness Under International Law* (Intersentia 2008) 31. See also Engan Isin and Peter Nyers, 'Introduction: Globalizing Citizenship Studies' in Engan Isin and Peter Nyers (eds), *Routledge Handbook of Global Citizenship Studies* (Routledge 2014) 4, where they note that citizenship can be 'a title or rank that separates, excludes, and hierarchizes.' ibid.

grounds on which discrimination in nationality law are prohibited by international law must therefore be enumerated. According to the UN Human Rights Committee, impermissible grounds for discrimination in granting nationality include "race, colour, sex, language, religion, political or other opinion, national or social origin, property, birth or other status."[57] At the same time, "[m]any post-independence political leaders have consequently been faced with the hard task of welding into a nation peoples diverse in language, ethnicity and religion."[58]

International law does not therefore prohibit discrimination against cross-border mobility, even when discriminatory effects based on race or language may arise. In fact, discrimination against cross-border mobility may, in some contexts, be regarded as one of the core functions of nationality law. While the creation of tiers of nationality based on ethnicity or tribal group within a country, such as practiced by Kuwait, is a violation of international law, or against persons of supposedly non-African ethnicity, like in Mali, may be impermissible discrimination, this chapter highlighted the fact that the postcolonial laws of many states adopted modes of belonging like residency and *jus sanguinis* that remain widely accepted under international norms and are not, usually, identified as discriminatory. Nevertheless, as Conklin puts it, "[t]he adoption of *jus sanguinis* by post-World War, newly independent states, has often had a discriminatory impact in favour of the dominant ethnic group on the states' territories."[59]

Relevant instruments to establishing when discrimination is a violation of international law include the Charter of the United Nations, the Universal Declaration of Human Rights, the International Covenant on Civil and Political Rights, the International Covenant on Economic, Social and Cultural Rights, and the International Convention on the Elimination of All Forms of Racial Discrimination.[60] Other laws that establish the principle of nondiscrimination include the International Labor Organization (ILO) Convention concerning Discrimination in Respect of Employment

[57] Human Rights Committee, 'CCPR General Comment No. 18: Non-discrimination' (1989).

[58] D Heater, *Citizenship: The Civic Ideal in World History, Politics and Education* (3rd edn, Manchester UP 2004) 133.

[59] W Conklin, *Statelessness: The Enigma of an International Community* (OUP 2014) 97–98.

[60] Charter of the United Nations (24 October 1945) 1 UNTS XVI; Universal Declaration on Human Rights (adopted 10 December 1948) 217 A(III) (UNGA); International Covenant on Economic, Social and Cultural Rights (adopted 16 December 1966, entered into force 3 January 1976) 993 UNTS 3; International Convention on the Elimination of All Forms of Racial Discrimination (adopted 21 December 1965, entered into force 4 January 1969) 660 UNTS 195.

and Occupation No. 111 of 1958,[61] the UNESCO Convention against Discrimination in Education of 1960,[62] the UNESCO Declaration on Race and Racial Prejudice of 1978,[63] and UN declarations such as the UN Declaration on the Elimination of All Forms of Intolerance and of Discrimination based on Religion or Belief of 1981.[64] Nondiscrimination is a founding principle of the Convention on the Rights of the Child in Article 2. It is also a principle of Article 5 of the Convention on the Rights of Persons with Disabilities,[65] the indigenous rights framework, ILO Convention 169,[66] and the 2007 Declaration on the Rights of Indigenous Peoples, Articles 15 and 22. Discrimination may be committed by all organs of government, including the police, courts, government agencies and others. Many experts consider the principle of nondiscrimination to be *jus cogens.*[67]

Several international treaties expressly prohibit discrimination in the granting of *nationality*. The International Convention on the Elimination of All Forms of Racial Discrimination guarantees a right to a nationality without racial prejudice in Article 5, though Article 1, paragraph 2 carefully preserves states' rights to set nationality law. Nondiscrimination on racial grounds is also prohibited when it applies to noncitizens.[68] The 1961 Convention on the Reduction of Statelessness prohibits the withdrawal of nationality for reasons of race, ethnicity, or religion or on political grounds.

Gender discrimination in nationality law, such as that practiced by Kuwait, is prohibited by the 1957 Convention on the Nationality of Married Women

[61] International Labour Organization, Discrimination (Employment and Occupation) Convention (adopted 25 June 1958, entered into force 15 June 1960) ILO Convention No 111, with 175 ratifications.

[62] United Nations Educational, Scientific and Cultural Organization, Convention against Discrimination in Education 1960, Paris, 14 December 1960.

[63] United Nations Educational, Scientific and Cultural Organization, Declaration on Race and Racial Prejudice, 27 November 1978.

[64] United Nations, Declaration on the Elimination of All Forms of Intolerance and of Discrimination Based on Religion or Belief, General Assembly resolution 36/55 of 25 November 1981.

[65] United Nations Convention on the Rights of Persons with Disabilities (adopted 13 December 2006, entered into force 3 May 2008) 2515 UNTS 3, with 182 parties.

[66] International Labour Organization, Convention (No 169) concerning Indigenous and Tribal Peoples in Independent Countries (adopted 27 June 1989, entered into force 5 September 1991) ILO Convention No 169, with twenty-three ratifications.

[67] Report of the International Law Commission, Sixty-sixth session, A/69/10 (2014).

[68] Committee on the Elimination of Racial Discrimination, General Recommendation 30, Discrimination against Non-citizens (Sixty-fourth session, 2004), UN Doc CERD/C/64/Misc.11/rev.3 (2004); Interights, 'Non-Discrimination in International Law: A Handbook for Practitioners' (2011); High Commissioner for Human Rights, 'Minority Rights: International Standards and Guidance for Implementation' HR/PUB/10/3 (2010). See also van Waas, *Nationality Matters* (n 56) 59; Alice Edwards, 'The Meaning of Nationality in international Law in an Era of Human Rights: Procedural and Substantive Aspects' in Alice Edwards and Laura van Waas (eds), *Nationality and Statelessness under International Law* (CUP 2014) 25.

and the Convention on the Elimination of All Forms of Discrimination against Women, which in Article 9 guarantees women equal rights with men in obtaining and maintaining their nationality, as well as passing it to their children.[69] The Convention on the Rights of Persons with Disabilities in Article 18 guarantees the right to a nationality without discrimination based on disability and mandates that states provide for "reasonable accommodation" to disabled persons.

Article 6 of the nonbinding 2007 UN Declaration on the Rights of Indigenous Peoples states that "every indigenous individual has the right to a nationality."[70] It goes on to protect indigenous ways of life and outlaw discrimination based on indigenous status. The Declaration on the Rights of Indigenous Peoples, in Article 2, prohibits discrimination against indigenous persons based on indigenous identity. The classification of nomadic peoples as indigenous peoples will be discussed in greater detail in chapter 5, but it is possible that some of the discrimination might be prohibited under the indigenous rights framework.

Nondiscrimination is also central to regional human rights law. It is contained within the African Charter on the Rights and Welfare of the Child and the Arab Charter on Human Rights and regional human rights courts, including the European Court of Human Rights, the Inter-American Court of Human Rights, and the African Commission and African Court on Human and Peoples' Rights, have handed down decisions on discrimination in the application of nationality.[71] Nondiscrimination in the granting and withdrawal of nationality has been also claimed before regional courts and treaty bodies with some success.[72] Chapter 1 noted the specific international commitments of Kuwait, Mali, Malaysia, and Côte d'Ivoire, but the next sections will look at the international prohibitions on discrimination in nationality law writ large to see if international law in its totality, if and when applied by states, protects nomadic peoples from statelessness resulting from the more indirect and implied types of discrimination discussed in this chapter.

[69] Human Rights Council, Twenty-third session, 'Report on discrimination against women on nationality-related matters, including the impact on children' A/HRC/23/23 (2013).

[70] United Nations Declaration on the Rights of Indigenous Peoples. See also Willem van Genugten, Anna Meijknecht and Bas Rombouts, 'Stateless Indigenous People(s): The Right to a Nationality, Including Their Own' (2014) 19 Tilburg L Rev 99.

[71] See for example *K2 v. United Kingdom* (2017) ECHR 4238/13.

[72] See generally Laura Bingham and L Gamboa, 'Litigating Against Statelessness' in Laura van Waas and Melenie Khanna (eds), *Solving Statelessness* (Wolf 2016) 129.

4.4.1 Discrimination against Nomadic Peoples in the Granting of Nationality for Reasons of Race, Ethnicity, National Origins, Historical Migration, Indigenous Status, and Other Status

Tiered systems of nationality based on race, sex, and religion, even when those categories are implied by the context in which laws are drafted, are nevertheless prohibited in many cases as impermissible discrimination. The type of tribal discrimination practiced by Kuwait would arguably be prohibited under international law as a form of ethnic discrimination and, potentially, the arbitrary deprivation of nationality. "[E]xclusion is often experienced in newly independent States that define citizenship in a manner that excludes persons belonging to certain minority groups who are considered as 'outsiders' despite long-standing ties to the territory of the new State."[73]

The fact that many of the Sama Dilaut were originally not Muslims might have contributed to their statelessness in ways that are prohibited under international law for reasons of religious discrimination in a context like Malaysia where Muslim identity is central to nationality under the law. However, more research is needed on this potential intersection between historical animism and present-day discrimination in Sabah.[74] Likewise, if the fact that the Tuareg were sometimes classified as "white" is a factor in their statelessness in Mali, which has previously adopted what could be argued is coded, racialized language in its nationality law, this would clearly violate international law as implicit discrimination.

There is much support in international law for the prohibition of these types of implicit ethnic, racial, and religious discrimination. For example, in *IHRDA v. Mauritania*, the African Commission on Human and Peoples' Rights held that impermissible racial discrimination was the true cause of the denationalization and expulsion of black Mauritanians from Mauritania that began in 1989 under a racially targeted program of "Arabization."[75]

[73] OHCHR, Fact Sheet No.18 (Rev.1) (Minority Rights, 1998) 4-6.

[74] Clifford Sather, 'Sulu's Political Jurisdiction over the Bajau Laut' (1971) 3 Borneo Res Bulletin 43, 61.

[75] *IHRDA and AMDH v. Mauritania* (2010) 242/01, African Commission on Human and Peoples' Rights.

"Equality in the international human rights framework . . . requires States to take action to combat intentional or purposeful racial discrimination, as well as to combat de facto or unintentional racial discrimination."[76]

Regional law also protects against discrimination leading to the failure to grant nationality to historical migrant groups and discrimination based on national origins. Regional courts have provided protections specifically to historical migrants, or populations whose ancestors migrated to what is now a postcolonial state, sometimes as part of coerced or forced colonial-era population transfers, who are also of different ethnicities or religions. This provides additional protections to groups being ostensibly excluded on the grounds of their past cross-border movement, rather than explicitly on the grounds of their ethnicity or race. This may be highly relevant to nomadic peoples who cross borders and are treated as immigrants or foreigners.

One example is *Yean and Bosico v. Dominican Republic* before the Inter-American Court of Human Rights, which is particularly relevant for cross-border populations like many nomadic peoples. The case concerned the Dominican Republic. The Inter-American Commission had previously argued that the government had violated the *jus soli* provision of its own constitution by denying birth certificates to qualifying children born in the territory of the state for improperly discriminatory reasons based on race.[77] The Inter-American Court of Human Rights addressed the issue of withdrawal of nationality from persons of Haitian descent whom the government had labeled as being the descendants of "transients" not permanently settled in the Dominican Republic, despite being born there. This case lends support for prohibitions in international law against discrimination in the granting of nationality based on a history of migration, though it does not expressly mention *mobility as a way of life* as protected from discrimination under international law. Its reasoning, however, could be applied to stateless Fulani born in Côte d'Ivoire.

A similar case of discriminatory nationality laws for reasons of national origins was brought before the African Committee of Experts and the Rights and Welfare of the Child, the treaty body for the African Charter on the Rights and Welfare of the Child, in 2011. The government of Kenya declared that the children of Nubians brought to the country by the British

[76] Report of the Special Rapporteur on contemporary forms of racism racial discrimination xenophobia and related intolerance, Human Rights Council, Thirty-eighth session (18 June–6 July 2018) 6.

[77] *Case of the Girls Yean and Bosico*, paras 111 and 112.

during the colonial period did not have an "ancestral homeland" in Kenya and, therefore, did not qualify as Kenyan nationals.[78] In this case, the government clearly pushed for a definition of nationality based on a combination of ethnic grounds and national origins. The Committee, however, rejected the argument that discrimination based on ethnicity and national origins is permissible under regional human rights law, holding that the migration history of the ancestors of the Nubian population was not a justification for their continued denial of nationality. This case provides support for nondiscrimination based on historical migration and national origins. "It is unacceptable to describe the alleged victims in this case as foreigners in transit, since those who live for 10, 15 or more years in a country cannot be described as transients."[79]

These cases, however, do not discuss the question of discrimination against nomadism and mobility as a way of life, and rely on the issue of place of birth and residence being settled questions and not up for debate, which is not the reality faced by many nomadic peoples.

Under the indigenous rights framework, discussed at length in chapter 5, nomadic peoples have a right to a nationality as indigenous peoples and the right to be protected from discrimination because of their status as indigenous peoples. Not all nomadic peoples are indigenous. The question of whether a particular nomadic community is not only nomadic but also indigenous is a complex topic and will be discussed at length in chapter 5, and the intersection between these two areas of law when it comes to the statelessness of nomadic peoples deserves to be explored in greater depth.

Under the Universal Declaration of Human Rights, Article 2 and the International Covenants, the inclusion of a category for "other status" as a prohibited grounds for discrimination has potentially opened protections from discrimination to a broader class of persons. Could nomadism be an "other status" under the Universal Declaration of Human Rights and a progressive interpretation of international law? This approach has had clear success when it comes to discrimination based on sexual orientation, in part

[78] *Institute for Human Rights and Development in Africa (IHRDA) and Open Society Justice Initiative (on behalf of Children of Nubian Descent in Kenya) v. the Government of Kenya* (2011) Decision No 002/Com/002/2009, African Committee of Experts on the Rights and Welfare of the Child, para 3.

[79] *Case of the Girls Yean and Bosico* (n 77) para 111.

because the United Nations has made a progressive interpretation of gender a focus of its work.[80]

Freedom of movement is a fundamental human right, so there is much already to support nomadic peoples and nomadism as an "other status" under antidiscrimination law. For example, the International Covenant on Civil and Political Rights guarantees freedom of movement in Article 12, including the right to enter and leave one's country. The Universal Declaration of Human Rights does so likewise in Article 13. Freedom of movement under international law, however, is often interpreted to mean the freedom to change residence. The American Declaration of 1948 in Article 8 guarantees that; "every person has the right to fix his residence within the territory of the state of which he's a national." Freedom of movement in the 1951 Refugee Convention is closely tied to the establishment of a residence in Article 26.

Though the right to freedom of movement, in the sense of changing residence, is well established in international law, the right to engage in a mobile lifestyle, and particularly a cross-border, mobile lifestyle, arguably is not.[81] Expert on nomadic rights Jérémie Gilbert notes that the right to freedom of movement is designed not to support a mobile lifestyle but to allow settled people to change residence. As Gilbert points out, "international law is fundamentally in favour of settled societies in supporting predominantly sedentarist States to the detriment of nomadic forms of organization."[82] Gilbert also notes that "[f]ree movement being the essence of nomadism, it is surprising how little the right to free movement has been associated with a nomadic lifestyle."[83]

As chapter 1 discussed on the topic of nationality as a social and cultural category, links between a community and land justify the exclusion of outsiders and validate *jus soli, jus sanguinis*, and habitual residence as ways to determine nationality. This creates a deep bias against mobile lifestyles, a bias that forms part of the generalized bias against nomadism that was summarized in chapter 2, and one that is embedded within nationality at a conceptual and systemic level, as well as being embedded within international law. This makes it difficult to apply principles like freedom of movement in the context of cross-border mobility to practice nomadism.

[80] J Gary and N Rubin, *Are LGBT Rights Human Rights? Recent Developments at the United Nations UN Matters* (Psychology International 2012).

[81] Human Rights Committee, 'General Comments Adopted by the Human Rights Committee Under Article 40' Addendum General Comment No 27(67): Freedom of Movement (1994), art 12.

[82] Jérémie Gilbert, *Nomadic Peoples and Human Rights* (Routledge 2014) 58.

[83] ibid 72.

Some areas of international law have taken steps to address these forms of implicit and systemic bias and discrimination. The International Labor Organization Recommendation 104 recommends that governments protect tribal rights to cross borders.[84] At the regional level, the Council of Europe Recommendations on Stateless Nomadic Peoples and Nomadic Peoples of Undetermined Nationality (R 83(1)) and on the Social Situation of Nomadic Peoples in Europe (R 75(13)) contain support for nomadism as a way of life, a right that is also supported by the freedom of movement generally enjoyed within the European Union and other laws.[85] Some support for the right to cross borders and maintain a mobile lifestyle as part of seasonal transhumance may also be found under the ECOWAS (Economic Community of West African States) framework, such as in the ECOWAS Protocol on Transhumance (1998) and supporting Regulation (2003), where it states that ECOWAS should take measures to "facilitate" transhumance.[86]

There has also been some acknowledgment of nomadic peoples' rights to cross international borders under bilateral treaties, such as the Jay Treaty between the United States and Canada.[87] The Council of Europe Recommendations are one of the few instruments that expressly mention a right to be nomadic, and therefore push back against the widespread and systemic bias against nomadism as a way of life in international nationality law. In general, however, the practice of nomadism and/or a mobile lifestyle lacks clear protections under both regional and international law. The rarity of such clauses points to a gap in international law on guaranteeing the right to be nomadic. This is not a coincidence but is related to the systemic bias against nomadism that is discussed as a thematic issue throughout this book, but particularly in chapter 2.

It is quite possible that a progressive interpretation of international law would find that nomadism is protected as a type of "other status," but this requires stronger articulation. In particular, any classification of nomadism

[84] ILO Recommendation 104, quoted in Gilbert, *Nomadic Peoples and Human Rights* (n 83) 82–83.

[85] Recommendation no 14 of the Committee of Ministers to member states on the movement and encampment of Travelers in Europe (2004), quoted in Gilbert, *Nomadic Peoples and Human Rights* (n 83) 77.

[86] Forty-ninth Session of the Council of Ministers, Regulation C/REG.3/01/03 Relating to the implementation of the regulations on Transhumance between the ECOWAS Member States (Dakar 26–28 January 2003) art 2(5).

[87] 'Border Crossing Issues and the Jay Treaty' Senate of Canada Standing Senate Committee on Aboriginal Peoples (June 2016). See also Jay Treaty (Treaty of Amity, Commerce, and Navigation, between His Britannic Majesty and the United States of America) (signed 19 November 1794, entered into force 29 February 1796).

as a protected status when granting nationality should be explicit under international law to combat the systemic bias against mobility in nationality law and the nation-state system. This systemic bias itself may be a form of discrimination, but, if so, this should be more clearly articulated. Strong, unequivocal support from UN organs in the recognition of nomadism as a protected cultural and economic practice is needed. In particular, a right to dual or multiple nationality for nomadic and mobile peoples, discussed in more detail in chapter 6, may be necessary in order to preserve and protect the right to be nomadic as part of nomadic peoples' special status or indigenous status. Dual and regional nationality are cited as possible solutions at many points in this book, and therefore deserve their own area of study as a solution to nomadic statelessness that would also preserve the right to be nomadic. There remains unaddressed in this book the question as to what extent nomadic peoples may need to be given unique access to regional nationalities, for example, or whether all human beings have the right to regional nationality to maintain a mobile lifestyle.

4.4.2 Discrimination against Nomadic peoples in the Granting of Nationality on the Basis of Their Statelessness

Statelessness itself is often used as a justification for discriminating against nomadic peoples in the granting of nationality because nomadic peoples are often classified as tribes that are naturally stateless, as discussed in chapter 2. This topic will be treated in greater detail in chapter 6.

4.4.3 Discrimination against Nomadic Peoples in the Granting of Nationality on the Grounds of Minority Status

Nondiscrimination in international law is also closely tied to minority rights. Minorities may be simply defined as "[a] group numerically inferior to the rest of the population of a State . . ."[88] or as "a non-dominant group of

[88] J Castellino and C Doyle, 'Who Are "Indigenous Peoples"? An Examination of Concepts Concerning Group Membership in the United Nations Declaration on the Rights of Indigenous Peoples' in J Hohmann and M Weller (eds), *The UN Declaration on the Rights of Indigenous Peoples: A Commentary* (OUP 2018) 16, quoting F Capotorti, Special Rapporteur, Study on the Rights of Persons Belonging to Ethnic, Religious and Linguistic Minorities, UN Doc E/CN.4/Sub.2/384/Rev 1 (1977).

individuals who share certain national, ethnic, religious or linguistic characteristics which are different from those of the majority population."[89]

As previous chapters explored, many nomadic peoples like the Bedouin, the Tuareg, the Sama Dilaut, and the Fulani were divided by colonial-era borders, leaving them as minorities in postcolonial states. Aggressive settlement tactics like those explored in chapter 3 have only shrunk many nomadic populations, further reducing them to minority status. International law offers protections to minorities that complement the antidiscrimination framework discussed in this chapter. Under the nonbinding United Nations Declaration on the Rights of Persons Belonging to National or Ethnic, Religious and Linguistic Minorities, minority status may be protected on grounds of nationality, ethnicity, culture, religion, or language.[90] As the Human Rights Council specified,

> the persons designed to be protected are those who belong to a group and who share in common a culture, a religion and/or language. Those terms also indicate that the individuals designed to be protected need not be citizens of the State party . . . migrant workers or even visitors in a State party constituting such minorities are entitled not to be denied the exercise of those rights.[91]

All these categories may apply to nomadic peoples who are frequently minorities based on their nomadic lifestyle because they were divided by colonial borders.[92] Nomadism, however, is a category lacking specific protections under minority rights. As with nondiscrimination law, minority rights could also be strengthened by specifically listing nomadism as a cultural practice, recognizing that their nomadic lifestyle is often central to the discrimination nomadic peoples face in obtaining a nationality. As well, the minority rights framework could do more to specifically prohibit discrimination in the granting of nationality to minorities.

[89] OHCHR, Fact Sheet No18 (Rev 1), Minority Rights.

[90] UN General Assembly, Declaration on the Rights of Persons Belonging to National or Ethnic, Religious and Linguistic Minorities, 3 February 1992, A/RES/47/135.

[91] Human Rights Committee General Comment No 23 (1994) on the rights of minorities, quoted in Note by the Secretary-General, Effective Promotion of the Declaration on the Rights of Persons Belonging to National or Ethnic, Religious and Linguistic Minorities, A/74/160 (15 July 2019) 16. See also ibid.

[92] A Bourgeot, *Les sociétés touarègues : Nomadism, identité, résistances* (Karthala 1995) 463–464.

4.4.4 Discrimination in Nationality against Nomadism as a Type of Mobility

One serious problem with the international laws prohibiting discrimination is that discrimination against nomadism is also baked into the structure of nationality law, which is predicated on border restrictions and settlement on land. The implicit requirement of settlement on land permeates all aspects of nationality law, creating a systemic barrier to nationality for nomadic peoples, both due to very real challenges in fitting nomadic peoples into this system and to the perceptions and biases explored in chapter 2.

Nationality under the law being predicated on settlement means that the concept of territorial sovereignty has influenced the common ways of establishing nationality at birth under the law, including *jus soli*, where the link between the individual and the state is formed via the individual's birth on territory exclusively controlled by the state, as well as *jus sanguinis*, where an individual is descended from ancestors who have connections to the territory of the state. *Habitual residence* on the territory of the state is also a common way to establish nationality.[93]

Nationality in the cultural or social sense, with its idea of rootedness in the soil,[94] also justifies and derives justification from the right of states to exclusively control an area of bounded land.[95] Historically, as international law expert Van Panhuys noted, the concepts of inhabitant, national, and subject were closely related and sometimes used interchangeably, demonstrating the historical relationship between residence on land and belonging.[96] As international law expert Ian Brownlie explains, "Territory, both socially and legally, is not to be regarded as an empty plot: territory . . . connotes population, ethnic groupings, loyalty patters, national aspirations, a part of humanity, or, if one is tolerant of the metaphor, an organism."[97]

[93] van Waas, *Nationality Matters* (n 56) 32–33. See also Ruth Donner, *The Regulation of Nationality in International Law* (2nd edn, Brill 1994) 31–34.

[94] Hannah Arendt, *The Origins of Totalitarianism* (Houghton Mifflin Harcourt 1973) 270.

[95] Thomas Baldwin, 'The Territorial State' in Hyman Gross and Ross Harrison (eds), *Jurisprudence: Cambridge Essays* (OUP 1992) 210–211; Donner (n 94) 5; A John Simmons, 'On the Territorial Rights of States' (2001) 35 Noûs 300–326; Anna Stilz, 'Why Do States Have Territorial Rights?' (2009) 1 Intl Theory 185, 188.

[96] J H F Van Panhuys, *The Role of Nationality in International Law* (A W Sijthoff 1959) 139–141.

[97] James Crawford, *Brownlie's Principles of Public International Law* (9th edn, OUP 2019) 435. See also Neil Walker, 'The Territorial Dimension of Citizenship in Recent Academic Literature' in A R Shachar, I Bloemraad and M Vink (eds) *The Oxford Handbook of Citizenship* (OUP 2017) 554–572; M Moretti, *Le Droit international public et les peuples nomades* (Publibook 2006) 134–137.

Philosopher Hannah Arendt called the link between government, population, and territory the "trinity of European statehood."[98] As international lawyer Gibran van Ert explains, in the context of state succession, "[t]he automatic change principle (of the transfer of nationality) is rooted in medieval theories of land conveyance, according to which people were appurtenances to land—quite literally corporeal hereditaments—title to which was disposed together with title to the territory."[99]

Colonial empires used nationality law to reinforce territorial sovereignty by, for example, settling their nationals on colonized land, while postcolonial states established their claims to land in border zones through the settlement of their nationals.[100] Yet international law does not consider this systemic bias against mobile lifestyles to be a form of discrimination. More recognition of this systemic issue for nomadic peoples might be needed to grapple with the full extent of the bias against nomadism in nationality law. The fact that settlement is often a predicate for nationality under the law also raises the question of the effectiveness for nomads of the current international system of nationalities, a topic discussed in greater detail in the work of Lindsey Kingston.

4.5 Conclusion and Recommendations

International and regional laws do provide protections against ethnic, religious, minority status, historical migrations, national origins, and race where these are relevant to nomadic peoples. Nomadism and cross-border mobility as a way of life, however, are not expressly protected under the frameworks discussed here. This book advocates that nomadism should be a protected class under antidiscrimination law and minority rights, alongside race, ethnicity, religion, national origins, and other types of status.

However, a deeper problem emerges from this analysis. Applying existing frames to counter discrimination against nomadic peoples, such as the framing of historical migration, may only reinforce the widely held and damaging view that nomadic peoples are foreigners or migrants because of their nomadism by conflating nomadism with immigration. While this framing

[98] Arendt (n 95) 282.

[99] Gibran van Ert, 'Nationality, State Succession, and the Right of Option: The Case of Québec' (1998) 36 Can YB Intl L 151, 156.

[100] Crawford (n 98) 318–319.

may be appropriate for some nomadic peoples, such as the Fulani, whose presence in northern Côte d'Ivoire largely postdates colonial independence, it is potentially harmful for indigenous groups like the Sama Dilaut. Labeling nomadic peoples as historical migrants, stateless persons, or persons of different national origins risks entrenching, rather than solving, their exclusion in a context where international law could do more to expressly center nomadism and mobile ways of life.

This discussion has illuminated an essential fact about nationality law that weakens the power of antidiscrimination laws and norms to resolve nomadic statelessness. Discrimination against mobility is deeply embedded in the structure of nationality law itself, and therefore mobility receives no obvious protection under international law. It is not an accident that diverse states around the world like Kuwait, Mali, and Malaysia have claimed nomadic groups to be "immigrants" because discrimination against migrant or immigrant groups is, in fact, a constituent part of nationality law, part of its main function within the international system of states. This fact arguably creates a major, systemic barrier to solutions for nomadic statelessness and has resulted in a form of structural discrimination, or bias, against nomadism that permeates not only nationality law at the individual country level but also international nationality law. The example of nomadic Fulani in Côte d'Ivoire perfectly illustrates one of the many ways in which the very structure of nationality law itself, even when the nomadic peoples themselves are not stateless, nevertheless creates a discriminatory burden on nomadic peoples because they need to be able to regularly cross borders in a way that most other peoples do not.

It is necessary here to also say a few words about the role nationality law can play in nomadic assimilation, an issue given the systemic bias in nationality law in favor of settled individuals and against nomadic forms of social organization and the lack of acknowledgment by, or recourse under, international law. Chapter 3 discussed the ways in which civil registration has been linked to forced settlement, which is part of this systemic bias, and chapter 2 discussed antinomadic bias in more general terms. Nationality, while remaining a basic human right, does not necessarily prevent nomadic assimilation and may accelerate it. Without better protections against nationality being used as a tool of nomadic assimilation and settlement, the purpose of antidiscrimination law to protect nomadism as a way of life risks getting lost in the push to obtain a nationality for the sake of accessing individual rights, resulting in an empty victory for some nomadic communities. This should be the topic of more research.

5

The Right to a Nationality for Indigenous Persons

5.1 Introduction

Chapter 5 will explore the right to a nationality for nomadic peoples as indigenous persons. The chapter interrogates the classification of nomadic peoples as indigenous under the nonbinding indigenous rights framework and other areas of international and regional law. Building on previous chapters, this chapter also explores how indigeneity is used to justify establishing nationality under the law, including the connections between indigenous land ownership, indigenous rights, and nationality. As part of this exploration, this chapter examines how concepts such as *terra nullius* intersect with nationality for nomadic peoples.

Chapter 5 will also explore the closely related concept of nomadic self-determination which, as Van Genugten, Meijknecht, and Rombouts put it, can be controversial.[1] It is necessary to note that this chapter does not discuss the concept of indigenous citizenship as a status independent from the existing nation-state structure, as this topic is beyond the scope of this book. This book focuses only on indigenous status as it relates to nation-state nationality.[2]

5.2 The Bedouin, the *Bidoon*, and Indigenous Status in Kuwait

This section will look at how the Kuwaiti government has defined its *bidoon* population as foreigners rather than as indigenous in a political context

[1] Willem van Genugten, Anna Meijknecht and Bas Rombouts, 'Stateless Indigenous People(s): The Right to a Nationality, Including Their Own' (2014) 19 Tilburg L Rev 99, n 4 (speaking of indigenous self-determination).

[2] For more on this topic, see Lindsey N Kingston, *Fully Human: Personhood, Citizenship, and Rights* (OUP 2019) 149.

The Nationality and Statelessness of Nomadic Peoples Under International Law. Heather Jean Alexander, Oxford University Press. © Oxford University Press 2025. DOI: 10.1093/9780197772362.003.0005

dominated by exclusive government control over the deserts containing Kuwait's massive oil wealth and the infrastructure and pipelines necessary to extract it.[3] Given the problems that the existence of a *bidoon* population has caused Kuwait, it would seem that the government has every incentive to grant them a nationality, yet the solutions put forth by the government in recent years have focused primarily on the removal of the *bidoon* not just from Kuwait, but from the entire region, including by relocating them to the Comoros islands or Sudan.[4] To explain the origins of the argument over the foreign status of the *bidoon*, this chapter will explore the question of *bidoon* indigeneity, Bedouin land rights, and how these topics relate to nationality in Kuwait.

As previous chapters discussed, many of the *bidoon* in Kuwait are the descendants of Bedouin tribes and are therefore indigenous to the region, though the division of Bedouin territories by colonial borders has created a (perhaps disingenuous) conceptual confusion over their supposed origins. The question of *bidoon* indigeneity is extremely important to the questions of *bidoon* nationality and also oil rights. Kuwait is both an oil-producing country and a rentier state, where distribution of the proceeds of the oil is limited to nationals, a fact which arguably provides the government with a financial incentive to exclude the *bidoon*.[5] The oil is located in Kuwait's desert, the traditional territory of the Bedouin, raising the stakes for British control of Kuwait Town and Kuwait's deserts.[6] Maintaining exclusive government rights to these resources has become a primary concern to the Kuwaiti government and was a major reason for the Gulf War between Kuwait and Iraq.[7]

As earlier chapters explained, in 1909, the Emir of Kuwait, then the acknowledged sovereign in the region, signed an exclusive agreement with Britain for oil exploration.[8] Once oil was discovered, the wealth of the desert went from being based on the caravan and pearl trades, traditional activities of the Bedouin, to oil and gas. The shift to an oil economy drove the decline

[3] At the end of this book are maps showing the location of oil and gas deposits in Malaysia, Mali, and Kuwait.

[4] 'Are Sudanese Passports the Bidoons' Solution?' Al Jazeera (2018) <https://www.aljazeera.com/news/2018/03/sudanese-passports-bidoons-solution-180311153502061.html> accessed 27 May 2024.

[5] Claire Beaugrand, *Stateless in the Gulf: Migration, Nationality and Society in Kuwait* (I B Tauris 2018) 29–31.

[6] A B Loewenstein, 'The Veiled Protectorate of Kowait': Liberalized Imperialism and British Efforts to Influence Kuwaiti Domestic Policy during the Reign of Sheikh Ahmad al-Jaber, 1938-50' (2000) 36 Middle E Stud 103, 115–118.

[7] P Carmichael, *Nomads* (Collins and Brown 1991) 129.

[8] Michael Casey, *The History of Kuwait* (Greenwood 2007) 58.

of pastoralism and caravan trade as key economic activities while exploding the wealth of Kuwait City to unimaginable heights.[9] As Anthony Toth, an expert on the Bedouin in Kuwait, summarizes,

> Bedouin have had to deal with droughts and economic fluctuations for centuries. However, the rise of states in the region, with their need to regularize such things as borders, laws, the monopoly on power, economic control and the allegiance of its citizens, brought new challenges to nomadic populations.[10]

While the political conception of Kuwait as a state had long meant Kuwait Town and its urban, merchant population, which Lund-Johansen calls the urban-centered conception of nationality,[11] by the 1960s, this conception of Kuwait as a city-state had to change to better reflect Kuwait as a territorial state consisting of town and desert, including the oil fields.[12] Kuwait has sought to justify and give legitimacy to its border. As Toth puts it, writing of the region more generally, "areas (in the Gulf) where ownership of the land or sovereignty was in question became hotly contested."[13] A map at the end of this book shows the location of oil and gas infrastructure in the deserts of Kuwait (Map 1), demonstrating to what extent former Bedouin areas are now extremely valuable to the Kuwaiti state.

The Indigenous versus foreign status of the Bedouin tribes, particularly those tribes with ties to Saudi Arabia and Iraq, became critically important to the Kuwaiti government following the Iraq war,[14] though more research is needed on possible connections between disputes over Kuwait's borders, Kuwait's exclusive control of its oil, and the status and history of the *bidoon*. Also important to the question of *bidoon* indigeneity is the extent to which the *bidoon* are seen by broader Kuwaiti society as being tribal, or *badu*. "Central governments, particularly in the Middle East, generally regard

[9] Beaugrand, *Stateless in the Gulf* (n 5) 70.

[10] Anthony Toth, 'Tribes and Tribulations: Bedouin Losses in the Saudi and Iraqi Struggles over Kuwait's Frontiers, 1918-1943' (2005) 32 Brit J Middle E Stud 145, 166.

[11] Marie Lund-Johansen, 'Fighting for Citizenship in Kuwait' (masters thesis, Oslo U 2014) 21.

[12] A N Longva, 'Citizenship in the Gulf States: Conceptualization and Practice' in N A Butenschon, U Davis and M Hassassian (eds), *Citizenship and the State in the Middle East: Approaches and Applications* (Syracuse UP 2000) 192–193 (on conceptions of nationality in Kuwait).

[13] Anthony Toth, 'Control and Allegiance at the Dawn of the Oil Age: Bedouin, Zakat and Struggles for Sovereignty in Arabia, 1916-1955' (2012) 21 Middle E Critique 60.

[14] Longva, 'Citizenship in the Gulf States' (n 12) 191–194.

non-sedentary populations as tribes, forming states within a state, and constituting a national problem."[15]

The societal view of *bidoon* as tribal echoes the widely held views in academia that nomadic peoples are both tribal and stateless, discussed in chapter 2.

> The term badu designates a socio-cultural category that refers less to an economic, nomadic or sedentarised dimension than social values and behaviors: badu share a set of images of themselves with regard to their active or real common lineage, values and attributes, including commonality of interests, the reciprocity of obligations, common residence that continues once settled and the importance placed on marriages and alliances.[16]

Over time, the idea that *badu* peoples are somehow not Kuwaiti has crystalized in the popular discourse. This discourse is widespread, even as Kuwait celebrates its Bedouin heritage in cultural and tourist spaces. As Kuwaiti Professor Farah Al-Nakib puts it,

> this interdependence between Kuwait's pre-oil sedentary and nomadic worlds has been replaced with a popular rhetoric that identifies the badū as antagonistic outsiders. The building of a fortified town wall (sur) in 1920 has become emblematic of this supposed conflict between town and desert.[17]

In recent decades, the question of *bidoon* inclusion in the nation-state of Kuwait has also become entwined and conflated with the problem of immigration, as attractive pay generated by the oil industry meant that immigrants from Saudi Arabia settled in Kuwait, sometimes at the Kuwaiti government's request.[18] By 1965, Kuwaiti nationals were a minority in Kuwait.[19] Large-scale

[15] Dawn Chatty, 'The Pastoral Family and the Truck' in Philip C. Salzman (ed), *When Nomads Settle* (Praeger 1980) 80 (citing Lawrence Krader, 'The Ecology of Nomadic Pastoralism' 11 *Int'l Social Science J* 499).

[16] Claire Beaugrand, 'Statelessness and Transnationalism in Northern Arabia: Biduns and State Building in Kuwait, 1959-2009' (PhD thesis, London Sch of Econ 2010) 70. See also A N Longva, 'Citizenship in the Gulf States: Conceptualization and Practice' (n 12) 186–187.

[17] Farah Al-Nakib, 'Revisiting Hadar and Badū in Kuwait: Citizenship, Housing, and the Construction of a Dichotomy' (2014) 46 Int J Middle E Stud 5, 8.

[18] Carmichael (n 7) 122.

[19] J S Ismael, *Kuwait: Dependency and Class in a Rentier State* (UP of Florida 1993) 117–122 (on demographic change in Kuwait post-Protected State).

immigration, combined with unclear statistics on the Kuwaiti *bidoon* population in the decades following the passage of the nationality law and a lack of civil registration and legal identity for Bedouin, as discussed in chapter 3, means that it is difficult today to establish the origins of many *bidoon* families and, therefore, to conclusively prove their indigenous status in Kuwait. The government today regularly conflates the distinction between nomadism and migration, and in popular Kuwaiti discourse, the term *bidoon* simply means foreigner.[20] The issue of whether or not *bidoon* are indigenous or foreign has become so contentious that at one point the government proposed genetic testing for the *bidoon* population.[21]

The war with Iraq would be devastating for public perception of the *bidoon,* cementing the association between them and Iraq, as well as the view of them as a potential security risk to the state. Because many *bidoon* lived to the north of Kuwaiti City near Al-Jahra, many families fled during the invasion.[22] The provisional government contained many *bidoon* and the Iraqi authorities also forced all *bidoon* to register for the army. These facts combined to paint a devastating picture of *bidoon* loyalty. Many who were displaced during the war were banned from returning to Kuwait, while others were fired from their jobs.[23] Some Iraqis also opted to stay as *bidoon* in Kuwait following the war. Despite a court ruling in 1998, that bidoon were stateless Indigenous people and not aliens, the government issued papers claiming the bidoon's origins as Iraqi and labeling them "illegal migrants."[24] While many naturalized Kuwaitis have achieved a lifestyle and standard of living similar to that of "original" Kuwaitis, life has only gotten more difficult for the *bidoon.* As Beaugrand points out, the Kuwaiti government frequently cites to the supposed "illegal" nature of the *bidoon* in Kuwait, many of whom have ancestors in the region dating back hundreds of years, as evidence not of a technical problem for the Kuwaiti government to solve, but of the *bidoon's* inherent criminality and statelessness.[25]

[20] Beaugrand, *Stateless in the Gulf* (n 5) 4 (on how the origins of the *bidoon* are presented and understood in Kuwait today). See also Lund-Johansen (n 11) 1. I am indebted to Professor Alwuhaib for his insights on this point.

[21] Beaugrand, 'Statelessness and Transnationalism in Northern Arabia' (n 16) 154.

[22] A N Longva, 'Citizenship in the Gulf States: Conceptualization and Practice' (n 12) 191–192. See also Lund-Johansen (n 11) 33.

[23] Beaugrand, *Stateless in the Gulf* (n 5) 172. See also Beaugrand, 'Statelessness and Transnationalism in Northern Arabia' (n 16) 152.

[24] Beaugrand, *Stateless in the Gulf* (n 5) 115–116. See also Beaugrand, 'Statelessness and Transnationalism in Northern Arabia' (n 16) 134–135.

[25] Beaugrand, 'Statelessness and Transnationalism in Northern Arabia' (n 16) 191, 227. See also Beaugrand, *Stateless in the Gulf* (n 5) 30–31.

5.3 Self-Determination and the Indigenous Status of Nomadic Peoples in Mali and Côte d'Ivoire

As chapter 3 explained, at decolonization, some Tuareg leaders pushed either for a separate, Tuareg state, for a semiautonomous region, or for the inclusion of the Tuareg areas of Niger and Mali with a North African state like Morocco.[26] During the decades since independence, various Tuareg independence movements have attempted to create an independent Tuareg state in the Sahel, one which would provide the Tuareg with their own nationality and control over their lands. While self-determination is not usually presented as a solution to statelessness, it might have provided a solution in the case of the Tuareg at colonial independence and could form part of a solution in the future. During decolonization, however, self-determination was rarely invoked as a right for nomadic peoples and most states in Africa resisted any changes in colonial borders.[27] Nomadic peoples appear to have fared particularly badly during the decolonization process, which would show "no consideration for the social, political and territorial integrity of the Tuareg and other (nomadic) societies like the Peul (Fulbe, Wodabee) or Berber (Imaziṙen), but in fact established their marginalization."[28]

The idea of shifting boundaries in the Sahara was not without precedent, as the French had moved boundaries and transferred territory throughout their tenure in West Africa.[29] Yet, neither the UN nor the Organization of African Unity endorsed self-determination for the Tuareg, instead allowing

[26] Créant une Organisation Commune des Régions Sahariennes Loi no 57-27 du 10 janvier 1957, *JORF*, 11 January 1957, 578. See also Baz Lecocq, 'Tuareg City Blues—Cultural Capital in a Global Cosmopole' in Ines Kohl and Anja Fischer (eds), *Tuareg Society within a Globalized World: Saharan Life in Transition* (Bloomsbury Press 2010) 47–52 (on attempts to create a semi-independent state in the Sahara); Hélène Claudot-Hawad, 'La question touarègue, quels enjeux?' in Michel Galy (ed), La guerre au Mali : Comprendre la crise au Sahel et au Sahara : enjeux et zones d'ombre (Découverte 2013) 133–135; Bruce Hall, *A History of Race in Muslim West Africa, 1600-1960* (CUP 2011) 299–300; P Boilley, *Les Touaregs Kel Adagh: dépendances et révoltes : du français au Mali contemporain* (Karthala 1999) 297–298.

[27] Sara R Dorman, 'Citizenship in Africa' in Isin EF and Peter Nyers (eds), *Routledge Handbook of Global Citizenship Studies* (Routledge 2014) 162. See also Malcolm Shaw, 'Peoples, Territorialism and Boundaries' (1997) 3 Eur J of In't L 478, 493; James Crawford, *Brownlie's Principles of Public International Law* (9th edn, OUP 2019) 108–122; Jérémie Gilbert, 'Nomadic Territories: A Human Rights Approach to Nomadic Peoples' Land Rights' (2007) 7 Hum Rts L Rev 681, 692–693; Mark Weller, 'Settling Self-determination Conflicts: Recent Developments' (2009) 20 Eur J Intl L 117; Suzanne Lalonde, *Determining Boundaries in a Conflicted World: The Role of Uti Possidetis* (McGill Queens 2012) 116–117; Malcolm Shaw, *International Law* (9th edn, CUP 2021) 230.

[28] Ines Kohl and Anya Fischer (eds), *Tuareg Society within a Globalized World: Saharan Life in Transition* (I B Tauris 2010) 5.

[29] Hall (n 27) 298 (citing the example of a transfer of territory from French Soudan to Mauritania during the colonial period).

decolonization, for the most part, to fall along existing borders. Ironically, this was done to promote stability,[30] though in the case of the Tuareg it would lead instead to war.

Many Tuareg did not appear to feel a common sense of purpose with southern Mali in the period leading up to independence, which was not helped by the fact that the new government did not celebrate Tuareg identity as an indigenous group but presented the Tuareg as a foreign threat to the Malian state.[31] The former chief of the Kounta Tuareg is quoted by Gabriel Féral as saying, "When you (the French) leave, it's Bamako who will rule, the settled peoples, the blacks . . . now, things are no longer done with the gun, with the *takoba (sword)*, all that is finished, it will be done with the vote, with the elections. But we, the nomadic peoples, are in the minority."[32]

As chapter 3 summarized, following the failed 1963 rebellion by Tuareg leaders, which led to a brutal campaign of government violence and repression,[33] the socialist Kieta government put into place aggressive policies to seize control of Tuareg lands for collectivization and the promotion of farming. The government granted the Tuareg the right to use, not own, their lands, and agriculture was favored over herding.[34] New restrictions were put in place to limit Tuareg migrations across what were now international borders.[35] This resembled the bias summarized in chapter 2 about nomadic peoples as lacking claims to land and about nomadic lands being available for government seizure. Advocacy to change Mali's borders was seen as evidence of foreign ties and disloyalty and the Tuareg were quickly branded by the Malian government as a foreign security threat to the state.[36] The Malian

[30] James Crawford has comprehensively addressed the creation of new states during the decolonization process in *The Creation of States in International Law* (2nd edn, OUP 2006) chs. 13, 14.

[31] See the discussion in J Keenan, *The Lesser Gods of the Sahara: Social Change and Contested Terrain amongst the Tuareg of Algeria* (Routledge 2004) 7–8. See also Boilley, *Les Touaregs Kel Adagh* (n 27) 284–285; T Benetti, 'Entwicklung des Verhältnisses zwischen Tuareg und staatlichen Strukturen in Mali' (masters thesis, U Vienna P 2008) 53–54; C O Diarrah, *Vers La IIIe République Du Mali* (L'Harmattan 1991) 33, 35; W J Foltz, *From French West Africa to the Mali Federation* (Yale UP 1965) 94, 119 (speaking generally of northern tribes); Hall (n 27) 308; Lecocq, 'Tuareg City Blues' (n 27) 43–52.

[32] Gabriel Féral, 'Administrations comparées en pays nomade' in E Bernus and others (eds), *Nomades et commandants: Administration et sociétés nomades dans l'ancienne AOF* (Karthala 1993) 111 (my translation).

[33] A Bourgeot, *Les sociétés touarègues: Nomadism, identité, résistances* (Karthala 1995) 406.

[34] C Gremont, 'Villages and Crossroads: Changing Territorialities among the Tuareg of Northern Mali' in J McDougall and J Scheele (eds), *Saharan Frontiers: Space and Mobility in Northwest Africa* (Indiana UP 2012) 135–137. See also Lecocq, 'Tuareg City Blues' (n 27) 160–164 (on government agricultural projects in the Sahel).

[35] Boilley (n 27) 361.

[36] ibid 307–310. See also Lecocq, 'Tuareg City Blues' (n 27) 48.

government often labeled the Tuareg as white, and they often labeled themselves in this way, as chapter 4 discussed, but for the Malian government, this label implied that they were therefore not indigenous. As Tuareg expert Aly put it, "It appears that the Malian government considers the recognition of indigenous peoples as a threat for the national unity."[37]

This debate over Tuareg indigenous status was taking place during a time when the Sahel, considered to be empty and unproductive by many French *commandants,* was found to contain valuable minerals. Mineral exploitation would quickly overtake agriculture as one of Mali's most important exports in the years following colonial independence. A period of brutal drought in the Sahel in the 1970s damaged both pastoralism and agriculture and led many Tuareg to leave the area;[38] at the same time, however, lucrative mining contracts in neighboring Niger and Algeria raised the stakes for ownership of the Sahel and highlighted the potentially serious economic repercussions of Tuareg independence.[39] Northern Mali contains large deposits of gold, iron, magnesium, copper, zinc, uranium, phosphates, salt, gypsum and oil, and tar sands, including the potentially lucrative Taoudeni Oil and Gas Basin in the far north of the country. A map at the end of this book (Map 2) shows the possible distribution of these valuable resources throughout Tuareg areas.

The question of land ownership in the Sahel for grazing and farming became more contentious in the 1980s and 1990s, when many Tuareg refugees returned to Mali from abroad.[40] During the decades of armed conflict, the Malian government claimed that Tuareg lands reverted to the state, and much of them had been parceled off to agricultural communities. The government and the international community also used the repatriation of refugees to promote Tuareg settlement, which exacerbated questions of land ownership for returned Tuareg, who were now considered foreigners. Settlement and land ownership would also be linked to registration and voting, meaning that returned Tuareg could only register to vote if they settled, and could

[37] Aly, Lahyerou AG, 42.

[38] Diarrah (n 32) 85–87.

[39] H Claudot-Hawad, 'La question touarègue, quels enjeux?' in M Galy (ed), *La guerre au Mali : Comprendre la crise au Sahel et au Sahara : enjeux et zones d'ombre* (Découverte 2013) 136–139, 145–147. See also Boilley (n 27) 307 (on northern Mali's proximity to oil in Algeria); Lecocq, 'Tuareg City Blues' (n 27) 49; Jane Whaley, 'Mali: A Country on the Cusp?' (GeoExpro 2008) <https://geoexpro.com/mali-a-country-on-the-cusp/> accessed 29 April 2024; International Business Publications, 'Mali Mineral & Mining Sector Investment and Business Guide' (2007) 44; World Nuclear Association, 'Uranium in Niger' (2023) <http://www.world-nuclear.org/information-library/country-profiles/countries-g-n/niger.aspx> accessed 29 April 2024.

[40] Ines Kohl and Anya Fischer, 'Tuareg Moving Global: An Introduction' in Ines Kohl and Anya Fischer (eds), *Tuareg Society within a Globalized World: Saharan Life in Transition* (I B Tauris 2010).

therefore influence Malian elections by settling and registering.[41] Younger Tuareg also often found themselves caught between the ideals of pastoral life and the allures of a more settled existence like the one they had experienced abroad.[42]

The fact that many Tuareg are returned refugees, combined with their historical association with nomadism, separatism, and cross-border migration, means that many non-Tuareg in Mali consider them not to be an indigenous group in Mali but foreign. The narrative of foreign Tuareg returning to steal Malian land became entrenched in Malian society. By 2012, the Tuareg resistance movement was heavily influenced by regional interests, including Algeria and Libya, which fueled the narrative that the Tuareg are foreign agents.[43]

Self-determination is today not the goal of many Tuareg in Mali, who instead want integration, though possibly with some autonomy.[44] The war over Tuareg separatism, however, has now metastasized into an international conflict involving a broad array of countries and actors. Instead of separatism, the government now fears a foreign takeover. The imposition of conservative Islamic law in northern Mali radically altered life for people living there and caused yet more displacement while cementing the widely held view that the Tuareg are linked to terrorism and foreign values. Recent events in Mali, with the introduction of multiple international actors in what was once a war of Tuareg independence, have only made a resolution of the conflict seem further away, while obscuring the origins of the conflict as one of Tuareg separatism. As one Tuareg individual put it, "Azawad is a dream."[45]

[41] D Badi, 'Genesis and Change in the Socio-political Structure of the Tuareg' in Anya Fischer and Ines Kohl (eds), *Tuareg Society within a Globalized World: Saharan Life in Transition* (I B Tauris 2010) 85.

[42] S Randall and A Guiffrida, 'Forced Migration, Sedentarization and Social Change: Malian Kel Tamasheq' in Dawn Chatty (ed), *Nomadic Societies in the Middle East and North Africa: Entering the 21st Century* (Brill 2006) 438–439.

[43] J Keenan, 'Resisting Imperialism: Tuareg Threaten US, Chinese and Other Foreign Interests' in Anya Fischer and Ines Kohl (eds), *Tuareg Society within a Globalized World: Saharan Life in Transition* (I B Tauris 2010) 221–223, 226–227. See also S Pezard and M Shurkin, *Toward a Secure and Stable Northern Mali: Approaches to Engaging Local Actors* (Rand Corporation 2013) 1, 6–7; Dona J Stewart, 'What's Next for Mali? The Roots of Conflict and Challenges to Stability' (US Army War College Strategic Stud Inst 2013) 37–38.

[44] Delphine Perrin, 'Tuaregs and Citizenship: "The Last Camp of Nomadism"' (2014) 6 Middle E L Governance 296.

[45] Quoted in Integrated Regional Information Networks, 'Separatists and Skeptics: refugees divided on future of northern Mali' (2014) <https://reliefweb.int/report/mali/separatists-and-sceptics-refugees-divided-future-northern-mali> accessed 29 April 2024.

The Ivoirian government, by contrast, at first encouraged Fulani to move into northern Côte d'Ivoire, as they brought their skills in raising cattle to the growing demand for beef among Ivoirian consumers. Drought and conflict also pushed both nomadic and sedentary Fulani communities to relocated to the relative stability of northern Côte d'Ivoire. The Fulani are not therefore considered to be, or consider themselves to be, an indigenous group in what is now northern Côte d'Ivoire, though they are indigenous to the wider region. Pastoral Fulani had always shifted migration routes in response to changes in the climate and cycles of drought, and in recent decades, more Fulani began migrating south in response to climate change, armed conflict, and anti-pastoral land use policies.[46]

However, the 1990s in Côte d'Ivoire saw huge changes in Ivoirian politics on cross-border migration and immigration, as Henri Konan Bédié, then president, began a new policy of *Ivoirité.* Foreigners could no longer vote or own land, even if they came from adjacent countries.[47] Government support for pastoralism in Côte d'Ivoire also ended, while a huge expansion of the agricultural sector greatly reduced the amount of land available to Fulani pastoralists for grazing. Customary law in Côte d'Ivoire does also not support Fulani grazing rights. "In colonial and post-colonial state law, livestock keepers are disadvantaged *vis-à-vis* farmers since customary rights to land are recognized, whereas pasture rights or territorial rights are not."[48]

Climate change and changing land use policies have fueled a new round of conflicts between Fulani pastoralists and farmers in Mali and Burkina Faso.[49] The dichotomy between indigenous farmers and foreign herders is now entrenched in the popular discourse both in West Africa and abroad, presenting Fulani pastoralists as non-indigenous, despite their long history in the region. The United Nations notes that,

> [i]n several coastal States, in addition, ideas of indigeneity (autochtonie) have become virulent, posing indigenous against settlers or autochtones against allogènes. The indigenous are generally the local farming

[46] T A Benjaminsen and B Ba, 'Fulani-Dogon Killings in Mali: Farmer-Herder Conflicts as Insurgency and Counterinsurgency' (2021) 14 Afr Sec 4, 4–26 (on the role of armed conflict, land use policy, and climate change in farmer-Fulani conflict in Mali).

[47] Loi no 98-750 du 23 décembre 1998 relative au domaine foncier rural (23 décembre 1998).

[48] Karin Nijenhuis 'Reconsidering Conflicts over Land in the Sahel as Conflicts over Power' (2009) Legal Anthropology from the Low Countries, Special Issue, Recht der Werkelijkheid 69, cited in Benjaminsen and Ba (n 47) 9.

[49] Stewart, 'What's Next for Mali?' (n 44) 5.

> communities, while migrant farmers and all herders are considered as settlers or strangers. It has become a widespread practice to negate strangers any secure access to natural resources such as land, and in some cases even to jobs, education and infrastructure. These beliefs exacerbate the social and economic marginalization of pastoralists, and further restrict their access to resources.[50]

The Ivoirian government officials interviewed in 2019 for this book spoke of the Fulani as an outsider, or foreign, group or ethnicity that is a danger to Côte d'Ivoire because they are associated with conflicts in Burkina Faso and Mali. All Fulani, including those born in Côte d'Ivoire and born abroad, who were interviewed for this book reported the perception that they are treated as foreigners and immigrants by both the authorities and the general population, even though Fulani pastoralism has been common in the wider region for hundreds of years and the border between Côte d'Ivoire and Burkina Faso is an arbitrary, colonial invention based largely on the location of local rivers that has never been formally recognized by either country.

Today, many younger, settled Fulani born in Côte d'Ivoire are stateless with sharply reduced opportunities, a fact that has the potential to negatively impact pastoralism in the region as it has traditionally been settled communities that have helped to negotiate access to land on behalf of nomadic pastoralists. Unable to shift southward to access better pastures in the face of climate change and conflict, pastoral Fulani have shrinking options to pursue pastoralism in the region. A regional problem of how to facilitate indigenous, pastoral migration across arbitrary, colonial borders has been reframed in Côte d'Ivoire as a black-and-white story of illegal immigration and security threats from dangerous foreign herders.

5.4 Malaysia and Sama Dilaut Indigenous Status

The question of Sama Dilaut indigenous status plays a small, but arguably vital, role in the larger question of Malaysian sovereignty over the border zone between Malaysia, the Philippines, and Indonesia, a zone of enormous

[50] M Leonhardt, 'Regional Policies and Response to Manage Pastoral Movements within the ECOWAS Region Study on behalf of the International Organization for Migration (IOM), within the framework of the Support to Free Movement of Persons and Migration in West Africa' (FMM West Africa Proj 2019) 8.

wealth from oil, fishing, and tourism. Even as the government of Malaysia has reframed the Sama Dilaut as a foreign threat, it is profiting from the massive amounts of oil under the oceans that were once the domain of the Sama Dilaut and other fishing communities. While during the colonial period, north Borneo was a remote part of the British Empire, a place where the BNBC struggled to make money, today, Sabah's offshore oil is a key driver of Malaysia's economy, and the federal government has only strengthened its exclusive control over offshore oil in recent decades.[51] The government of Malaysia now derives a significant portion of its wealth from oil exploitation in the Sulu Sea, as well as fishing and tourism in its marine parks, even as it has pushed the Sama Dilaut out of their traditional fishing zones and branded them as illegal migrants.

The federal government is focusing heavily on exploration in Sabah and Sarawak, with oil fields pushing up against the maritime boundaries with Brunei and the Philippines, which, in turn, have their own off-shore wells.[52] Western Sabah, for example, houses the Sabah Oil and Gas Terminal (SOGT), the Sabah-Sarawak Integrated Oil and Gas Project, and the Sabah-Sarawak Gas Pipeline.[53] A map at the end of this book shows the location of present-day and future drilling sites in Malaysia and the Philippines, demonstrating the value of Sama Dilaut oceans to both governments (Map 3).

The desire to claim the oceans off the coast of Sabah for its exclusive use for oil exploration, national parks, and large-scale fishing has raised the stakes for the legitimacy of the government of Malaysia's sovereignty over the region. Concerns over immigration, changing demographics, and breakaway movements have led the government to securitize the border and push out any groups it views as destabilizing or having ties to foreign states like the Philippines.[54] The Sama Dilaut fall into this category of so-called undesirable

[51] Goh Beng Lan, 'Dilemma of Progressive Politics in Malaysia: Islamic Orthodoxy versus Human Rights' in Wendy Mee and Joel Kahn (eds), *Questioning Modernity in Indonesia and Malaysia* (Nus Press 2012) 302–306, 340.

[52] US Energy Information Administration, 'Malaysia: International Energy Data and Analysis' (2020) <http://www.eia.gov/beta/international/analysis.cfm?iso=MYS> accessed 30 April 2024. See also H Singh, *South Asia Defense and Strategic Year Book* (2nd edn, Pentagon 2015) 218.

[53] US Department of Commerce International Trade Administration, 'Malaysia—Oil and Gas' (2017) <https://www.trade.gov/market-intelligence/malaysia-energy-doing-business-petronas-0> accessed 30 April 2024. See also Gregory Poling, 'The South China Sea in Focus: Clarifying the Limits of Maritime Dispute' (Center for Strategic and International Studies 2013); E S Fernandez, 'Philippine-Malaysia Dispute over Sabah: A Bibliographic Survey' (Philippine E-J 2007) 55; V M Hooker, *A Short History of Malaysia: Linking East and West* (Allen and Unwin 2003) 221–222.

[54] A Nah, 'Globalisation, Sovereignty and Immigration Control: The Hierarchy of Rights for Migrant Workers in Malaysia' (2012) 40 Asian J Sco Sci 486, 491–492, 498–499.

groups, as the question of Sama Dilaut indigenous status is linked to broader questions in Malaysia about national identity and borders.

As chapter 3 discussed, Malaysia is a country united by a common experience with British colonization, which has proven to be a difficult idea around which to organize a nation-state. The centrality of the Malay nation, or *bangsa*, sits uneasily with the idea of a universal, Malaysian nationality law for the country's ethnic, religious, and culturally diverse population.[55] Malaysian history had multiple cycles of immigration and emigration in an area dominated by the long-distance, seafaring trade by Arab, European, and Chinese traders.[56] Sabah has also been the site of several independence movements, raising the specter of separatism, and incursions by armed groups from the Philippines.[57]

The struggle to differentiate between indigenous and immigrant populations in Malaysia can be seen in successive governments' attempts to develop census categories over the decades. In Borneo, while early censuses included the indigenous peoples in the general category of Malay, starting in the 1921 census, the British government began to apply the term "Bajau" to the inhabitants occupying the coastal areas of North Borneo and Sarawak rather than the term "Malay."[58] Bajau, however, was also an indigenous, ethnic category in the Philippines. In 1969, by contrast, the Malaysian government included all indigenous peoples in Malaysia in the category of *bumiputra*, or sons of the soil, validating their indigenous status and granting

[55] Nagatsu Kazufumi, 'Pirates, Sea Nomads or Protectors of Islam? A Note on "Bajau" Identifications in the Malaysian Context' (2001) 1 Asian Afr Area Stud 212, 218–219. See also William Guinee, 'Race, Ethnicity, and Ethnic Relations: A Malaysian Case Study: A Curriculum Project for the Fulbright-Hays Seminar Abroad: Malaysia and Singapore' (Westminster College 2005); N M Saleeby, 'Studies in Moro History, Law and Religion' (Proj Gutenberg Ebook 2013, Philippines Dept of the Int 1905) 158; V Sinnadurai, 'Nationality and International Law in the Perspective of the Federation of Malaysia' in Ko Swan Sik (ed), *Nationality and International Law in Asian Perspective* (Martinus Nijhoff 1990) 313.

[56] C Hirschman, 'The Meaning and Measurement of Ethnicity in Malaysia' (1987) 46 J Asian Stud 558. See also Tom Harrisson, 'The Prehistory of Borneo' (1970) 13 Asian Persp 17, 37–39 (note the contested nature of this period of Borneo history).

[57] Kassim A and Haji Mat Z R, 'Policy on Irregular Migrants in Malaysia: An Analysis of its Implementation and Effectiveness' (Philippine Inst for Dev Stud 2011) , 16. See also 'Esscom Ops against Illegal Immigrants in Kudat' Borneo Post (15 May 2015) (accessed July 2020); Harjeet Singh, *South Asia Defense and Strategic Year Book* (Pentagon 2015) 222; A Kassim and Z R Haji Mat, 'Policy on Irregular Migrants in Malaysia: An Analysis of Its Implementation and Effectiveness' (Philippine Inst for Dev Stud 2011) 20; Fernandez (n 54).

[58] Kazufumi (n 56) 219. See also Hirschman (n 57) 567; Wendy Mee and Joel Kahn, 'Islam and Capitalism in the Frontiers and Borderlands' in Wendy Mee and Joel Kahn (eds), *Questioning Modernity in Indonesia and Malaysia* (Nus Press 2012) 49; F Barlocco, *Identity and the State in Malaysia* (Routledge 2014) 35.

them special privileges over the descendants of immigrant populations.[59] The creation of the *bumiputra* category was specifically designed to bond Malays with the so-called native populations of the Borneo territories.

In the 1980s, the government began to employ the term *pribumi* in the census for all indigenous groups in Sabah and Sarawak, a term also used in Indonesia. This prompted a backlash in Sabah, as it appeared to include Indonesian and Filipino immigrants as part of the native population. In the 1990s, the Malaysian government attempted to do away with racial classifications altogether. Instead, it introduced a single national identity of Bangsa Malaysia, reaffirming this approach with the 1Malaysia, and Vision 2020 campaigns and programs. Yet, the government continues to face the same issues in creating a unified nationality identity to help protect against separatism and foreign claims in a multiethnic federation where many nationals share an ethnicity with peoples in neighboring states, particularly in Borneo.

Further confusing the question of indigenous status is the fact that the aboriginal peoples of Peninsular Malaysia, some of whom are nomadic but do not cross borders, were not included in the *bumiputra* category, while non-Malays in the Borneo states, such as the Bajau/Sama, Kadazan, and Dusun groups, are included. As a result, the aboriginal peoples of peninsular Malaysia were treated under a different set of laws from the indigenous peoples of Borneo.[60] These classifications have serious repercussions under the law. While the land rights of aboriginal groups in peninsular Malaysia are protected by the Aboriginal Peoples' Act of 1954,[61] it has been left to the courts, citing indigenous rights cases in Australia, Canada, and the United States, to uphold the land rights of certain indigenous groups in Sabah and Sarawak on an ad hoc basis. The debate over indigenous versus immigrant status is also very relevant to voting and political power in Malaysia. The topic of phantom voters is a constant political issue and, at one point,

[59] M Clark and J Pietsch, *Indonesia-Malaysia Relations: Cultural Heritage, Politics and Labour Migration* (Routledge 2014) 162. See also Hwok-Aun Le, 'Affirmative Action in Malaysia and South Africa: Contrasting Structures, Continuing Pursuits' (2015) 50 J Asian Afr Stud 615, 616. See also Anja Frank, 'Negotiation Borders: Everyday Corruption and Immigration Policing in Malaysia' (2014) ISA Working Paper 2; Barlocco (n 59) 53; Hooker (n 54) 233, 260.

[60] Ramy Bulan, 'Native Title in Malaysia: A "Complementary" Sui Generis Proprietary Right under the Federal Constitution' (2007) 11 Austral Indigenous L R 54, 56–57. See also Barbara Watson Andaya and Leonard Y Andaya, *A History of Malaysia* (2nd edn, Palgrave Macmillan 2001) 341–432; Hooker (n 54) 23, 227.

[61] Malaysia Aboriginal Peoples Act, *Malaysia Act* (1954, 1974), 134. Aboriginal is defined in Malaysia's Constitution as limited to Aboriginal peoples of the Malay Peninsula. Constitution of Malaysia (1957) art 160(2).

triggered a Royal Commission of Inquiry tasked with looking into the question of fraudulent documents issued to irregular migrants.[62]

By contrast, the government regularly classifies the Sama Dilaut as an immigrant population, along with the descendants of Chinese and Indian immigrants. Today, many officials hold the entrenched view that all Sama Dilaut are from the Philippines and are not indigenous to Sabah.[63] Undocumented people and populations labeled "immigrants" in Malaysia, including the Sama Dilaut, as well as persons of Chinese and Indian descent, have faced intergenerational statelessness in Malaysia despite protections against statelessness written into Malaysia's laws.[64]

The classification of Sama Dilaut as a foreign population has had serious consequences for their rights. Foreign and stateless workers, including Sama Dilaut, are routinely deported during economic downturns or in response to security incidents. Immigration to Sabah is now considered to be an issue of national security as it is taking place across an international border, arbitrarily set during the colonial period, but whose placement has serious repercussions for oil exploration. The debate over the origins of the Sama Dilaut can be seen in local media, which frequently presents the Sama Dilaut as coming from the Philippines[65] or lacking a homeland.[66] The typical position toward the Sama Dilaut in Malaysia can be seen by this quote from a local newspaper *The Star*: "Another census on the Palau people or sea gypsies of Semporna will be done in August amid allegations they act as the 'eyes and ears' of cross border criminals, such as kidnappers."[67]

The rhetoric on the Sama Dilaut, however, frequently goes beyond simply classifying them as illegal immigrants. They are frequently discussed as being naturally stateless. Their historic fishing zones are now under the exclusive

[62] Tan Sri Datuk Amar Steve Shim Lip Kiong (Chairman) and Commissioners, Royal Commission of Enquiry, 'Report of the Commission of Enquiry on Immigrants in Sabah' (2012) 3.

[63] Helen Brunt, 'Stateless Stakeholders: Seen but Not Heard? The Case of the Sama Dilaut in Sabah, Malaysia' (masters thesis, U Sussex 2013) 35–36.

[64] C Allerton, 'Contested Statelessness in Sabah, Malaysia: Irregularity and the Politics of Recognition' (2017) 15 J Imm and Refugee Stud 250–251. See also Tamara Duraisingam, 'Chronology of Policies Affecting Potentially Stateless Persons and Refugees in Malaysia' (2016) Statelessness Working Paper Series No 2016/07.

[65] See for example 'Poor and Stateless: Sabah's 50,000 undocumented children denied access to education, health care' The Malay Mail Online (30 April 2015) (accessed April 2024); 'Look into the Plight of the Sama Dilaut Urges NGO' *The Star Online* (7 July 2015) (accessed April 2024); Qin Xie, 'Last of the Sea Gypsies: Fascinating Images of the Nomadic Borneo Tribe Who Spend Their Lives on the Water' *Daily Mail* (8 February 2016) (accessed April 2024).

[66] Cris Majors and J Swiecicka, 'Missing the Boat?' *Inside Indonesia* (24 July 2007) (accessed 21 April 2024).

[67] Muguntan Vanar, 'ESSCOM to Hold Another Census' *The Star Online* (11 July 2015).

ownership of the Malaysian government as they are regularly deemed to have no territorial rights in the region. In litigation before the International Court of Justice with Indonesia, for example, the Malaysian government drew a careful distinction between "wandering . . . sea gypsies" who in precolonial times were "effectively beyond the jurisdiction of any of the States in the region, including the Sultan of Sulu" and other peoples in northern Borneo who have land rights.[68] This framing of the Sama Dilaut as stateless has a long history in Malaysia. From precolonial times, origin myths of the Sama Dilaut that were popular on the mainland framed the group as having been cast out of Islam and regular society.

In 2016, Malaysia created the Tun Mustapha Park, the largest ocean park in Malaysia, at the northern tip of Sabah.[69] The creation of the park has not stopped oil exploration in the oceans off Sabah, but it has greatly impacted Sama Dilaut fishing rights. As stateless people, the Sama Dilaut have no legal standing to challenge their removal from park areas or to change government policy. Meanwhile, the government still markets the Sama Dilaut as a tourist attraction based on their "traditional" lifestyle as a nomadic people.[70] In an example of the sometimes contradictory attitude of governments toward nomadic peoples, one that simultaneously presents them as indigenous and foreign, Part Ten of the report on the creation of the nearby Semporna Islands Park, which also occupies Sama Dilaut fishing zones, contains the following paragraph:

> The high percentage of non-Malaysian citizens living in the proposed park should not be seen as an obstacle. The questions of citizenship can be addressed later, but in the meantime, it is important to establish the park and introduce management strategies for resource use and other activities... The nomadic Sama Dilaut have a unique lifestyle and have been using the area for hundreds of years. They should be allowed into some parts of the

[68] *Case Concerning Sovereignty Over Pulau Ligitan and Pulau Sipandan (Indonesia v Malaysia)* (Merits) International Court of Justice, ICJ Rep 625 ICGJ 54 (ICJ 2002) (17 December 2002). See also R Haller-Trost, *The Territorial Dispute between Indonesia and Malaysia over Pulau Sipadan* (IBRU 1995).

[69] R Jumin and K Kassem, 'Ecosystem-based Management in a Proposed Marine Protected Area: Tun Mustapha Park' (World Wildlife Fund Malaysia 2011); Coral Triangle Initiative, 'Valuation Study of the Proposed Tun Mustapha Park' (2011). I am indebted to Helen Brunt for her comments on this point.

[70] See for example the Malaysia government tourism website at Malaysia Truly Asia, 'Regatta Lepa 2023' 2023 <https://www.malaysia.travel/events/regatta-lepa-2023> accessed 30 April 2024.

park, where they will be required to comply with all regulations concerning resource use.[71]

5.5 Nomadic Indigenous Status

Nationality is an individual right, but, as the examples showed, it is also important at the community level, particularly for nomadic peoples to protect their unique way of life by accessing and controlling their lands, either as a minority group within a state, or their own state pursuant to self-determination.[72] Yet, natural resource extraction incentivizes governments to seize nomadic lands for their own use, while falling back on tropes about nomadic peoples as foreign or stateless. As anthropologist and expert on Malaysia James Scott noted,

> The sovereign state is now busy projecting its power to its outermost territorial borders and mopping up zones of weak or no sovereignty. The need for the natural resources of the "tribal zone" and the desire to ensure the security and the productivity of the periphery has led, everywhere, to strategies of "engulfment."[73]

One common theme that emerges from the examples in this chapter is that some governments have reclassified their nomadic populations as dangerous foreigners or stateless populations without rights rather than as indigenous peoples.[74] Often, this reclassification of nomadic populations as dangerous to the state is occurring in a very real climate of border disputes and terrorism, but it is hard to avoid the observation that nomadism, itself, as a way of life is being targeted. As nationality law expert Audrey Macklin puts it, speaking more generally of minorities, "Investing in mechanisms that enable the conversion or reversion of risky people to the status of foreigner simplifies the equation of state

[71] Semporna Islands Project, 'Management Plan for the Semporna Islands Park (Draft: 1-2001) Part 10: Legal Aspects and Regulations' (2010) 133.

[72] *African Commission of Human and Peoples' Rights v The Republic of Kenya (the Ogiek case)* (2017) African Court on Human and Peoples' Rights, App No 006/2012.

[73] James C Scott, *The Art of Not Being Governed: An Anarchist History of Upland Southeast Asia* (Yale UP 2010) xxi, 5–6.

[74] For more on this theme in the African context, see Jérémie Gilbert, Litigating Indigenous Peoples' Rights in Africa: Potentials, Challenges and Limitations (2017) 66 Intl Comp L 657 (on the concept of nomadic peoples as indigenous in African litigation).

security."[75] Being classified by their governments as foreign populations places nomadic peoples in the same category as other historical migrant groups, as having no right to a nationality or self-determination.

Today, it is nomadic lands, rather than nomadic livelihoods, that are vital to the economic and political security of many states. Governments are eager to deem these lands empty and ripe for exploitation. Branding nomadic communities as stateless or foreign, rather than indigenous, removes a moral justification for nomadic rights to land and justifies their relocation and exclusion. It justifies maintaining arbitrary colonial borders and the removal of "foreign" or "stateless" nomadic populations from their lands for security reasons. As the *Segovia Declaration of Nomadic and Transhumant Pastoralists* points out, the nationalization of nomadic lands has been a widespread, global problem.[76] Nationalization, often for natural resource extraction, continues the long-standing practice of governments branding nomadic regions as empty, discussed in chapter 2, and, therefore, under exclusive state control. As Manby points out in the African context, statelessness, migration, colonial policy, conflict, and land expropriation are "linked."[77] Modern nationalization of nomadic lands echoes colonial policies on *terra nullius*.[78] "Indigenous communities have in so many cases been pushed out of their traditional areas to give way for the economic interests of other more dominant groups and to large scale development initiatives that tend to destroy their lives and cultures rather than improve their situation."[79]

Finally, the case of the Fulani exposes another issue for nomadic peoples as indigenous peoples, that of the global tendency to frame indigenous status as existing at the national, rather than the regional, level, particularly in regions where borders are arbitrary and bisect nomadic lands. What is clear from the examples is that the intersection between nomadic statelessness

[75] Audrey Macklin, 'The Securitization of Dual Citizenship' in T Faist and P Kivisto (eds), *Duel Citizenship in Global Perspective: From Unitary to Multiple Citizenship* (Palgrave Macmillan 2007) 42.

[76] Segovia Declaration of nomadic and transhumant pastoralists, La Granja, Segovia (14 September 2007).

[77] Bronwen Manby, 'Trends in Citizenship Law and Politics in Africa since the Colonial Era' in Engin Isin and Peter Nyers (eds), *Routledge Handbook of Global Citizenship Studies* (Routledge 2014) 172.

[78] M Moretti, *Le Droit international public et les peuples nomades* (Publibook 2006) 130–137.

[79] *Centre for Minority Rights Development (Kenya) and Minority Rights Group International on behalf of Endorois Welfare Council v. Kenya* (2010) African Commission on Human and Peoples' Rights, Communication No 276/2003 para 247, quoting Report of the African Commission's Working Group on Indigenous Populations/Committees (2005) 20. See also Genugten, Meijknecht and Rombouts (n 1) 102; Nick McDonell, *The Civilization of Perpetual Movement: Nomads in the Modern World* (Hurst 2016).

at the community level, land rights, and indigenous status requires further study. Based on the information here, however, the next sections will look specifically at the protections offered against statelessness to nomadic persons under international law in the area of indigenous rights and self-determination.

5.6 The Right to a Nationality and Indigenous Status under International Law

Over the last few decades, international law has increasingly recognized collective rights, or the rights of groups to make claims against their governments on a group basis, including under the nonbinding indigenous rights framework, as expressed in the United Nations Declaration on the Rights of Indigenous Peoples.[80] As previous chapters discussed, indigenous peoples are protected from discrimination and guaranteed access to nationality under this area of soft law, making the recognition of nomadic peoples as indigenous an additional potential tool to resolve their statelessness. Indigenous status, when combined with civil rights and nationality, has helped nomadic groups around the world gain recognition and rights, including land rights, through public advocacy and the courts. To access these protections, however, a nomadic community must first be defined as indigenous. The examples discussed in this chapter demonstrate how difficult it can be for cross-border, nomadic populations to establish their indigenous status, particularly given the long history of branding nomadic peoples as both naturally stateless and foreign. The next section will discuss how indigenous status is determined under international law.

5.6.1 Defining Nomadic Peoples as Indigenous under International Law

As the examples in this chapter showed, nomadic peoples have often struggled to establish their indigeneity. Many countries use the rhetoric that nomadic peoples are migrants or foreigners to justify their exclusion from

[80] UN Declaration on the Rights of Indigenous Peoples. See also Crawford, *Creation of States in International Law* (n 31) 112; Genugten, Meijknecht and Rombouts (n 1) 98.

nationality.[81] While international soft law has established the right to a nationality for indigenous persons, it has arguably not done enough to regulate and discourage this use of the concept of indigeneity to exclude groups and justify statelessness. The lack of a clear definition of "indigenous" under international law has arguably contributed to this problem. There is no settled definition of indigenous under regional or international law, or methods by which such disputes could be settled. A general weakness of using the indigenous rights framework as a pathway to a solution for nomadic statelessness is that it carries the risk that the right to a nationality for nomadic peoples gets lost in a debate over the status of nomadic peoples as indigenous persons.

In an attempt to bring more specificity to indigeneity, experts have offered varying opinions on how to define indigenous status. Self-identification, as discussed, is often an important component. This is the approach taken by ILO Convention 169, which emphasizes state recognition of indigenous or tribal status.[82] The United Nations Development Group, which guides mainstreaming the sustainable development goals, cites a variety of factors that may be relevant to the identification of indigenous peoples, including, most importantly, self-identification but also historical continuity with precolonial societies, priority in time, a strong link to particular territories and natural resources, distinct social systems and culture from the majority population, and a history of discrimination.[83]

The international rights framework provides specific guidance on the question of indigenous status for nomadic peoples, as nomadism as an indigenous practice may be framed as a protected cultural practice and/or as a traditional economic activity protected under Articles 3, 5, and 20 of the Declaration on the Rights of Indigenous Peoples and under Article 27 of the International Covenant on Civil and Political Rights (ICCPR). Some scholars argue, however, that historical occupancy of land lies at the heart of the concept of indigenous, though others dispute this claim.[84] The examples

[81] For a discussion of the weaponization of nomadism in the European context, see generally Claudia Tavani, *Collective Rights and the Cultural Identity of the Roma: A Case Study of Italy* (Brill 2020).

[82] Convention (No 169) concerning Indigenous and Tribal Peoples in Independent Countries, art 1.

[83] UN Development Group, 'Guidelines on Indigenous Peoples' Issues' (2009) 8–9. See also Gilbert, 'Nomadic Territories' (n 28) 692–704 (on nomadic peoples and indigenous land rights).

[84] J Castellino and C Doyle, 'Who Are "Indigenous Peoples"? An Examination of Concepts Concerning Group Membership in the United Nations Declaration on the Rights of Indigenous Peoples' in J Hohmann and M Weller (eds), *The UN Declaration on the Rights of Indigenous Peoples: A Commentary* (OUP 2018) 17–24.

showed how problematic the link between indigenous status, land occupation, and ownership can be for nomadic communities. Some other definitions of indigenous status appear to adopt the view that European colonization is a necessary precondition,[85] a problem in parts of the world where indigenous nomadic peoples are seeking greater independence not from settler societies but from other indigenous groups, like in the examples highlighted for this book. The indigenous rights framework is arguably designed for states where the majority population have European origins, but this is not the case in many parts of the world where nomadic peoples live.[86] The case of the *bidoon* also demonstrates how changes to group identity over time have complicated the question of their indigenous status, which presupposes a level of group cohesion that has simply been impossible for many nomadic communities to maintain and ironically disadvantages the most marginalized nomadic peoples.[87]

There is also the question of indigenous status at the regional level, a question raised by the problems confronting Fulani nomadic peoples in northern Côte d'Ivoire. Greater, and more specific, recognition under international law of indigenous status as a regional status would be helpful to many cross-border nomadic communities. At the regional level in Africa, the indigenous status of pastoralists finds support in pastoral charters and regional and bilateral agreements, such as the ECOWAS (Economic Community of West African States) Protocol on Transhumance (1998) and supporting Regulation (2003), the N'Djamena Declaration on the contribution of pastoral livestock herding to the security and development of the Saharo-Sahelian areas, the African Union Commission Department of Rural Economy and Agriculture, Policy Framework for Pastoralism in Africa, and the bilateral protocol between Mali and Niger to regulate cross-border pastoralism.[88]

[85] Statement of the former United Nations Special Rapporteur on Discrimination against Indigenous Populations, José Martínez Cobo at http://indigenousfoundations.web.arts.ubc.ca/global_actions/.

[86] See the discussion in T Bloom, 'Members of Colonized Groups, Statelessness and the Right to Have Rights' in T Bloom, K Tonkiss and P Cole (eds), *Understanding Statelessness* (Routledge 2017) 155–156. See also Gilbert's discussion on indigenous land rights, Gilbert, 'Nomadic Territories' (n 28) 695 and Jérémie Gilbert, *Nomadic Peoples and Human Rights* (Routledge 2014) 57. See also S Imai and K Buttery, 'Indigenous Belonging: A Commentary on Membership and Identity in the United Nations Declaration on the Rights of Indigenous People' (2013) 49 York UP Working Paper.

[87] See the discussion in Bloom'Members of Colonized Groups' (n 87) 166. See also *Endorois* (n 80) para 161.

[88] ECOWAS Protocol on Transhumance and supporting Regulation, 42 Official Journal (1998, 2003) art 2; Protocole d'accord en matière de transit du bétail entre la République du Niger et la République du Mali, *Bamako* (1988); Solomon Beyene, *Securing, Protecting and Improving the Lives, Livelihoods and Rights of Pastoralist Communities* (African Union Dept of Rural Economy and Agriculture 2010).

Yet these agreements have not been widely implemented and have not led to meaningful change in the rights of pastoral communities, in large part because, as the examples showed, indigenous status in both Africa and the Middle East and Asia is sometimes framed as being limited to the borders of a particular nation-state. Instead of being recognized as indigenous, nomadic peoples are often labeled "non-indigenous" foreigners or naturally stateless people.

In all the examples discussed in this chapter, internationally sponsored rhetoric on nomadic peoples being bad for the environment, reflecting the bias against nomadism that can be found throughout academia, has further damaged nomadic claims to indigeneity by seeming to place them in opposition to the natural world. Such framings demonstrate more gaps between the ideals of indigenous rights, and the realities of the debate over indigeneity for many nomadic communities.

Perhaps most problematically for nomadic communities, indigenous status is sometimes conceptualized as requiring that the indigenous group was present in a location first, under the concept of "first in time."[89] "[P]articular importance is always placed on the requirement that the group . . . must have occupied and used a fairly definable territory before present day state borders."[90]

This implies that important rights, such as land rights and nationality, are somehow justified following a historical analysis of a group's location on a particular piece of land prior to an arbitrary date. The intersection between indigenous rights, rights to land, and rights to nationality in a specific state has raised the stakes for nomadic peoples in many countries to prove such historical occupations of land and created incentives for governments to rebrand nomadic peoples as foreign or naturally stateless. It is therefore worth asking if linking rights to arguments over first in time is sometimes doing more harm than good for nomadic peoples.

Recent jurisprudence suggests that indigenous rights may be moving away from its classical framing of first in time, European colonization, and some of the other problematic framings discussed here to a framework that focuses instead on state oppression.[91] For example, the Inter-American

[89] Genugten and others (n 1) 100.
[90] *Endorois* (n 80) 139, 159–160. See also M Ahren, 'The Provisions on Lands, Territories and National Resources in the UN Declaration on the Rights of Indigenous Peoples: An Introduction' cited in Castellino and Doyle (n 85) 30.
[91] *Endorois* (n 80) para 154–160.

Court of Human Rights extended indigenous status to a group descended from African slaves brought to Suriname in *Saramaka v Suriname*. This broadened the definition of indigenous to groups that arrived to what is now Suriname during the colonial period.[92] Speaking of the African context, indigenous rights experts Montes and Cisnero, quoted by Castellino and Doyle say, "It is not the issue of aboriginality, who came first, that is a fundamental aspect of the definition of indigenous peoples, as suggested by the states, but rather the current relations of oppression within those African societies."[93]

The extension of indigenous rights to groups that were not first in time shows a possible way forward for some nomadic peoples who struggle to establish first in time because of the recent placement of borders dividing their territories and a history of mobility that has too often been weaponized against them. A progressive interpretation of indigeneity as based on state oppression of mobility as a unique cultural practice may make the indigenous rights framework helpful to a broader class of nomadic peoples in general.

5.6.2 Minority Status as an Alternative or Complement to Indigenous Status for Nomadic Peoples

As Castellino and Doyle point out, other international frameworks, such as minority rights, discussed in chapter 4, might be more appropriate for nomadic peoples seeking a solution to statelessness.[94] It is worth revisiting here the framing of nomadic rights as a type of minority rights, not only for antidiscrimination law but also to access human rights more broadly.[95] Under the 1992 United Nations Declaration on the Rights of Persons Belonging to National or Ethnic, Religious and Linguistic Minorities, minorities have the right to fully exercise their human rights and to take appropriate measures under the law to protect their cultures, languages, religions, traditions, and

[92] See generally Fergus MacKay, *The Rights of Maroons in International Human Rights Law* (2010).

[93] Castellino and Doyle (n 85) quoting A Regino Montes and G Torres Cisneros, 'The United Nations Declaration on the Rights of Indigenous Peoples: The Foundation of a New Relationship between Indigenous Peoples, States and Societies' in Claire Charters and Rodolfo Stavenhagen (eds), *Making the Declaration Work: The United Nations Declaration on the Rights of Indigenous Peoples* (International Work Group for Indigenous Affairs 2009) 29.

[94] Castellino and Doyle (n 85) 25–27.

[95] See the discussion in Jérémie Gilbert, 'Still No Place to Go: Nomadic Peoples Territorial Rights in Europe' (2004) 4 Eur YB Minority Issues 141, 144–145, 159.

customs.[96] Particularly important for nomadic peoples, cross-border minorities have the right to participate in decision-making on both the national and regional level and maintain contact with one another across borders. Minority rights also include special rights to protect against assimilation.

The rights available to nomadic peoples as minorities, however, could be more explicitly articulated under international law, particularly given the challenges nomadic peoples face in accessing their rights as indigenous peoples, and the fact that nomadic peoples are frequently minorities. The relationship between minority status and indigenous status under international law could also be better articulated, given the arguably stronger protections offered to indigenous peoples when it comes to the specific issues facing many nomadic peoples, which include the linked issues of land rights and access to nationality. Perhaps most importantly for the subject of this book, there is no particular right to a nationality for minorities, something that international law could remedy to offer stronger protections against statelessness for minorities, including many nomadic peoples.

5.6.3 The Tuareg and the Right to Self-Determination

It is necessary to say a few words about the right to self-determination, which guarantees, among other things, the right to an independent, group, or collective nationality. In the Tuareg context, for example, self-determination would provide them with land rights, status as an indigenous people, and a nationality of their own.[97] Though not expressly in the United Nations Charter, the right to self-determination is guaranteed by several important human rights treaties including the International Covenant on Civil and Political Rights and the International Covenant on Economic, Social and Cultural Rights. Before decolonization, the principle of self-determination had been successfully invoked in limited cases by the League of Nations in the *Aland Islands* case.[98] In 1960, the UN General Assembly passed Resolution 1514 on the Granting of Independence to Colonial Countries and Peoples as existing political groups, enshrining the territorial approach

[96] Declaration on the Rights of Persons Belonging to National or Ethnic UN General Assembly, Religious and Linguistic Minorities, A/RES/47/135 (3 February 1992) art 4.

[97] Genugten and others (n 1) 99.

[98] *Aaland Islands Case* [1920] LNOJ Spec. Supp. No. 3.

to decolonization. Resolution 1514 expressly applied self-determination only to "(t)rust and non-self-governing territories or all other territories which have not yet attained independence."[99] Self-determination at decolonization was, therefore, limited to existing political and territorial units. As a result, the decolonization process left many peoples and nations without states of their own.[100]

In 1970, the UN General Assembly passed the Declaration on Friendly Relations and Cooperation Among States to prevent self-determination claims that would "dismember . . . sovereign and independent states conducting themselves in compliance with the principle of equal rights and self-determination of peoples."[101] The International Court of Justice affirmed the right to independence from colonization for former colonies in the Namibia Opinion of 1971.[102] As a result, while the right to self-determination from European colonization is arguably *jus cogens,* the right to self-determination by minorities and indigenous peoples within postcolonial states does not find similar support under international law unless recognized by the United Nations and usually following a referendum.

As well, the principle of self-determination under international law has not always recognized a concurrent right to a nationality. For example, Article 1 of both the ICCPR and the International Covenant on Economic, Social and Cultural Rights did not expressly include a right to a nationality, arguably missing the intersection between the two. The focus of the decolonization process was much more on stabilizing borders and regulating relations between the new states than on establishing a nationality for all or registering the population.

Nomadic communities, however, have had difficulties qualifying for self-determination. The 1975 *Western Sahara* case provided a rare example of a nomadic group successfully advocating for their own state. The case

[99] Declaration on the Granting of Independence to Colonial Countries and Peoples, GA Res 1514 (XV) (14 Dec. 1960).

[100] Shaw, *International Law* (n 28) 282–233. See generally the discussion in Ingrid Barnsley and Roland Bleiker, 'Self Determination: From Decolonization to Deterritorialization' (2008) 20 Global Change, Peace and Security 121. See also Craig Scott, 'Indigenous Self-Determination and Decolonization of the International Imagination: A Plea' (1996) 18 HR Q 814; Crawford, *Creation of States in International Law* (n 31) 120.

[101] Declaration on Principles of International Law concerning Friendly Relations and Co-operation among States in accordance with the Charter of the United Nations (24 October 1945) 1 UNTS XVI.

[102] *Legal Consequences for States of the Continued Presence of South Africa in Namibia (South West Africa) notwithstanding Security Council Resolution 276* [1970] ICJ Rep 16.

provided nomadic groups in the western Sahara region with independence from both European states and earlier colonization by Morocco. The decision recognized that nomadic peoples were "socially and politically organized,"[103] pushing back against the systemic bias against nomadic peoples that conceptualizes them as naturally stateless and without a homeland. The case also rejected the concept of *terra nullius* for nomadic peoples. While *Western Sahara* could have provided a blueprint for other nomadic states, however, it has not been followed by a wave of nomadic independence and statehood but instead remains something of an outlier. Self-determination as a solution to nomadic statelessness requires further study, but the political challenges involved and the lack of support from major international actors, may make other solutions to nomadic statelessness more accessible.

5.7 Conclusion and Recommendations

This chapter showed how indigenous status is a double-edged sword for nomadic communities. On the one hand, it has the potential to offer additional protections from statelessness to nomadic peoples under the indigenous rights framework. On the other hand, states may use it to justify the exclusion and statelessness of nomadic peoples by rebranding them as non-indigenous immigrants or naturally stateless tribes, often to justify seizing nomadic peoples' lands. As the examples observed, the removal of nomadic peoples from their lands and their rebranding as dangerous foreigners or stateless persons is sometimes accompanied by resource extraction or tourism in what could be categorized as a modern application of *terra nullius.*

This has allowed states to place stateless nomadic peoples within the context of irregular migration and border security to justify their continued exclusion. The indigenous rights framework arguably injects more discord into the debate over nomadic statelessness due to the lack of a clear definition of indigenous and the requirement that indigenous peoples have strong, provable, and long-standing connections to land. Other frameworks, such as the minority rights framework, or a modern reenvisaging of indigenous rights around the idea of ongoing oppression rather than the idea of first in time, may be more helpful to nomadic peoples, in securing their rights both to land and to a nationality.

[103] *Western Sahara* (Advisory Opinion) [1975] ICJ Rep 12.

Finally, the biased view of nomadic peoples as naturally stateless and the framing of nomadic groups as non-indigenous are factors in their difficulties in claiming the right to self-determination, though more research is needed on this crucial issue. Modern debates over nomadic nationality, self-determination, and their relationship to land often mirror debates stretching back to the early colonial period over the extent to which nomadic communities form states or tribes, as discussed in chapter 2. Because of this history, while this book does not endorse the right to self-determination as a solution for nomadic statelessness, nomadic peoples would benefit from more explicit protections under international, one that moved away from indigenous status as the normative justification for rights.

6

Identifying Nomadic Persons as Stateless for the Purposes of a Solution under International Law

6.1 Introduction

Drawing on the examples from chapters 2 through 5, this chapter discusses solutions under international law that require that a nomadic person be identified as stateless. The identification of statelessness may be followed by an automatic grant of nationality or facilitated naturalization. These solutions are heavily promoted by the UN High Commissioner for Refugees (UNHCR) and other international actors for stateless migrants and children born stateless, including by encouraging states to enact statelessness determination procedures and ratifying the statelessness conventions. Identifying nomadic individuals as stateless may open the door to some powerful solutions, yet it also carries risks. This chapter will first discuss the international laws for identifying children born stateless, which leads to the automatic granting of nationality or facilitated naturalization. Under international law, it will look at the possibility of individualized or group statelessness determination procedures, followed by facilitated naturalization.

In looking at these possible solutions, chapter 6 also discusses how stateless people can establish they are in their own country, the difficulties stateless people face in establishing their statelessness, and the dangers associated with labeling nomadic individuals as stateless. It, therefore, builds on the discussions in previous chapters around the history of nomadism, indigenous status, and the centrality of place of birth and residency to establishing nationality.

The Nationality and Statelessness of Nomadic Peoples Under International Law. Heather Jean Alexander, Oxford University Press. © Oxford University Press 2025. DOI: 10.1093/9780197772362.003.0006

6.2 The Risks to Nomadic Peoples of the Statelessness Label

The solutions in this chapter require that individual nomadic people be first labeled as stateless to access a solution, usually facilitated naturalization. Chapters 2 through 5, however, have highlighted some of the serious risks to nomadic individuals of labeling them as stateless, as well as the long history of labeling nomadic peoples as a class or group as naturally or intrinsically stateless. Some nomadic peoples are already officially labeled by their states as stateless, including many former Bedouin in Kuwait, who have received the official status of *bidoon*. In these cases, statelessness is clearly established and passed down through the generations under a type of negative *jus sanguinis*. In this way, statelessness has become a type of nationality status itself, except it excludes people from rights and traps them in a cycle of illegality.[1] Other nomadic communities have received identity documents that imply their statelessness, such as the Sama Dilaut in Malaysia, where many hold various forms of ID that attest to their non-national status.[2] As Arendt points out, "[t]he stateless person, without right to residence and without the right to work, had of course constantly to transgress the law."[3] For these reasons, this book does not advocate for this solution for nomadic peoples. It is worth interrogating in the abstract, however, if a formal recognition of statelessness might assist some nomadic peoples to obtain a nationality under international law in the hypothetical case of full state adoption and implementation of international norms.

6.3 The International Laws Applicable to Children Born Otherwise Stateless

This section will look at solutions available under international law that rely on the identification of nomadic children at birth who are born stateless. As the examples showed, particularly in chapter 4, the feasibility and

[1] Amal De Chickera and J Whiteman, 'Addressing Statelessness through the Right to Equality and Non-discrimination' in M. Khanna and Laura van Waas (eds), *Solving Statelessness* (Wolf 2017) 103–104. See also Neil Partrick, 'Nationalism in the Gulf States' in D Held and K Ulrichsen (eds), *The Transformation of the Gulf* (Routledge 2011) 57 (discussing the 'politics of descent' in Kuwait).

[2] 'Stop Scapegoating Sabah to Push for Fed Constitution Citizenship Amendments that Affect Statelessness, Undocumented Indigenous Communities of East Malaysia—CSO Platform for Reform' Malay Mail (23 November 2023). Note that at the time of writing, Malaysia was debating a new bill that might worsen access to documents for some Sama Dilaut.

[3] Hannah Arendt, *The Origins of Totalitarianism* (Houghton Mifflin Harcourt 1973) 286.

appropriateness of rapid and strict adoption of *jus sanguinis* by numerous postcolonial states was never questioned during the decolonization process, despite the arguably high risk of creating statelessness. International law mandates, however, that children born otherwise stateless in the territory of the state be granted a nationality. The central treaty supporting this norm is the Convention on the Reduction of Statelessness of 1961, Article 1. To help states understand how to apply this norm, UNHCR has issued Guidelines on Ensuring Every Child's Right to Acquire a Nationality through Articles 1–4 of the 1961 Convention on the Reduction of Statelessness.[4] Though the Convention has not been widely adopted, this section will consider its effectiveness as a possible solution for nomadic children.

In addition to the Convention, regional treaties and court decisions support limits on *jus sanguinis* in order to prevent statelessness, including the American Convention on Human Rights, the African Charter on the Rights and Welfare of the Child,[5] the European Court of Human Rights, which has recognized that nationality was an integral part of a child's identity, and the African Committee of Experts on the Rights and Welfare of the Child in *Nubian Children*.[6]

The requirement that states grant nationality to a child born otherwise stateless may be automatic under Article 1(1)(a), or subject to conditions, like habitual residence, under Article 1(1)(b). According to UNHCR, the condition of habitual residence cannot continue longer than five years and, in a clause that is very helpful to families suffering from intergenerational statelessness, lawful residence is not required.[7] UNHCR permits states, however, to give children a designation of "undetermined nationality" during the adjudication process, though some regional treaties prohibit this approach. Civil registration also plays a central role in implementing Article 1, as it is necessary to establish that the child was born in the territory of the state, on the one hand, and is not the national of another state, on the other hand, complicating this solution for nomadic individuals who lack

[4] American Convention art 20(2); African Charter art 6(4). See also the Convention to Reduce the Number of Cases of Statelessness, 13 September 1973, ICCS Convention No 13.

[5] Pact of San José American Convention on Human Rights, Costa Rica, 1144 UNTS 123 (came into force 18 July 1978). For a list of state parties see: https://treaties.un.org/pages/showdetails.aspx?objid=08000002800f10e1; African Charter on the Rights and Welfare of the Child Organization of African Unity (OAU), CAB/LEG/24.9/49 (11 July 1990). For a list of state parties, see https://au.int/sites/default/files/treaties/36804-sl-AFRICAN%20CHARTER%20ON%20THE%20RIGHTS%20AND%20WELFARE%20OF%20THE%20CHILD.pdf.

[6] *Menesson v France* (2014) ECHR 65192/11, 5e sect.

[7] UNHCR Guidelines on Statelessness Nos 4, 6, 8, 9.

civil registration, as discussed in chapter 3. It is not clear, therefore, that this individualized solution for children born otherwise stateless provides an effective solution for ending intergenerational statelessness for nomadic families.

As noted in chapter 1, Malaysia has protections against statelessness written into its nationality law that are similar to those in Article 1 of the 1961 Convention, including a provision guaranteeing nationality at birth to persons born in Malaysia who would be otherwise stateless.[8] The experience of stateless children in Malaysia, however, demonstrates the gaps in this approach. Beginning in 2010, a number of court cases have been brought to establish Malaysian nationality for stateless children adopted by Malaysian parents.[9] Yet, these cases have struggled in the courts because the procedures and evidence required for establishing statelessness under Malaysian law are unclear. In 2017, a Federal Court in Malaysia granted the right of appeal to five stateless and adopted children, including two stateless foundlings, who were petitioning for Malaysian nationality under Article 15(a) of the Constitution. The court rejected the applications of the stateless foundlings because while they had proven they were born in Malaysia, they had not proven they were stateless. Some of the children were later granted citizenship because they could furnish documents demonstrating that they did not have access to another nationality.

Though Malaysia's law provides for nationality to be granted in "special circumstances" where nationality is unclear or contested, this vague provision does nothing to specify a mechanism or a set of standards to establish when such circumstances exist. These cases show the very real barriers that may be faced by the Sama Dilaut and other nomadic peoples in trying to use these types of limits on *jus sanguinis* that rely on a finding that the individual is stateless. According to UNHCR, the sorts of disputes between states over whether a child is stateless, or the unregistered national of a neighboring state, should not prevent states from granting a stateless child a nationality.

> A Contracting State must accept that a person is not a national of a particular State if the authorities of that State refuse to recognize that person as a national. . . A Contracting State to the 1961 Convention cannot avoid

[8] Malaysian Const art 15(a).

[9] See for example Immigration and Refugee Board of Canada, Malaysian nationality law, and the case of M. Navin. Goh Siu Lin, 'In the Case of M. Navin, the Guiding Criteria for Article 15A' (Association of Women Lawyers (2016).

> the obligations to grant its nationality to a person who would otherwise be stateless under Articles 1 and 4 based on its own interpretation of another State's nationality laws where this conflicts with the interpretation applied by the State concerned.[10]

When countries do not have bilateral relations with the necessary states or when relations are strained, the process of establishing that a child is stateless for the purposes of Article 1 of the 1961 Convention, or similar laws, risks becoming snarled in international relations and red tape. As the examples showed, some nomadic peoples live in contested border zones, so the lack of clarity under international law in determining when a child is stateless in these circumstances is a serious gap.

6.4 The Burden of Proving Statelessness

Identifying statelessness for nomadic peoples also raises the question of who carries the burden of proof to establish statelessness. This question is often far from straightforward but has been addressed by both UNHCR and national courts. According to the UNHCR Handbook on the Protection of Stateless Persons, the burden of proof to prove statelessness is "shared," part of a "collaborative" effort, and statelessness should be established to a "reasonable" degree.[11] In a case where a government has a long history of policies stating that nomadic families are foreign without ties to the state due, in part, to their historical migrations, shifting the burden of proof to the government to establish that a child is not stateless would strengthen the solutions offered under the 1961 Convention, and international law already provides some support for the principle that states carry the burden of proof for the country where the child is born.[12]

For stateless children, the human rights norm of the "best interests of the child" would seem to favor an even lower standard of proof for stateless and nomadic children. As UNHCR stipulates, to comply with the Convention on the Rights of the Child, the burden placed on the family to provide evidence of a child's statelessness must be reasonable. In an environment of

[10] UNHCR Guidelines on Statelessness Nos 4, 4.

[11] UNHCR Guidelines on Statelessness Nos 4, 5. See also Handbook, 2014, 34–35.

[12] William T Worster, 'The Obligation to Grant Nationality to Stateless Children under Treaty Law' (2019) 24 Tilburg L Rev 204, 208.

bias against nomadic peoples, alongside concrete problems with providing documentary evidence, shifting the burden of proof entirely to the government would go much further toward resolving intergenerational statelessness for nomadic peoples and counteract the bias against them described in chapter 2.

There is the additional problem of types of proof, which tend to involve documents that nomadic peoples may struggle to provide. The UNHCR Handbook, section D, lists the types of evidence used to establish statelessness, including responses from foreign governments on nationality, identity documents, travel documents, immigration documents, employment documents, and school records. On the list of forms of evidence, only the testimony of the applicant, neighbors, and community members are things that some nomadic peoples may be able to provide or that are culturally appropriate. Some of the solutions proposed in Chapter 3 might help in these circumstances, demonstrating the importance of reforming and strengthening international law for nomadic peoples in a holistic way, so that the various areas of international law discussed in this book work more effectively together.

Court cases in Australia have shown that despite the guidance from UNHCR, the burden often falls on stateless persons to establish their own statelessness. In *Re DLSV and Minister for Immigration and Border Protection,* the Australian Administrative Appeals Tribunal held that while a child was eligible for nationality in the country of nationality of their parents, the policies of the authorities of that country had made it impossible for the child to obtain proof of this nationality even after repeated attempts and, as a result, the Court held that child was stateless.[13] This case placed a burden on the family to furnish considerable evidence of the attempts made on the child's behalf to establish its nationality.

In *Hoti v Croatia,* the European Court of Human Rights determined the applicant to be stateless based on a thorough investigation into his various attempts to establish his status in multiple countries following the dissolution of the former Yugoslavia.[14] The court thoroughly reviewed the individual's documentation and interactions with various authorities. What

[13] *Re DLSV and Minister for Immigration and Border Protection* (2017) AATA 2999. See also Kim Rubenstein and Elizabeth Harris, 'Case Note: Re DLSV and Minister for Immigration and Border Protection (2017) AATA 2999 (27 November 2017)' (2019) 1 Statelessness and Citizenship Rev 177

[14] *Hoti v Croatia* (2008) 26 ECHR App No 63311/14. See also Katja Swider, 'Hoti v Croatia, European Court of Human Rights, First Section, App No 63311/14 26, Case Note' (2018) 1 Statelessness and Citizenship Rev 184.

is notable about this case is the high burden of proof placed on the stateless person to prove their own statelessness. The applicant interacted with various consulates and government agencies in multiple countries, creating an administrative trail courts could evaluate. This example brings our discussion back to the nomadic experiences with documents and civil registration considered at length in chapter 3.

UNHCR has advocated for limiting to five years the period that a state has to establish the child's nationality in another country.[15] Such limitations should be codified in international law to provide clear limits on the ability of states to drag out the process through burdensome litigation. There is also the question of whether the standard of proof should be lower for certain groups like nomadic peoples. The UN Committee on the Elimination of Discrimination Against Women has noted that naturalization procedures may be particularly burdensome on specific groups or categories of persons.[16] This book notes, however, the long and problematic history of labeling nomadic peoples as stateless and, therefore, the risks of this approach for nomadic communities, whether at birth or later in life.

6.5 The Identification of Stateless Nomadic Persons Leading to Their Facilitated Naturalization

This section will discuss how the identification of stateless nomadic persons may be followed by their facilitated naturalization under the 1954 Convention relating to the Status of Stateless Persons, Article 32, as informed by the soft law guidance of the UNHCR Handbook on the Protection of Stateless Persons and case law.[17] This solution also finds support under the Protocol to the African Charter on Human and Peoples' Rights on the Specific Aspects of the Right to a Nationality and the Eradication of Statelessness in Africa and the Draft Articles on the Protection of Stateless Persons and the

[15] UNHCR Guidelines on Statelessness No 6.

[16] UN Committee on the Elimination of Discrimination against Women, General Recommendation No 32 on the gender-related dimensions of refugee status, asylum, nationality and statelessness of women, CEDAW/C/GC/32 (5 November 2014).

[17] Gerard-Rene De Groot and Oliver Willem Vonk, *International Standards on Nationality Law: Texts, Cases and Materials* (Wolf Legal 2015) 25–26. See also Laura van Waas, *Nationality Matters: Statelessness under International Law* (Intersentia 2008) ch 6; Ruth Donner, *The Regulation of Nationality in International Law* (2nd edn, Brill 1994) 247–282.

Facilities for their Naturalization.[18] The Draft Articles provide, among other benefits, the removal of residency and language requirements for stateless persons in order that they may naturalize, changes that would prove useful for nomadic peoples who struggle to prove residency.

> The duty to "facilitate" acquisition of nationality is a term used in other international treaties that involves at least making such acquisition significantly easier than for foreigners generally, for example by reaching out to communities known to be lacking documentation of nationality, by providing a non-discretionary process of acquisition, such as those known in different countries as declaration, registration or option, or by reducing the period of residence required.[19]

UNHCR advises, however, that formal statelessness determination procedures (SDPs) "may only be appropriate for the minority of the world's stateless persons who are in a migratory situation" and "a different approach is called for in the case of stateless persons who are in their own country, recognizing their profound connection with that State through, for example, birth or longstanding residence."[20] According to UNHCR guidance, *in situ* populations, like many nomadic peoples, should instead be treated as de facto nationals. However, the category of being a de facto national is not defined under international law and does not lead to a straightforward procedure for a solution in the same way that a statelessness determination does. The identification of stateless nomadic persons, followed by facilitated naturalization, however, is not advocated as a solution by this book because of the negative consequences of labeling nomadic communities as stateless, even when it might, in theory, lead to a solution. A clearer definition of de facto national under international law might provide a way forward.

[18] Draft Articles on the Protection of Stateless Persons and the Facilities for their Naturalization, UNHCR (February 2017). Protocol to the African Charter on Human and Peoples' Rights on the Specific Aspects of the Right to a Nationality and the Eradication of Statelessness in Africa: Explanatory Memorandum, para 48.

[19] Protocol to the African Charter on Human and Peoples' Rights on the Specific Aspects of the Right to a Nationality and the Eradication of Statelessness in Africa: Explanatory Memorandum, para 48.

[20] Handbook, 2014, 1, 3, 25–26, 57. See also European Network on Statelessness, 'Statelessness Determination and the Protection Status of Stateless Individuals' (2013) 5, citing UNHCR Guidelines; Caia Vlieks, 'Contexts of statelessness: the concepts "statelessness in situ" and "statelessness in the migratory context"' in Tendayi Bloom, Katherine Tonkiss and Philip Cole (eds), *Understanding Statelessness* (Routledge 2017) 40–42 (on the concept of own country).

6.6 Identifying De Facto Nationality for the Purposes of a Targeted Nationality Campaign

UNHCR generally does not recommend that statelessness determination be used for *in situ* populations, which this book agrees with. The concept of de facto nationals, however, is currently undefined as a concept under international law[21] but could be used as part of a solution. As this book demonstrated, many nomadic individuals, like many border populations more generally, are stateless because of the decolonization process.[22] This section will explore the extent to which modern norms of statelessness identification might be applied to nomadic communities to identify them as de facto nationals, creating a duty on the part of the state to facilitate their naturalization as part of a targeted nationality campaign. Such campaigns, as described in the UNHCR Handbook, have been used for rural indigenous and aboriginal populations in Malaysia.[23]

What standards qualify an individual as a de facto national under international law? As chapters 3 and 4 explained, many nomadic communities suffer from intergenerational statelessness due to the decolonization process. At the time of decolonization, the United Nations and the international community did not pay enough attention to the risk of statelessness for cross-border groups like the four nomadic communities profiled in this book. As a result, as states never registered many nomadic people, today, many states claim their border-zone nomadic minorities are foreigners rather than *in situ* stateless groups. The use of strict *jus sanguinis* in some countries subsequently locked the descendants of unregistered border-zone nomadic communities out of a nationality, leading to intergenerational statelessness.

Today, states label many of these populations as being of foreign origin, meaning that a targeted naturalization campaign of the kind used for unregistered, rural populations in Malaysia, one that the government runs, may not be possible for a supposedly foreign population like the Sama Dilaut. International law could do more to define the concept of being a de facto

[21] While the concept of de facto statelessness is also undefined under international law, it has arguably received more attention as a definitional category by experts. See for example Carol Batchelor, 'Statelessness and the Problem of Resolving Nationality Status' (1998) 10 Intl J Refugee L 156, 172–174.

[22] See for example the Draft Protocol on the avoidance of statelessness in relation to state succession, Council of Europe, Strasbourg, 19.V.2006. See also W Conklin, *Statelessness: The Enigma of an International Community* (OUP 2014) 19.

[23] UNHCR Handbook para 59. See also Human Rights Commission of Malaysia, 'Human Rights and Statelessness in Peninsular Malaysia' (2023) 232–233.

national to create a duty on the part of an individual state to facilitate the naturalization of a stateless, nomadic community.[24]

To create a duty on the part of a state to resolve nomadic statelessness, it might be helpful to refer to the right to a nationality at decolonization under the laws relating to the succession of states, including the Draft Articles on the Succession of States in Respect of Treaties of 1974, which specifically refer to decolonization in the Commentaries to Article 8.[25] While it should be noted that decolonization is not a classic example of a succession of states because colonies were not predecessor states under the meaning usually given to that term, the norms of nationality acquisition under international law during a succession of states arguably provide essential guidance to a determination of de facto nationality for nomadic, border populations.[26]

The international laws governing the norms of nationality acquisition during a succession of states are primarily found in soft law. Nonbinding instruments on nationality at state succession include the Venice Declaration on the Consequences of State Succession for the Nationality of Natural Persons of 1996, and the Draft Articles on Nationality of Natural Persons in Relation to the Succession of States of 1999.[27] The Committee on the Elimination of All Forms of Racial Discrimination in 2004, in General Recommendation 30, advised states to "[r]egularize the status of former citizens of predecessor States who now reside within the jurisdiction of the State party."[28] Regional laws include the Convention on the Avoidance of Statelessness in Relation to State Succession by the Council of Europe of 2009, and the 2024 Protocol to the African Charter on Human and Peoples' Rights

[24] van Waas (n 17) 122; Paul Weis, *Nationality and Statelessness in International Law* (Brill 1979) 165–172.

[25] Draft Articles on the Succession of States in Respect of Treaties of 1974, International Law Commission, Twenty-sixth session, General Assembly, YB Intl Law Commission, 1974, vol II, pt One. (1974), Art 8, Commentaries.

[26] But see contra Francesco Costamagna, 'Statelessness in the Context of State Succession: An Appraisal under International Law' in Alessandra Annoni and Serena Forlati (eds), *The Changing Role of Nationality in International Law* (Routledge 2013) 40–48, where he does not specifically address the problem of statelessness as a result of decolonization. See also the discussion in James Crawford, *The Creation of States in International Law* (2nd edn, OUP 2006) 330–373, 383.

[27] Draft articles on nationality of natural persons in relation to the succession of States with commentaries (1999), vol II, pt Two, Articles 5, 11, 14, 20, 28, 40 and Commentaries; Venice Declaration on the Consequences of State Succession for the Nationality of Natural Persons of 1996 (adopted at its 28th Plenary Meeting, Venice, 13–14 September 1996).

[28] Committee on the Elimination of All Forms of Racial Discrimination 64th Session General Recommendation 30 Discrimination against Non-Citizens, CERD/C/64/Misc.11/rev.3 (23 February–12 March 2004).

on the Specific Aspects of the Right to a Nationality and the Eradication of Statelessness in Africa.[29]

The general rule establishing nationality during state succession has long been that nationality follows sovereignty.[30] It should be noted that experts widely acknowledge the automatic transfer of nationality during state succession to be *jus cogens* if it is necessary to prevent statelessness.[31] Facilitated naturalization drives could be employed to settled cases of disputed nationality for nomadic border populations that never received identity documents, something that was not done at the time, arguably in contravention of international norms. In 1949, the United Nations commissioned a study on stateless refugees and displaced stateless persons,[32] but it took little note of *in situ* populations, even though the risk of continued statelessness during decolonization was noted at the time by experts such as Hannah Arendt.[33]

Subsequent developments in international law also neglected the problem of *in situ* statelessness as a result of decolonization. While the International Court of Justice ruled on the nationality status of persons in Mandate territories like South-West Africa,[34] it was not asked to decide cases of disputed nationality between sovereign states. In 1954, the Convention Relating to the Status of Stateless People mandated in Article 10 that treaties of state succession contain protections against statelessness. For state succession without a treaty, however, the problem of statelessness did not receive enough attention. Given that few cases of disputed nationality at decolonization were governed by treaty,[35] this left many border populations, including nomadic peoples, at risk of statelessness, but without a legal procedure to challenge their exclusion.

Those nomadic peoples who had received colonial-era nationality, like some Tuareg, arguably should have automatically received a nationality in their postcolonial state under international law. In such cases of international

[29] Council of Europe Convention on the Avoidance of Statelessness in Relation to State Succession (adopted 19 May 2006, entered into force 1 May 2009) CETS No 200, with seven state parties.

[30] James Crawford, *Brownlie's Principles of Public International Law* (9th edn, OUP 2019) 656. See also Costamagna (n 26) 36; van Waas (n 17) 126; Ineta Ziemele, 'State Succession and Issues of Nationality and Statelessness' in Alice Edwards and Laura van Waas (eds), *Nationality and Statelessness under International Law* (CUP 2014) 217.

[31] Crawford, *Brownlie's Principles* (n 30) 52–53.

[32] UN Ad Hoc Committee on Refugees and Stateless Persons, 'A Study of Statelessness' (United Nations, 1 August 1949, Lake Success, New York) UN Docs E/1112 and E/1112/Add.1.

[33] Arendt (n 3) 297.

[34] See International Court of Justice, International Status of South-West Africa, (1950) ICJ Rep quoted in Weis (n 24) 24.

[35] Weis (n 24) 158–159.

litigation or facilitated naturalization organized by the United Nations, the burden would be on the state to prove the invalidity of the documents of persons with documents from the predecessor state, as was the case for some Tuareg families. A program of facilitated naturalization for Tuareg families with colonial-era documents would correct a gap produced by previous failures to apply international law during decolonization.

As the Commentaries to the 1999 Draft Articles point out that, however, even in the soft law, reasonable measures to prevent statelessness do not obligate each state to provide a nationality to every person at risk of statelessness that may result from the succession. van Waas also points out that there is also no clear duty on the predecessor state to refrain from withdrawing nationality until possible cases of statelessness have been resolved.[36] Given that there was a rush to withdraw colonial forms of nationality and lay the problem squarely on the shoulders of the new states, this gap in international law left many people, including nomadic peoples, vulnerable to statelessness. The extent to which predecessor states, including the former colonial powers, may have been required to take a more active role in preventing statelessness is under-addressed in international law, even in soft law, and could be revisited today as part of a United Nations-led, facilitated naturalization program, or through litigation before the International Court of Justice to resolve border disputes.

The law is also vague regarding the measures required to identify persons at risk of statelessness during state succession. For example, Article 4 of the Draft Articles of 1999 and Article 3 of the Council of Europe Convention places an express duty on states to take "appropriate measures" to prevent statelessness during the succession of states for persons with a nationality in the predecessor state. Many nomadic peoples who live in contested border areas that arose from the decolonization process need to maintain their cross-border mobility, complicating their claims to nationality even when they hold colonial-era documents. As the breakup of states is likely to continue, international law could do more to clarify what "appropriate measures" means in such cases.

The most serious gap in the right to a nationality for nomadic peoples during decolonization, however, was the lack of specificity even in the soft law as to how to identify which state had an obligation to resolve the status of stateless persons at decolonization for nomadic groups like the Sama Dilaut

[36] van Waas (n 17) 132.

who had no documents at all. This is not only a problem for nomadic peoples, but is perhaps more acute for them, given their frequent cross-border mobility and ties to multiple states. The Draft Articles, for example, only address the status of persons who had the nationality of the predecessor state, yet the examples cited in this book showed that many nomadic persons were already stateless under the colonial system.

The 1961 Convention does not address how a state should determine if it, rather than the adjacent state, is the appropriate actor to resolve cases of statelessness, though the Draft Convention on the Reduction of Future Statelessness of 1954 places an affirmative duty on states to prevent and resolve cases of statelessness during succession even though neighboring states may also have a duty to those individuals.[37] An earlier draft of the 1961 Convention, prepared by the International Law Commission, also placed a duty on states to avoid statelessness for their "inhabitants," but this clause was removed from the final version.[38] This analysis demonstrates that international law contained at the time, and continues to contain, serious gaps when it came to creating a specific duty on the part of a state to regularize the nationality status of border populations during a succession of states in the absence of documentary evidence. Filling such gaps with stronger treaty norms on stateless nomadic, cross-border populations would help to create a better international environment for a negotiated solution.

This discussion raises the question of why nomadic persons must choose between the nationalities of adjacent states during an event like decolonization in the first place. The following section will explore solutions for stateless nomadic peoples that either do not involve this binary choice which, as the examples showed, particularly the example of the Fulani, is not conducive to the nomadic way of life

6.7 The Right of Option

The right to a nationality for nomadic peoples during the decolonization process also raises the issue of the right of option under international law, or

[37] Draft Article on the Elimination or Reduction of Future Statelessness UN General Assembly, A/RES/896 (4 December 1954), Art 10.

[38] YB Intl Law Commission, International Law Commission sixth session (1954) submitted to the GA para 25, 1954, vol II UN Conference of Plenipotentiaries on the Status of Refugees and Stateless Persons, Summary Record of the Nineteenth Meeting, A/CONF.9/C.1/SR.9 (26 November 1951) 2.

the right to choose nationality. This is particularly relevant to stateless nomadic peoples with links to two or more post-colonial states for whom mobility is a way of life. At the time of decolonization, the right of option was far from being a universally accepted principle of law in cases of state succession. A right of option was sometimes included in treaties of cession, though it was not always open to all classes of people.[39]

As Weis noted, traditionally the right of option, or election, was limited to "the right to decline the nationality of the acquiring State implicitly by leaving the transferred territory after the change in sovereignty had taken place."[40] It did not traditionally include the right of positive, or affirmative, option, whereby an individual would go through an administrative or judicial process to elect nationality. Soft law has long provided some support for an affirmative right of option, but traditionally it was only for persons with the nationality of the predecessor state.[41]

The Council of Europe Convention and the African Charter on Human and Peoples' Rights on the Specific Aspects of the Right to a Nationality and the Eradication of Statelessness in Africa also provide an affirmative right of option.[42] The African Court on Human and Peoples' Rights has also recommended that states observe an affirmative right of option in cases of state succession.[43] A right of option, however, would not fully resolve the nationality status of cross-border, mobile and nomadic persons whose way of life is constrained by a binary choice between nationalities, as the example of the Fulani so starkly highlighted. In conclusion, international law should strengthen the laws regulating nationality during the succession of states to prevent statelessness in general and specifically for nomadic and cross-border populations. Doing so would provide firmer guidance to states

[39] See for example Treaty of Peace with Austria (signed 10 September 1919, entered into force 16 July 1920) 226 CTS 8, arts 70–82; Convention franco-viêtnamienne du 16 août 1955 sur la nationalité (signed 16 August 1955, entered into force 30 June 1956) Recueil des traités et accords de la France 62; Burma Independence Act (1947) 11 & 12 Geo 6. c. 3; and Article 47 of the Yugoslav Citizenship Law (No. 33/96) Law No. 40/1993 of 29 December 1992 on the acquisition and loss of citizenship of the Czech Republic, *No. 33/96* (29 December 1992).

[40] Weis (n 24) 160. See also G Van Ert, 'Nationality, State Succession, and the Right of Option: The Case of Québec' (1998) 36 Can YB Intl L 151, 160 and sub.

[41] See the discussion in Weis (n 24) 159–164.

[42] Venice Declaration (n 27) para 13. Protocol to the African Charter on Human and Peoples' Rights on the Specific Aspects of the Right to a Nationality and the Eradication of Statelessness in Africa, art 20.

[43] African Commission on Human and Peoples' Rights, 'The Right to Nationality in Africa' (May 2014) para 47.

attempting to identify and resolve cases of intergenerational statelessness among their nomadic populations.

6.8 Dual Nationality

A right to dual, or multiple, nationality under international law may provide the best solution as part of facilitated naturalization for stateless and nomadic individuals in the post-colonial context. Dual, or multiple, nationality would prevent the need for a binary choice for nomadic individuals, as well as the need for a right of option. Nomadic individuals identified as stateless would, therefore, receive the nationality of all states relevant to their nomadism, and previous chapters in this book have mentioned dual, or multiple, nationality as a potential solution for nomadic peoples who must traverse borders to secure their way of life. While dual nationality is now permitted under international law, it is far from a right.[44] Far from promoting a right to dual nationality, international law has often adopted a conservative approach to dual nationality. For example, the 1930 Hague Convention on Certain Questions relating to the Conflict of Nationality Laws codified the general principles in cases where dual nationality is allowed, but the Convention falls well short of establishing a right to dual nationality and, indeed, one of the goals of the Convention was to reduce dual nationality.[45] Paul Weis exemplified the opinion of the mid-twentieth century when he categorized dual nationality as a type of conflict of laws.[46]

The Draft Articles on Nationality of Natural Persons in relation to the Succession of States of 1999 also adopted the position that dual nationality on a large scale is not something that international law wishes to promote.[47] "Historically, exclusivity has been an essential characteristic of nationality... [i]n the absence of any international legal mechanism to regulate nationality

[44] Kim Rubenstein and Niamh Lenagh-Maguire, 'More or Less Secure? Nationality Questions, Deportation and Dual Nationality' in Alice Edwards and Laura van Waas (eds), *Nationality and Statelessness under International Law* (Cambridge University Press 2014) 266–271. See also Rainer Bauböck, 'The Trade-Off Between Transnational Citizenship and Political Autonomy' in T Faiset and P Kivisto (eds), *Dual Citizenship in Global Perspective: From Unitary to Multiple Citizenship* (Palgrave 2007) 84–85; Van Ert (n 40) 152; Donner (n 17) 204–212.

[45] Convention on Certain Questions relating to the Conflict of Nationality Law (signed 12 April 1930, entered into force 1 July 1937) 179 LNTS 89, art 3. See also Weis (n 24) 185.

[46] Weis (n 24) 165.

[47] Draft Articles, Article 9, Commentary to Article 1, Commentary (6), 28.

in a comprehensive way, dual nationality attracted various legal responses in the international and domestic spheres."[48]

More could be done by international law to require dual, or multiple, nationality as a solution to intergenerational statelessness for nomadic individuals whose statelessness is the result of the decolonization process. This would remove the need to identify one state as responsible for resolving the problem. While the non-binding 2007 Declaration on the Rights of Indigenous Peoples states that indigenous peoples separated by borders have the right to "develop contacts" across borders, it does not mention dual nationality.[49] Many states, including Malaysia and Kuwait, do not recognize dual nationality. The complexities faced by the Fulani, in particular, showed reasons why international law should recognize a right to dual or multiple nationality for nomadic peoples. A regional nationality for nomadic peoples in West Africa at the time of decolonization would have prevented many cases of statelessness.

Finally, it is worth saying a few more words about the role bilateral and regional treaties may play in resolving cases of intergenerational statelessness for nomadic peoples as part of a recognition of their de facto nationality. A Memorandum of Understanding has been signed by Malaysia, Indonesia and the Philippines, for example, to look into the matter of cross-border statelessness.[50] Increasingly, regional organizations have also been exploring the use of tripartite agreements and regional action plans to resolve statelessness.[51] The Banjul Plan of Action for the ECOWAS (Economic Community of West African States) system, of which Mali had been until recently a member and Côte d'Ivoire remains a member, contains clauses pertaining to the nationality status of persons living in disputed border regions and those who became stateless as a result of the succession of states.[52] Such clauses, if

[48] Rubenstein and Lenagh-Magquire (n 44) 265–266.

[49] UN Office of the High Commissioner for Human Rights, 'The United Nations Declaration on the Rights of Indigenous Peoples' (August 2013 HR/PUB/13/2) art 36. See also Protocol to the African Charter on Human and Peoples' Rights on the Specific Aspects of the Right to a Nationality and the Eradication of Statelessness in Africa: Explanatory Memorandum, discussing the increasing acceptance of dual nationality in Africa, para 77.

[50] Kristy Inus, 'Malaysia, Indonesia to Tackle Sabah Stateless Issue' *Star Online* <https://www.thestar.com.my/news/nation/2023/09/07/stateless-issue-in-sabah-suhakam-renews-mou-with-its-counterparts-in-indonesia-and-philippines>.

[51] See for example the Action Plan of the International Conference on the Great Lakes Region (ICGLR) on the Eradication of Statelessness 2017-2019 and the Banjul Plan of Action of the Economic Community of West African States (ECOWAS) on the Eradication of Statelessness 2017–2024.

[52] Economic Community of West African States (ECOWAS), 'Plan of Action on Eradication of Statelessness Economic Community of West African States (ECOWAS), 2017–2024 (Banjul Plan of Action)' (2017) Objective 5.3.

implemented, may provide a roadmap to a negotiated, regional solution for stateless nomadic individuals.

6.9 Discrimination against Nomadic People as Stateless People

Discrimination as a cause of statelessness was the topic of chapter 4, but this section will discuss the specific problem of discrimination against stateless people on account of their statelessness, which, as the example of the *bidoon* shows, is a very real risk for nomadic peoples who are identified as stateless. Protections against discrimination based on statelessness finds support in Article 29 of the International Convention on the Protection of the Rights of All Migrant Workers and Members of Their Families, which prohibits discrimination against migrants and protects their children's right to a nationality.[53] The Committee on the Elimination of All Forms of Racial Discrimination in General Recommendation 30 recommended that states ensure non-citizens and stateless persons were also protected from racial discrimination and advised states to remove discrimination against groups with regard to access to nationality and naturalization.[54] Article 32 of the Convention relating to the Status of Stateless Persons mandates states to facilitate the naturalization of stateless persons and remove unreasonable barriers to naturalization for long-term residents. Finally, international law mandates that states protect the fundamental human rights of nonnationals and stateless persons.[55]

As De Chickera and Whiteman point out, however, prohibiting discrimination against stateless persons does not find the same level of obvious support in international law as race, ethnicity, and other factors.[56] The Statelessness Conventions lack a treaty body of their own, meaning that the

[53] International Convention on the Protection of the Rights of All Migrant Workers and Members of Their Families (adopted 18 December 1990, entered into force 1 July 2003) 2220 UNTS 3, with fifty-five state parties.

[54] Committee on the Elimination of All Forms of Racial Discrimination, 64th Session, General Recommendation 30, Discrimination against Non-Citizens, CERD/C/64/Misc.11/rev.3 (23 February–12 March 2004).

[55] See generally the Basic Principles and Guidelines on the Right to a Remedy and Reparation for Victims of Gross Violations of International Human Rights Law and Serious Violations of International Humanitarian Law, GA Res 60/147 (16 December 2005). See also van Waas (n 17) 15, 28, 36, 40, 50; J H W Verzijl, *International Law in Historical Perspective. v 5: Nationality and Other Matters relating to Individuals* (Martinus Nijhoff 1998) 48.

[56] De Chickera and Whiteman (n 1) 111.

issue of discrimination against stateless persons must be addressed through other treaty bodies, such as the Committee on the Rights of the Child. As the Office of the High Commissioner for Human Rights has observed, freedom from discrimination against stateless persons does not require that the state grant stateless persons a nationality, only that they be given the same treatment as other nonnationals.[57] Rather than necessarily providing a pathway to a solution, this area of law places many nomadic peoples in the same position as other foreigners, reinforcing their status not as de facto nationals but as foreign.

As well, as this book has made clear, labeling nomadic peoples as stateless risks perpetuating the view that they are "naturally stateless" and unable to form or participate in states, a view that dates from the colonial period or even earlier in some regions, and that has done incalculable damage to nomadic peoples. Chapter 2 identified a systemic bias against nomadism in academia, which arguably influenced government policy from the early colonial period to the present day and could constitute a form of discrimination against nomadic peoples. The idea that nomadic peoples form tribes and not states may arguably be prohibited as discrimination under international law, but explicit protections from this very nomadic-specific form of discrimination are needed, as chapter 4 discussed. There are, therefore, serious risks associated with the identification of nomadic individuals as stateless, risks that may outweigh the usefulness of many of the solutions discussed in this chapter.

6.10 Conclusion and Recommendations

Chapter 6 discussed the identification of nomadic individuals as stateless or as de facto nationals for the purposes of accessing a solution, such as facilitated naturalization. This chapter first discussed the dangers of labeling nomadic peoples as stateless, a practice with a long and troubling history. In recommending against identifying individual nomadic peoples as stateless, it discussed how the statelessness label has negatively affected the *bidoon* in Kuwait. Chapter 6 next explored the solution under international law for children born otherwise stateless, looking at the experiences of stateless children under laws of Malaysia as an example. This analysis exposed

[57] OHCHR, Fact Sheet No 18 (Rev 1).

how difficult it can be for individuals to prove their statelessness in a political environment where states are eager to instead classify persons, including nomadic peoples, as foreign.

Chapter 6 also looked at the emerging norms of statelessness determination, facilitated naturalization, and naturalization for de facto nationals, recommending that international law better define the concept of being a de facto national. In seeking to develop a definition, it looked at other relevant areas of law, such as the norms of nationality at state succession, bilateral and regional treaties, the right of option and dual nationality, and the role of international courts and the United Nations. The concept of de facto nationality under international law remains underdeveloped and could benefit from fresh thinking and newer approaches to bring relevant areas of international law into conversation with one another. Finally, chapter 6 looked at discrimination against stateless people, finding that once again, as chapter 4 noted, the international norms against discrimination in the granting of nationality could be further developed to better protect stateless nomadic persons not only as nomadic persons but as stateless persons.

7
Conclusion

This book explored the experiences with nationality, statelessness, civil registration, and legal identity of four nomadic, or previously nomadic, communities: the Bedouin in Kuwait, the Tuareg (Kel Tamasheq) in Mali, the Fulani (Foulbé) in Côte d'Ivoire, and the Sama Dilaut (Bajau Laut) in Malaysia. This book treated nomadic peoples as a specific class of persons with specific needs regarding the protections offered by international law against statelessness. It interrogated the solutions to statelessness available under international law, looking at the hypothetical case of full state adoption of norms, including soft law, and applying a progressive approach.

As this book shows, international law, if and when applied, offers nomadic peoples much protection against statelessness, particularly in antidiscrimination law. Still, much more needs to be done to recognize that specific protections are needed under international law for nomadic peoples as nomadic peoples. More also needs to be done to protect stateless persons more generally and to harmonize different areas of international law that are not often effectively brought into conversation with one another. This book exposed not only the usefulness of international law in providing solutions to statelessness but also the gaps and the dangers to nomadic peoples of both statelessness and of nationality itself under an international system that too often pits nationality and rights against nomadism as a way of life.

The ability of nationality law and statelessness to serve as weapons of assimilation and coercive and forced settlement of nomadic peoples emerged as a strong, cautionary finding of this book. The histories compiled in this book shed some light on how nationality under the law is fraught for some nomadic communities, pitting their way of life against their membership in a nation-state. This book also used the lens of the nomadic experience to demonstrate how its usefulness sometimes outweighs the negatives of statelessness for states as a form of exclusion of so-called problematic groups, particularly in border areas, and particularly in an age of massive resource extraction in previously remote areas where nomadic peoples live, like oceans and deserts.

The Nationality and Statelessness of Nomadic Peoples Under International Law. Heather Jean Alexander, Oxford University Press. © Oxford University Press 2025. DOI: 10.1093/9780197772362.003.0007

This book looked beyond a narrow, legal analysis to incorporate information from anthropology, history, philosophy, geography, and other fields. By adopting this approach, this book has contextualized its legal analysis with information from other disciplines to explore some of the reasons why nomadic statelessness occurs and why it persists to better inform the analysis of solutions and to provide a more complete picture of the political and social forces that have driven nomadic exclusion. This approach has allowed this book to provide a broader overview of the causes of nomadic statelessness than that usually offered by a strict, legal analysis, in recognition of the fact that "(a)ll of us relate to states, the political units into which the world is divided, by means of both law and emotion."[1]

Chapter 2 discussed the pervasive bias in academia against nomadism as a way of life. As anthropologist Dawn Chatty put it, "[h]istory is written from the perspective of the settled."[2] This bias persists to this day and perhaps unavoidably influences this book. Chapter 3 examined the creation of the colonial system of borders and governance that marginalized nomadic peoples and leaders, vesting political and administrative power in cities, while enacting policies to settle nomadic peoples. Coercive settlement policies continued in Kuwait, Mali, Côte d'Ivoire, and Malaysia, even when they caused intercommunal tension and environmental degradation.

Chapter 3 next looked at the right to be registered at birth, the laws regulating civil registration, and the creation of a legal identity under international law. It traced the history of government registration and identity documents in Kuwait, Mali, Malaysia, and Côte d'Ivoire, showing how governments faced barriers in registering nomadic peoples under administrative systems designed to privilege settled and urban communities while also weaponizing registration as another tool to encourage nomadic settlement, with serious consequences for the nationality of nomadic peoples at decolonization.

The division of their lands by borders and linking civil registration to settlement and assimilation would create a serious barrier for nomadic peoples to gain a nationality within existing nation-states. Chapter 3 argues against requiring more forms of civil registration under international law

[1] Nina G Schiller, 'Transborder Citizenship: An Outcome of Legal Pluralism within Transnational Social Fields' in K. Von Benda-Beckmann and A Griffiths (eds), *Mobile People, Mobile Law: Expanding Legal Relations in a Contracting World* (Routledge 2005) 30.

[2] Dawn Chatty, 'Negotiating Authenticity and Translocality in Oman: The 'Desertscapes' of the Harasiis Tribe' in Steffen Wippel (ed), *Regionalizing Oman: Political, Economic and Social Dynamics* (Springer 2013) 129.

besides birth certificates because identity documents have often been weaponized to entrench, rather than resolve, nomadic statelessness. Rather, chapter 3 focused on narrower reforms to international law, including defining the concept of residency in a way favorable to nomadic peoples and more expressly prohibiting discrimination against nomadic peoples in applying for documents. Chapter 3 also acknowledged, however, that because governments have long tied registration to settlement and assimilation, this link likely cannot be completely broken by the revisions to international norms proposed by this book.

Chapter 4 looked at the prohibitions under international law against discrimination in the granting of nationality under the law, looking at the various ways in which the laws and policies of Kuwait, Mali, Côte d'Ivoire, and Malaysia discriminated against the Bedouin, the Tuareg, the Fulani, and the Sama Dilaut. Antidiscrimination law has much to offer nomadic peoples to protect them from statelessness and to resolve existing cases of statelessness. Yet, gaps remain for nomadic peoples, as the laws and norms to prohibit discrimination, even under soft law, lack specificity for them and may sometimes be contrary to their needs. It is not always easy to link the statelessness of nomadic peoples to their status as ethnic, religious, linguistic, or racial groups without acknowledging the centrality of nomadism as the cause of their exclusion. Language expressly protecting nomadism as a way of life and prohibiting discrimination against nomadic peoples, including in the granting of nationality, should be included in an international treaty or other binding instrument of law, and nomadism should be more clearly defined as a protected class by itself.

For many nomadic peoples, certain framings in antidiscrimination law, such as those prohibiting discrimination against historical migration, risk perpetuating the stereotype that nomadic peoples are immigrants or migrants, rather than a class of indigenous persons practicing mobility as a way of life. Because discrimination against mobility is a primary function of nationality law, much more clarity and specificity in international law to protect nomadic peoples as a specific class is needed to avoid perpetuating harmful stereotypes and problematic framings. International law should be more proactive in protecting nomadism as a way of life, to protect nomadic peoples who otherwise too often find their nomadism reclassified as immigration, migration, smuggling, piracy, or other harmful stereotypes. Solutions that require framing nomadic peoples as indigenous, foreign, immigrants, or stateless all carry very real risks of achieving not nomadic inclusion and empowerment but further discrimination and exclusion.

Building on the observations in previous chapters, chapter 5 explored the intersection between the indigenous rights framework, nomadic nationality, and nomadic land rights. International law could do much more to examine and make precise the concept of indigenous status concerning nomadic peoples. International law should move away from relying on the concept of first in time, which is difficult for some nomadic peoples to establish, and toward a framework of marginalization. International law should better recognize that indigenous rights, nomadic land rights, and the right to a nationality for nomadic peoples go hand in hand and might require protection under a joint framework that better reflects this intersection. The right to self-determination for nomadic peoples should be more explicit within international law and any special requirements for nomadic peoples, such as cross-border rights. At the same time, this book advocates against designing an entirely separate framework of nomadic rights, suggesting instead that nomadic rights be based as much as possible on existing norms and frameworks.

Finally, chapter 6 found that the framework to identify stateless persons and provide them with facilitated naturalization carries the risk of further stigmatizing nomadic peoples as naturally stateless persons, foreigners, or immigrants. This book agrees with United Nations High Commissioner for Refugees (UNHCR) that statelessness determination procedures should not be used for *in situ* populations, where *in situ* is defined at the country and regional levels. Instead, chapter 6 advocated creating a presumption of de facto nationality under international law. As an underdeveloped concept in international law, chapter 6 further proposed that de facto nationality might draw from other related areas of law, like the right to a nationality during the succession of states, where decolonization, the cause of much nomadic statelessness, is treated as a kind of state succession. This solution requires much more attention and development and should be the focus of further study and research. Finally, chapter 6 noted that powerful tools like dual or multiple nationality find little current support in international law but could do much to offer solutions for nomadic peoples.

This book also acknowledges the limits of the solutions proposed here. Nationality law has proven to be, in and of itself, an engine of nomadic assimilation and settlement, as the link between nomadic nationality and nomadic land ownership greatly raises the stakes for many governments in recognizing nomadic nationality rights. In contrast, the long, sordid history of labeling nomadic peoples as naturally stateless means that otherwise obvious-seeming solutions may be dangerous for many nomadic peoples. More research is needed, particularly comparative research, on nomadic nationality and statelessness in different regions and countries to explore this intersection properly. Nationality alone will not solve the many rights violations nomadic peoples face, particularly when nomadism so regularly requires transcending state borders and bureaucracy.

Underestimating the potential of nationality to preserve nomadism, however, would also be a mistake, and what emerges from this book is not an easy answer to the question of nomadic nationality within existing nation-state systems as either good or bad, but rather that nationality in an internationally recognized nation-state remains a valuable asset that many nomadic peoples may employ to protect their rights, offering them access to court systems and the power to vote. While nationality has a powerful, assimilating effect and can be yet another cause of nomadic settlement and the end of nomadism as a way of life, it would be a great disservice to nomadic peoples to ignore the very real power nationality under the law can bring to help them enforce and protect their rights. "[I]n a world on the move . . . Citizenship or nationality of a state . . . has thus become the basis for equal protection, solidarity and a democratic voice in the norms by which citizens feel bound."[3]

The fixes to international law proposed in this book may help to ameliorate some of the more dangerous aspects of nationality law for some nomadic peoples, but these fixes cannot resolve the deeper tension between nomadism as a way of life and the nation-state system that has done so much to destroy it. As anthropologist Baz Lecocq, an expert on the Tuareg, observed, "it is hard to underpin exactly why nomadic existence is found so disturbing by those who are not nomads."[4] Anh Nga Longva, an expert on nationality in Kuwait, argues that because the word "citizenship" derives from the Latin word for city, it is "at heart an urban phenomenon."[5] There remains something profound that is missing from the pages of this book, something that is perhaps beyond the power of international law, with its framework based in the bounded, territorial nation-states of the Westphalian system, to fix.

[3] E M H Hirsch Ballin, *Citizen's Rights and the Right to be a Citizen* (Brill 2014) 65.

[4] B Lecocq, 'Tuareg City Blues—Cultural Capital in a Global Cosmopole' in Ines Kohl and Anya Fischer (eds), *Tuareg Society within a Globalized World: Saharan Life in Transition* (Bloomsbury 2010) 132.

[5] A N Longva, 'Citizenship in the Gulf States: Conceptualization and Practice' in N A Butenschon, U Davis and M Hassassian (eds), *Citizenship and the State in the Middle East: Approaches and Applications* (Syracuse UP 2000) 181.

Maps

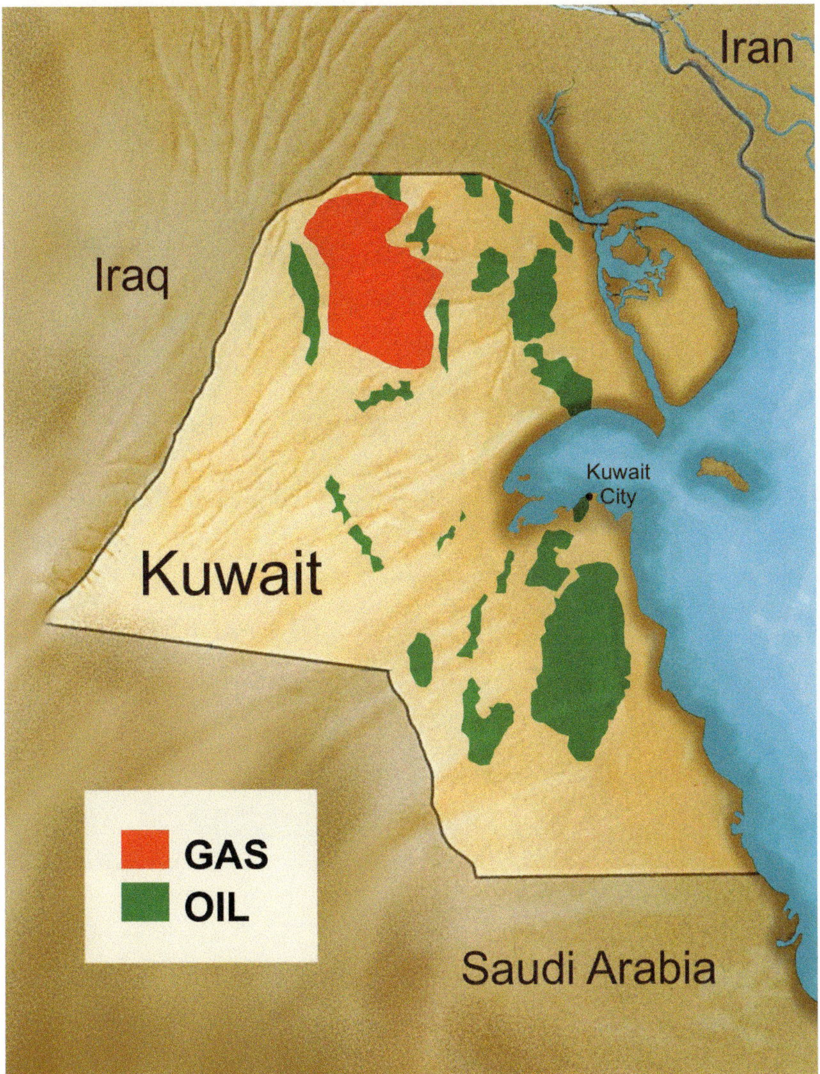

Map 1 Kuwait

Map 2 Mali

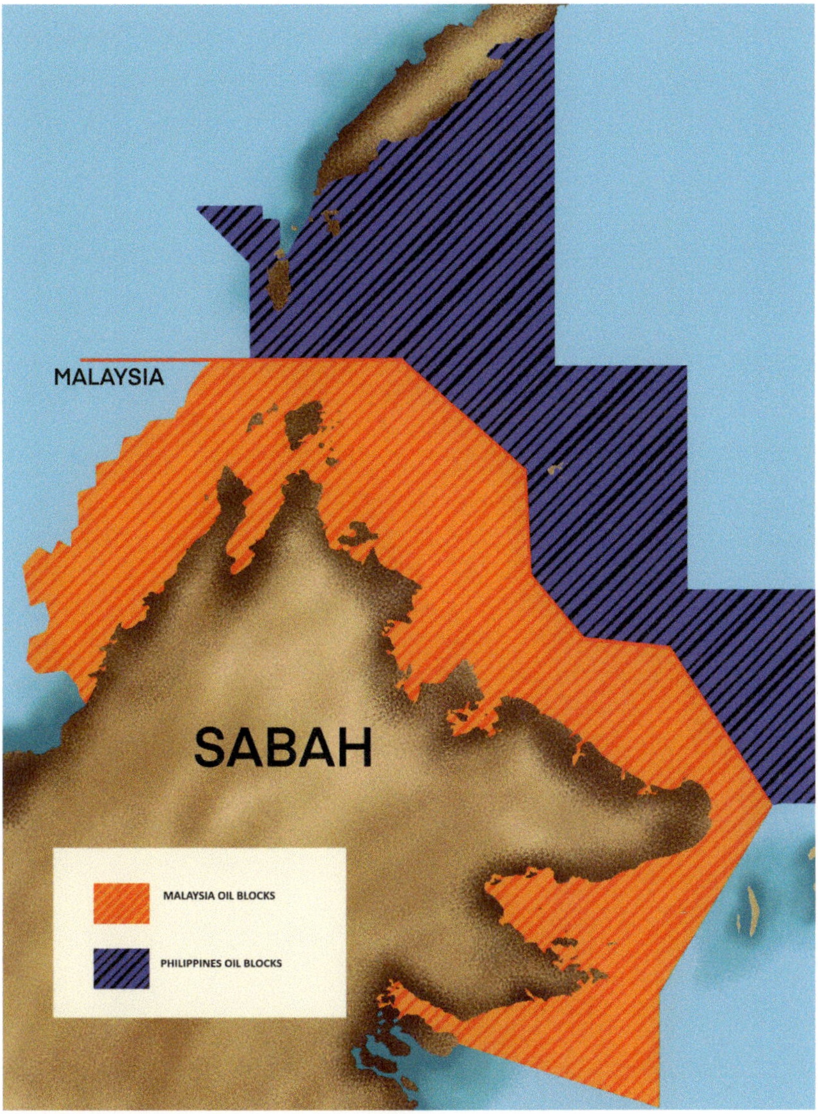

Map 3 Malaysia

Bibliography

Books

Al-Dekhayel A, *Kuwait: Oil, State and Political Legitimization* (Ithaca Press 2000)
Andaya B and Andaya L, *A History of Malaysia* (2nd edn, Palgrave Macmillan 2001)
Anscombe F, *The Ottoman Gulf, the Creation of Kuwait, Saudi Arabia and Qatar* (Columbia University Press 1997)
Arendt H, *The Origins of Totalitarianism* (Houghton Mifflin Harcourt 1973)
Ballin E H, *Citizen's Rights and the Right to Be a Citizen* (Brill 2014)
Barlocco F, *Identity and the State in Malaysia* (Routledge 2014)
Beaugrand C, *Stateless in the Gulf: Migration, Nationality and Society in Kuwait* (I B Tauris 2018)
Boilley P, *Les Touaregs Kel Adagh : dépendances et révoltes : du français au Mali contemporain* (Karthala 1999)
Bourgeot A, *Les sociétés touarègues : Nomadism, identité, résistances* (Karthala 1995)
Bury J B, *The Idea of Progress: An Inquiry into its Origin and Growth* (Macmillan 1932)
Busch B, *Britain and the Persian Gulf: 1894-1914* (California UP 1967)
Carmichael P, *Nomads* (Collins and Brown 1991)
Casey M, *The History of Kuwait* (Greenwood 2007)
Chatty D, *Mobile Pastoralists: Development Planning and Social Change in Oman* (Columbia UP 1996)
Cheng C B, *Malaysia: The Making of a Nation* (Institute of Southeast Asian Studies 2002)
Chipman J, *French Power in Africa* (Basil Blackwell 1989)
Chou C, *The Orang Suku Laut of Riau, Indonesia: The Inalienable Gift of Territory* (Routledge 2010)
Clark M and Pietsch J, *Indonesia-Malaysia Relations: Cultural Heritage, Politics and Labour Migration* (Routledge 2014)
Commins D, *The Gulf States: A Modern History* (I B Tauris 2012)
Conklin W, *Statelessness: The Enigma of an International Community* (OUP 2014)
Cooper F, *Nationality between Empire and Nation, Remaking France and French Africa 1945-1960* (Princeton UP 2014)
Crawford J, *The Creation of States in International Law* (2nd edn, OUP 2006)
Crawford J, *Brownlie's Principles of Public International Law* (9th edn, OUP 2019)
De Groot G-R and Vonk O, *International Standards on Nationality Law: Texts, Cases and Materials* (Wolf Legal 2015)
Diallo Y, *Nomads des espaces interstitiels: Pastoralisme, identité, migrations (Burkina Faso–Cote d'Ivoire)* (Rüdiger Köppe Verlag 2008)
Diarrah C O, *Vers La IIIe République Du Mali* (L'Harmattan 1991)
Dicken S N and Pitts F R, *Introduction to Cultural Geography: A Study of Man and His Environment* (Ginn 1970)
Donner R, *The Regulation of Nationality in International Law* (2nd edn, Brill 1994)
Eklöf S, *Pirates in Paradise, A Modern History of Southeast Asia's Maritime Marauders* (NUS Press 2006)
Foltz W J, *From French West Africa to the Mali Federation* (Yale UP 1965)

Fransman L, *Fransman's British Nationality Law* (3rd edn, Bloomsbury Professional 2011)
Gaudio A, *Le Mali* (2nd edn, Karthala 1988)
Gilbert J, *Nomadic Peoples and Human Rights* (Routledge 2014)
Grotius H, *Mare Liberum Sive De Jure Quod Batavis Competit Ad Indicana Commercia Dissertatio* (Elsevier 2014)
Habermas J, *The Postnational Constellation: Political Essays* (MIT Press 2001)
Hall B, *A History of Race in Muslim West Africa, 1600-1960* (CUP 2011)
Haller-Trost R, *The Territorial Dispute Between Indonesia and Malaysia over Pulau Sipadan: A Study in International Law* (IBRU 1995)
Hamani D, *Au carrefour du Soudan et de la Berbérie : Le Sultanat Touareg de l'Ayar* (L'Harmattan 1989)
Heater D, *Citizenship: The Civic Ideal in World History, Politics and Education* (3rd edn, Manchester UP 2004)
Hiskett M, *The Development of Islam in West Africa* (Longman 1984)
Hooker V M, *A Short History of Malaysia: Linking East and West* (Allen and Unwin 2003)
Ismael J S, *Kuwait: Dependency and Class in a Rentier State* (UP of Florida 1993)
Jault-Seseke F Barbou des Places S and Corneloup S, *Droit de la nationalité et des étrangers* (Presses universitaires de France 2015)
Kane O, *Beyond Timbuktu: An Intellectual History of Muslim West Africa* (Harvard UP 2016)
Keenan J, *The Lesser Gods of the Sahara: Social Change and Contested Terrain amongst the Tuareg of Algeria* (Routledge 2004)
Khazanov A M, *Nomads and the Outside World* (2nd edn, U Wisconsin P 1994)
Kingston L, *Fully Human: Personhood, Citizenship, and Rights* (OUP 2019)
Lagarde P, *La Nationalité Française* (2nd edn, Dalloz 1989)
Lalonde S, *Determining Boundaries in a Conflicted World: The Role of* Uti Possidetis (McGill Queens 2012)
Lauterpacht H Weller M and Bethlehem D, *The Kuwait Crisis: Basic Documents* (CUP 1991)
Lecocq B, *Disputed Desert: Decolonisation, Competing Nationalisms and Tuareg Rebellions in Northern Mali* (Brill 2010)
Manby B, *Citizenship in Africa: The Law of Belonging* (Hart 2018)
McDonell N, *The Civilization of Perpetual Movement: Nomads in the Modern World* (Hurst 2016)
Miller D, *On Nationality* (OUP 1995)
Moretti M, *Le Droit international public et les peuples nomades* (Publibook 2006)
Parolin G, *Citizenship in the Arab World* (Amsterdam UP 2009)
Sack R, *Human Territoriality: Its Theory and History* (CUP 1986)
Sather C, *The Bajau Laut: Adaptation, History, and Fate in a Maritime Fishing Society of South-eastern Sabah* (OUP 1997)
Scott J C, *The Art of Not Being Governed: An Anarchist History of Upland Southeast Asia* (Yale UP 2010)
Shaw M, *International Law* (9th edn, CUP 2021)
Singh H, *South Asia Defense and Strategic Year Book* (2nd edn, Pentagon 2015)
Slot B, *Mubarak Al-Sabah: Founder of Modern Kuwait: 1896-1915* (Arabian 2005)
Smith L, *Making Citizens in Africa: Ethnicity, Gender and National Identity in Ethiopia* (CUP 2013)
Swan Sik K, *Nationality and International Law in Asian Perspective* (Martinus Nijhoff 1990)
Tavani C, *Collective Rights and the Cultural Identity of the Roma: A Case Study of Italy* (Brill 2020)
Trimingham J S, *Islam in West Africa* (Clarendon 1959)
Verwilghen M, *Conflits de nationalités : plurinationalité et apatridie* (Brill 1999)
Verzijl J H W, *International Law in Historical Perspective. Vol 5: Nationality and Other Matters relating to Individuals* (Martinus Nijhoff 1998)
Van Panhuys J H F, *The Role of Nationality in International Law* (A W Sijthoff 1959)

van Waas L, *Nationality Matters: Statelessness under International Law* (Intersentia 2008)
Warren J, *The North Borneo Chartered Company's Administration of the Bajau, 1878-1909: The Pacification of a Maritime, Nomadic People* (Ohio UP 1971)
Warren J, *The Sulu Zone: 1768-1898* (Singapore UP 1981)
Weil P, *Qu'est-ce qu'un français? Histoire de la nationalité française depuis la Révolution* (Grasset 2002, 2004)
Weis P, *Nationality and Statelessness in International Law* (Brill 1979)
Young K Bussink W C F and Hasan P, *Malaysia: Growth and Equity in a Multiracial Society* (Johns Hopkins UP 1980)
Zatzépine A, *Le Droit de la Nationalité des Républiques Francophones d'Afrique et de Madagascar* (LGDJ 1963)

Book Chapters

Ag Alfarouk R, 'La politique coloniale d'affaiblissement de la confédération Kel Denneg de 1900 à 1949' in Bernus E, Boilley P, Clauzel J and Triaud J-T (eds), *Nomades et commandants : Administration et sociétés nomades dans l'ancienne AOF* (Kathala 1993)
Ag Litny I, 'La première école de l'Adagh' in Bernus E and others (eds), *Nomades et commandants : Administration et sociétés nomades dans l'ancienne AOF* (Karthala 1993)
Alexander H, 'The Open Sky or a Brick and Mortar School? Statelessness, Education and Nomadic Children' in Instutue on Statelessness and Inclusion (ed), *The World's Stateless Children* (Wolf 2017)
Aronson D, 'Must Nomads Settle? Some Notes Toward Policy on the Future of Pastoralism' in Salzman P C (ed), *When Nomads Settle: Processes of Sedentarization as Adaptation and Defense* (Praeger 1980)
Badi D, 'Genesis and Change in the Socio-political Structure of the Tuareg' in Fisher A and Kohl I (eds), *Tuareg Society within a Globalized World: Saharan Life in Transition* (I B Tauris 2010)
Baldwin T, 'The Territorial State' in Gross H and Harrison (eds), *Jurisprudence: Cambridge Essays* (OUP 1992)
Al Barazi Z and Tucker J, 'Challenging the disunity of statelessness in the Middle East and North Africa' in Bloom (ed), *Understanding Statelessness* (Routledge 2017)
Barba J-F, 'L'administration en zone frontalière algero-soudanaise' in Bernus E and others (eds), *Nomades et commandants : Administration et sociétés nomades dans l'ancienne AOF* (Karthala 1993)
Bernus E, 'Dates, Dromedaries, and Drought: Diversification in Tuareg Pastoral Systems' in Galaty J and Johnson D L (eds), *The World of Pastoralism: Herding Systems in Contemporary Perspective* (Guilford 1990)
Bingham L and Gamboa L, 'Litigating against Statelessness' in Khanna M and van Waas L (eds), *Solving Statelessness* (Wolf 2016)
Bloom T, 'Members of Colonized Groups, Statelessness and the Right to Have Rights' in Bloom T, Tonkiss K and Cole P (eds), *Understanding Statelessness* (Routledge 2017)
Bocco R, 'The Settlement of Pastoral Nomads in the Arabe Middle East: International Organizations and Trends in Development Policies, 1950-1990' in Chatty D (ed), *Nomadic Societies in the Middle East and North Africa: Entering the 21st Century* (Brill 2006)
Castellino J and Doyle C, 'Who Are "Indigenous Peoples"? An Examination of Concepts Concerning Group Membership in the United Nations Declaration on the Rights of Indigenous Peoples' in Hohmann J and Weller M (eds), *The UN Declaration on the Rights of Indigenous Peoples: A Commentary* (OUP 2018)
Chatty D, 'The Pastoral Family and the Truck' in Salzman P C (ed), *When Nomads Settle* (Praeger 1980)

Chatty D, 'Negotiating Authenticity and Translocality in Oman: The "Desertscapes" of the Harasiis Tribe' in Wippel S (ed), *Regionalizing Oman: Political, Economic and Social Dynamics* (Springer 2013)

Chatty D and Colchester M, 'Introduction' in Chatty D and Colchester M (eds), *Conservation and Mobile Indigenous Peoples: Displacement, Forced Settlement and Sustainable Development* (Berghahn 2002)

De Chickera A and van Waas L, 'Unpacking Statelessness' in Bloom and others (eds) *Understanding Statelessness* (Routledge 2017)

Claudot-Hawad H, 'La question touarègue, quels enjeux?' in Galy M (ed), *La guerre au Mali : Comprendre la crise au Sahel et au Sahara: enjeux et zones d'ombre* (Découverte 2013)

Clifton J, 'Achieving Congruence between Conservation and Community: The Bajau Ethnic Group and Marine Management within the Wakatobi and South-East Asia' in Clifton J, Unsworth R and David S (eds), *Marine Research and Conservation in the Coral Triangle: The Wakatobi National Park* (Nova 2010)

Cole P, 'Introduction: "Border Crossings"—The Dimensions of Membership' in Calder G, Cole P and Seglow J (eds), *Citizenship Acquisition and Natural Belonging Migration, Membership and the Liberal Democratic State* (Palgrave Macmillan 2010)

Combelles H, 'La scolarisation et les écoles nomades au Mali' in Bernus E and others (eds), *Nomades et commandants : Administration et sociétés nomades dans l'ancienne AOF* (Karthala 1993)

Costamagna F, 'Statelessness in the Context of State Succession: An Appraisal Under International Law' in Annoni A and Forlati S (eds), *The Changing Role of Nationality in International Law* (Routledge 2013)

Crystal J, 'Public Order and Authority: Policing Kuwait' in Dresch P and Piscatori J (eds), *Monarchies and Nations: Globalisation and Identity in the Arab States of the Gulf* (I B Tauris 2005)

De Chickera A and Whiteman J, 'Addressing Statelessness through the Right to Equality and Non-discrimination' in Khanna M and van Waas L (eds), *Solving Statelessness* (Wolf 2017)

De Geyer d'Orth, M, 'Les actions de développement' in Bernus E and others (eds), *Nomades et commandants : Administration et sociétés nomades dans l'ancienne AOF* (Karthala 1993)

Dorman S R, 'Citizenship in Africa' in Engin I and Nyers P (eds), *Routledge Handbook of Global Citizenship Studies* (Routledge 2014)

Dumbrava C, 'Bloodlines and Belonging: Time to Abandon Ius Sanguinis?' in Bauböck R (ed), *Debating Transformations of National Citizenship* (SpringerLink 2018)

Edwards A, 'The Meaning of Nationality in International Law in an Era of Human Rights: Procedural and Substantive Aspects' in Edwards A and van Waas L (eds), *Nationality and Statelessness under International Law* (CUP 2014)

Féral G, 'Administrations comparées en pays nomade' in Bernus E and others (eds), *Nomades et commandants : Administration et sociétés nomades dans l'ancienne AOF* (Karthala 1993)

Fischer A, 'Research and Nomads in the Age of Globalization' in Fischer A and Kohl I (eds), *Tuareg Society Within a Globalized World: Saharan Life in Transition* (I B Tauris 2010)

FitzGerald D S, 'The History of Racialized Citizenship' in Shachar A and others (eds), *The Oxford Handbook of Citizenship* (OUP 2017)

Frémeaux J, 'La mise en place d'une administration aux marges sahariennes de l'A.O.F. (1891-1930)' in Bernus E and others (eds), *Nomades et commandants : Administration et sociétés nomades dans l'ancienne AOF* (Karthala 1993)

Gremont C, 'Villages and Crossroads: Changing Territorialities among the Tuareg of Northern Mali' in McDougall J and Scheele J (eds), *Saharan Frontiers: Space and Mobility in Northwest Africa* (Indiana UP 2012)

Gyulai G, 'The Determination of Statelessness and the Establishment of a Statelessness-Specific Protection Regime' in Edwards A and van Waas L (eds), *Nationality and Statelessness under International Law* (CUP 2014)

Harding J, 'Matters Colonial, Consular and Curious' in Hinchcliffe P, Ducker J T and Holt M (eds), *Without Glory in Arabia: The British Retreat from Aden* (I B Tauris 2013)
Hole F, 'Pastoral Mobility as an Adaptation' in Szuchman J (ed), *Nomads, Tribes, and the State in the Ancient Near East: Cross-disciplinary Perspectives* (Chicago UP 2009)
Isin E and Nyers P, 'Introduction: Globalizing Citizenship Studies' in Isin E and Nyers P (eds), *Routledge Handbook of Global Citizenship Studies* (Routledge 2014)
Keenan J, 'Resisting Imperialism: Tuareg Threaten US, Chinese and Other Foreign Interests' in Fischer A and Kohl I (eds), *Tuareg Society within a Globalized World: Saharan Life in Transition* (I B Tauris 2010)
Khazanov A, 'Pastoralists in the Contemporary World: The Problem of Survival' in Ginat J and Khazanov A (eds), *Changing Nomads in a Changing World* (Sussex 1998)
Khazanov A, 'Nomads in the History of the Sedentary World' in Wink M and Khazanov A (eds), *Nomads in the Sedentary World* (Curzon 2001)
Kingston L, 'Worthy of Rights: Statelessness as a Cause and Symptom of Marginalisation' in Bloom T and others (eds), *Understanding Statelessness* (Routledge 2017)
Lan G B, 'Dilemma of Progressive Politics in Malaysia: Islamic Orthodoxy versus Human Rights' in Mee W and Kahn J (eds), *Questioning Modernity in Indonesia and Malaysia* (NUS Press 2012)
Lecocq B, 'Tuareg City Blues—Cultural Capital in a Global Cosmopole' in Kohl I and Fischer A (eds), *Tuareg Society within a Globalized World: Saharan Life in Transition* (Bloomsbury 2010)
Lecocq B and Niang A, 'Identités sahéliennes en temps de crise : histoires, enjeux, et perspectives' in Lecocq B and Niang A (eds), *Identités sahéliennes en temps de crise : histoires, enjeux, et perspectives* (LIT Verlag 2019)
Longva A N, 'Citizenship in the Gulf States: Conceptualization and Practice' in Butenschon N A, Davis U and Hassassian M (eds), *Citizenship and the State in the Middle East: Approaches and Applications* (Syracuse UP 2000)
Longva A N, 'Neither Autocracy nor Democracy' in Dresch P and Piscatori J (eds), *Monarchies and Nations: Globalisation and Identity in the Arab States of the Gulf* (I B Tauris 2005)
Macklin A, 'The Securitization of Dual Citizenship' in Faist T and Kivisto P (eds), *Dual Citizenship in Global Perspective: From Unitary to Multiple Citizenship* (Palgrave Macmillan 2007)
Manby B, 'Trends in Citizenship Law and Politics in Africa Since the Colonial Era' in Isin E and Nyers P (eds), *Routledge Handbook of Global Citizenship Studies* (Routledge 2014)
Manly M, 'UNHCR's mandate and activities to address statelessness' in Edwards A and van Waas L (eds), *Nationality and Statelessness under International Law* (CUP 2014)
Maury J, 'Nationalité. Théorie générale du français' in De LaPradelle A G and Niboyet J-H-P (eds), *Répertoire de droit international* (Sirey 1931)
Mazrui A, 'Francophone Nations and English-Speaking States: Imperial Ethnicity and African Political Formations' in Rothchild D and Olorunsola VA (eds), *State Versus Ethnic Claims: African Policy Dilemmas* (Routledge 1983)
McDougall J, 'Frontiers, Borderlands, and Saharan/World History' in McDougall J and Scheele J (eds), *Saharan Frontiers: Space and Mobility in Northwest Africa* (Indiana UP 2012)
Mee W and Kahn J, 'Islam and Capitalism in the Frontiers and Borderlands' in Mee W and Kahn J (eds), *Questioning Modernity in Indonesia and Malaysia* (NUS Press 2012)
Odinkalu C A, 'Natives, Subjects, and Wannabes: Internal Citizenship Problems in Postcolonial Nigeria' in Howard-Hassmann R E and Walton-Roberts M (eds), *The Human Right to Citizenship: A Slippery Concept* (Pennsylvania UP 2015)
O'Fahey R S, 'Islamic Hegemonies in the Sudan: Sufism, Mahdism and Islamism' in Brenner L (ed), *Muslim Identity and Social Change in Subsaharan Africa* (Indiana UP 1994)
Partrick N, 'Nationalism in the Gulf States' in Held D and Ulrichsen K (eds), *The Transformation of the Gulf* (Routledge 2011)

Payen J-M, 'Le recensement et l'impôt' in Bernus E and others (eds), *Nomades et commandants: administration et sociétés nomades dans l'ancienne AOF* (Karthala 1993)

Power G, 'The Difficult Development of Parliamentary Politics in the Gulf' in Held D and Ulrichsen K (eds), *The Transformation of the Gulf: Politics, Economics and the Global Order* (Routledge 2012)

Randall S and Giuffrida A, 'Forced Migration, Sedentarization and Social Change: Malian Kel Tamasheq' in Chatty D (ed), *Nomadic Societies in the Middle East and North Africa: Entering the 21st Century* (Brill 2006)

Rubenstein K and Lenagh-Maguire N, 'More or Less Secure? Nationality Questions, Deportation and Dual Nationality' in Edwards A and van Waas L (eds), *Nationality and Statelessness under International Law* (CUP 2014)

Salzman P C, 'Introduction' in Salzman P C (ed), *When Nomads Settle: Processes of Sedentarization as Adaptation and Response* (Praeger 1980)

Schiller N G, 'Transborder Citizenship: An Outcome of Legal Pluralism within Transnational Social Fields' in Von Benda-Beckmann F, Von Benda-Beckmann K and Griffiths A (eds), *Mobile People, Mobile Law: Expanding Legal Relations in a Contracting World* (Routledge 2005)

Sinnadurai V, 'Nationality and International Law in the Perspective of the Federation of Malaysia' in Swan Sik K (ed), *Nationality and International Law in Asian Perspective* (Martinus Nijhoff 1990)

Sperfeldt C, 'Statelessness and Governance at the Periphery: "Nomadic" Populations and the Modern State in Thailand, Côte d'Ivoire, and Lebanon' in Bloom T and Kingston L (eds), Statelessness and Governance: Rights, Identity, Citizenship (Manchester UP 2021)

Staples K, 'Recognition, nationality, and statelessness: State-based challenges for UNHCR's plan to end statelessness' in Bloom T and others (eds), *Understanding Statelessness* (Routledge 2017)

Szuchman J, 'Integrating Approaches to Nomads, Tribes, and the State in the Ancient Near East' in Szuchman J (ed), *Nomads, Tribes, and the State in the Ancient Near East: Cross-disciplinary Perspectives* (Chicago UP 2009)

Ting H, 'Malaysian History Textbooks and the Discourse of Ketuanan Melayu' in Goh D and others (eds), *Race and Multiculturalism in Malaysia and Singapore* (Routledge 2009)

Toth A, 'Last Battles of the Bedouin and the Rise of Modern States in Northern Arabia: 1850-1950' in Chatty D (ed), *Nomadic Societies in the Middle East and North Africa: Entering the 21st Century* (Brill 2006)

Tymowski M, 'The Origins and Structures of Political Institutions' in Tymowski M and Claessen HJM (eds), *Pre-Colonial Black Africa; Dynastic Monarchy, Taxes and Tributes, War and Slavery, Kinship and Territory* (Edwin Mellen 2009)

Vlieks C, 'Contexts of Statelessness: The Concepts "Statelessness *in situ*" and "Statelessness in the Migratory Context"' in Bloom T and others (eds), *Understanding Statelessness* (Routledge 2017)

van Waas L, 'The U.N. Statelessness Conventions' in Edwards A and van Waas L (eds), *Nationality and Statelessness under International Law* (CUP 2014)

Walker, N 'The Territorial Dimension of Citizenship in Recent Academic LIteratrure' in Shachar A and others (eds) *The Oxford Handbook of Citizenship* (OUP 2017)

Young K, 'Malay Social Imaginaries: Nationalist and Other Collective Identities in Indonesia' in Mee W and Kahn J (eds), *Questioning Modernity in Indonesia and Malaysia* (NUS Press 2012)

Ziemele I, 'State Succession and Issues of Nationality and Statelessness' in Edwards A and van Waas L (eds), *Nationality and Statelessness under International Law* (CUP 2014)

Journal Articles

Acciaoli G, 'Archipelagic Culture' as an Exclusionary Government Discourse in Indonesia' (2001) 2 Asia Pac J Anthro 1

Acciaoli G, Brunt H and Clifton J 'Foreigners Everywhere, Nationals Nowhere: Exclusion, Irregularity, and Invisibility of Stateless Bajau Laut in Eastern Sabah, Malaysia' (2017) 15 J Imm Refugee Stud 232

Alexander H, 'Nomads and the Struggle for a Legal Identity' (2020) 2 Statelessness and Citizenship Rev 338

Alexander H and Simon J, 'No Port, No Passport: Why Submerged States Can Have No Nationals' (2016) 26 Wash Intl L J 307

Alhajeri A M, '"The Bedoun": Kuwaitis without an Identity' (2015) 51 Middle E Stud 17

Allerton C, 'Contested Statelessness in Sabah, Malaysia: Irregularity and the Politics of Recognition' (2017) 15 J Imm Refugee Stud 250

Al-Nakib F, 'Revisiting Hadar and Badū in Kuwait: Citizenship, Housing, and the Construction of a Dichotomy' (2014) 46 Intl J Middle E Stud 5

Arkell T, 'The Decline of Pastoral Nomadism in the Western Sahara' (1991) 76 Geography 162

Aukot E, 'Am I Stateless Because I Am a Nomadic?' (2009) 32 Forced Migration Rev 18

Azarya V, 'Pastoralism and the State in Africa: Marginality or Incorporation?' (1996) 38 Nom Peoples 11

Barnsley I and Bleiker R, 'Self Determination: From Decolonization to Deterritorialization' (2008) 20 Global Change, Peace and Sec 121

Bassett T J, 'Fulani Herd Movements' (1986) 76 Geographical Rev 233

Batchelor C, 'Statelessness and the Problem of Resolving Nationality Status' (1998) 10 Intl J Refugee L 156

Bauman Z, 'Soil, Blood and Identity' (2008) 40 Socio Rev 675

Beaugrand C, 'Statelessness and Administrative Violence: Biduns' Survival Strategies in Kuwait' (2011) 101 The Muslim World, 228

Beaugrand C 'Framing Nationality in the Migratory Context: The Elusive Category of Biduns in Kuwait' (2014) 6 Middle E L Governance 1

Benjaminsen T A and Ba B, 'Fulani-Dogon Killings in Mali: Farmer-Herder Conflicts as Insurgency and Counterinsurgency' (2021) 14 Afr Sec 4

Bourgeot A, 'Sahara: espace géostratégique et enjeux politiques (Niger)' (2014) 31 NAQD: Revue d'Etudes et de Critique Sociale 153

Brownlie I, 'Relations of Nationality in Public International Law' (1963) 39 Brit YB of Intl L 284

Brubaker R, 'Citizenship Struggles in Soviet Successor States' (1992) 26 Intl Migration Rev 269

Bulan R, 'Native Title in Malaysia: A "Complementary" Sui Generis Proprietary Right under the Federal Constitution' (2007) 11 Austral Indigenous L R 54

Coquery-Vidrovitch C, 'Nationalité et Citoyenneté en Afrique Occidentale Français: Originaires et Citoyens dans le Sénégal Colonial' (2001) 42 J Afr Hist 285

De Bruijn M and Dijk H, 'Changing Population Mobility in West Africa: Fulbe Pastoralists in Central and South Mali' (2003) 102 Afr Affairs 285

Decheix P, 'Le Code de la Nationalité Malienne' (1963) 697 Penant 300

Fletcher R, '"Between the Devil of the Desert and the Deep Blue Sea": Reorienting Kuwait: 1900-1940' (2015) 50 J Hist Geo 51

Gilbert H, '"This Is Not Our Life, It's Just a Copy of Other Peoples": Bedouin and the Price of "Development" in South Sinai' (2011) 15 Nom Peoples 7

Gilbert J, 'Still No Place to Go: Nomadic Peoples Territorial Rights in Europe' (2004) 4 Eur YB on Minority Issues 141

Gilbert J, 'Nomadic Territories: A Human Rights Approach to Nomadic Peoples' Land Rights' (2007) 7 Hum Rts L Rev 681

Gilbert J, 'Litigating Indigenous Peoples' Rights in Africa: Potentials, Challenges and Limitations' (2017) 66 Intl Compar L 657

Gilbert J and Clench B, 'Mapping for Rights: Indigenous Peoples, Litigation and Legal Empowerment' (2018) 11 Erasmus L Rev 6

Guy N, 'Communautés islamiques et collectivité nationale dans trois États d'Afrique occidentale' (1981) 250 Revue française d'histoire d'outre-mer 156

Harrisson T, 'The Prehistory of Borneo' (1970) 13 Asian Persp 17
Hirschman C, 'The Meaning and Measurement of Ethnicity in Malaysia' (1987) 46 J Asian Stud 555
Kazufumi N, 'Pirates, Sea Nomads or Protectors of Islam? A Note on "Bajau" Identifications in the Malaysian Context' (2001) 1 Asian Afr Area Stud 212
Kingston L, 'Statelessness as a Lack of Functioning Citizenship' (2014) 19 Tilburg L Rev 127
Kingston L, 'Conceptualizing Statelessness as a Human Rights Challenge: Framing, Visual Representation, and (Partial) Issue Emergence' (2019) 11: 1 J H R Prac 52
Koessler M, 'Subject, Citizen, National and Permanent Allegiance' (1946) 56 Yale L J 58
Le H-A, 'Affirmative Action in Malaysia and South Africa: Contrasting Structures, Continuing Pursuits' (2015) 50 J Asian Afr Stud 615
Lenhart L, 'Recent Research on Southeast Asian Sea Nomadic Peoples' (1995) 36 Nom Peoples 245
Loewenstein A B, 'The Veiled Protectorate of Kowait': Liberalized Imperialism and British Efforts to Influence Kuwaiti Domestic Policy during the Reign of Sheikh Ahmad al-Jaber, 1938-50' (2000) 36 Middle E Stud 103
Manby B, 'Case Note: Anudo Ochieng Anudo v. Tanzania (Judgement) (African Court on Human and Peoples Rights, APP No. 012/2015, 22 March 2018)' (2019) 1 Statelessness and Citizenship Rev 170
Manderscheid A, 'Decline and Re-emergence of Nomadism: Tibetan Pastoralists Revive a Nomadic Way of Life and Production' (2001) 53 GeoJournal 173
Manly M and van Waas L, 'The State of Statelessness Research' (2014) 19 Tilburg L Rev 3
Mathews T, 'Is Malaysia's Mykad the 'One Card to Rule Them All'? The Urgent Need to Develop a Proper Legal Framework for The Protection of Personal Information in Malaysia' (2004) 28 Melbourne U L Rev 15
Nah A, 'Globalisation, Sovereignty and Immigration Control: The Hierarchy of Rights for Migrant Workers in Malaysia' (2012) 40 Asian J Soc Sci 486
Nijenhuis K, 'Reconsidering Conflicts Over Land in the Sahel as Conflicts over Power' (2009) Recht der Werkelijkheid Special Issue 69
Oxby C, 'Will the 2010 "Code Pastoral" Help Herders in Central Niger? Land Rights and Land Use Strategies in the Grasslands of Abalak and Dakoro Departments' (2011) 15 Nom Peoples 53
Pedersen S, 'The Coastal Sámi of Norway and Their Rights to Traditional Marine Livelihood' (2012) 3 Arctic Rev L Pol 51
Perrin D, 'Tuaregs and Citizenship: "The Last Camp of Nomadism"' (2014) 6 Middle E L Governance 296
Razali R M, Nordin R and Duraisingam T J, 'Migration and Statelessness: Turning the Spotlight on Malaysia' (2015) 23 Pertanika J Soc Sci Human 19
Rubenstein K and Harris E, 'Case Note: Re DLSV and Minister for Immigration and Border Protection (2017) AATA 2999 (27 November 2017)' (2019) 1 Statelessness and Citizenship Rev 177
Sadiq K, 'When States Prefer Non-Citizens Over Citizens: Conflict over Illegal Immigration Into Malaysia' (2005) 49 Intl Stud Q 101
Salih K, 'Kuwait Primary (Tribal) Elections 1975-2008: An Evaluative Study' (2011) 38 Brit J Middle E Stud 141
Sather C, 'Commodity, Trade, Gift Exchange, and the History of Maritime Nomadism in Southeastern Sabah' (2002) 6 Nom Peoples 20
Scott C, 'Indigenous Self-Determination and Decolonization of the International Imagination: A Plea' (1996) 18 H R Q 814
Senghor L S, 'Balkanization ou Federation?' (1956) 2 Afrique Nouvelle 180
Shaw M, 'Peoples, Territorialism and Boundaries' (1997) 3 Eur J Intl L 478
Shiblak A, 'The Lost Tribes of Arabia' (April 2009) 32 Forced Migration Rev 37
Simmons A J, 'On the Territorial Rights of States' (2001) 35 Noûs 300

Stenning D J, 'Transhumance, Migratory Drift, Migration; Patterns of Pastoral Fulani Nomadism' (1957) 87 J Royal Anthropological Inst Great Britain Ireland 57

Stilz A, 'Why Do States Have Territorial Rights?' (2009) 1 Intl Theory 185

Swider K, 'Hoti v Croatia, European Court of Human Rights, First Section, Application No 63311/14 26, Case Note' (2018) 1 Statelessness and Citizenship Rev 184

Turner M D, 'Livestock Mobility and the Territorial State: South-Western Niger (1890–1920)' (2017) 87 Africa: J Intl Afr Inst 578

Van Ert G, 'Nationality, State Succession, and the Right of Option: The Case of Québec' (1998) 36 Can YB Intl L 151

Van Genugten W, Meijknecht A and Rombouts B, 'Stateless Indigenous People(s): The Right to a Nationality, Including Their Own' (2014) 19 Tilburg L Rev 99

Waldie A, 'Contesting an Elastic Constitution: British Nationality and Protection in the Mandates' (2023) 16 Britain World 168

Warren C, 'Consciousness in Social Transformation: The Sama Dilaut of East Malaysia' (1980) 5 Dialectical Anthro 227

Warren J, 'Looking Back on "The Sulu Zone": State Formation, Slave Raiding and Ethnic Diversity in Southeast Asia' (1996) 69 J Malaysian Branch Royal Asiatic Soc 21

Weller M, 'Settling Self-determination Conflicts: Recent Developments' (2009) 20 Eur J Intl L 117

Wilkinson J C, 'Traditional Concepts of Territory in Southeast Arabia' (1983) 149 Geographic J 306

Worster W T, 'The Obligation to Grant Nationality to Stateless Children under Treaty Law' (2019) 24 Tilburg L Rev 204

Yelpaala K, 'Western Anthropological Concepts in Stateless Societies: A Retrospective and Introspective Look at the Dagaaba' (1992) 17 Dialectical Anthro 431

Websites and Newspaper Articles

'Are Sudanese passports the Bidoons' solution?' *Al Jazeera* (2018) <https://www.aljazeera.com/news/2018/03/sudanese-passports-bidoons-solution-180311153502061.html> accessed 22 October 2024

Chou C T and Gooch L, 'Malaysia's Invisible Children' *Al Jazeera* (2015) <https://www.aljazeera.com/features/2016/7/5/malaysias-invisible-children> accessed 23 October 2024

International Organization for Migration, 'Northern Côte d'Ivoire Crisis Response Plan' (2024) <https://crisisresponse.iom.int/response/northern-cote-divoire-crisis-response-plan-2024> accessed 4 September 2024.

IRI Networks, 'Separatists and Skeptics: Refugees Divided on Future of Northern Mali' (2014) <https://reliefweb.int/report/mali/separatists-and-sceptics-refugees-divided-future-northern-mali> accessed 22 October 2024

Malaysia Travel, 'Regatta Lepa 2023' (2023) <https://www.malaysia.travel/events/regatta-lepa-2023> accessed 22 October 2024

Malaysian NRD Website (2025) <https://www.commissionerforoaths.com.my/service-category/national-registration-department-jpn-malaysia/> accessed 22 October 2024

Macdonald, A, 'ECOWAS Agrees to Accelerate Implementation of ENBIC Regional ID Card for Stronger Integration' Biometric Update (1 October 2024) <https://www.biometricupdate.com/202410/ecowas-agrees-to-accelerate-implementation-of-enbic-regional-id-card-for-stronger-integration> accessed 22 October 2024

OHCHR, 'Ratification Status for Kuwait' (2024) <http://tbinternet.ohchr.org/_layouts/TreatyBodyExternal/Treaty.aspx?CountryID92&LangĒN> accessed 27 May 2024

Refugees Deeply, 'In Limbo: Malian Refugees in Burkina Faso' (20 April 2016) <https://deeply.thenewhumanitarian.org/refugees/community/2016/04/20/in-limbo-malian-refugees-in-burkina-faso> accessed 27 May 2024

Reliefweb, 'Thousands to Receive Birth Certificates in Mali' (2015) <https://reliefweb.int/report/mali/thousands-receive-birth-certificates-mali> accessed
UNESCAP, 'Get Everyone in the Picture' (2019) <https://www.getinthepicture.org/> accessed 22 October 2024
UNESCO, 'Guide to International Procedures Available in Cases of Human Rights Violations in Africa' (2024) <http://www.claiminghumanrights.org/mali.html> accessed 22 October 2024
UNHCR, 'Ending Statelessness in Malaysia' (2024) <https://www.unhcr.org/my/ending-statelessness-malaysia> accessed 22 October 2024
UNHCR, 'Mali Situation: UNHCR Regional Update, December 2015-2016' Reliefweb (2016) <https://reliefweb.int/report/mali/mali-situation-unhcr-regional-update-december-2015-february-2016> accessed 22 October 2024
UNICEF, 'Ending Statelessness for a Bright Future for Every Child: The Right to a Nationality for Every Child' (2025) <https://www.unicef.org/thailand/livesuntold> accessed 22 October 2024
US Energy Information Administration, 'Malaysia: International Energy Data and Analysis' (2020) <http://www.eia.gov/beta/international/analysis.cfm?iso = MYS> accessed 22 October 2024
US International Trade Administration, 'Malaysia - Oil and Gas' (2017) <https://www.trade.gov/market-intelligence/malaysia-energy-doing-business-petronas-0> accessed 22 October 2024
Vanar M, 'Sabah Set to Issue Foreigner Cards for Refugees, Stateless People' *The Star* (2022) <https://www.thestar.com.my/news/nation/2022/06/02/sabah-set-to-issue-foreigner-cards-for-refugees-stateless-people> accessed 23 October 2024
Whaley J, 'Mali: A Country on the Cusp?' *GeoExpro* (2008) <https://geoexpro.com/mali-a-country-on-the-cusp/> accessed 22 October 2024
World Bank, 'Country Diagnostic Burkina Faso' (2025) <https://documents.worldbank.org/pt/publication/documents-reports/documentdetail/653431522763079651/id4d-country-diagnostic-burkina-faso> accessed 22 October 2024
World Nuclear Association, 'Uranium in Niger' (2023) <http://www.world-nuclear.org/information-library/country-profiles/countries-g-n/niger.aspx> accessed 22 October 2024

Reports, Working Papers, and Policy Documents

Adjami M, 'Statelessness and Nationality in Côte d'Ivoire—A Study for UNHCR' (UNHCR 2016)
Alexander H, 'Identité juridique et préservation du nomadisme comme mode de vie : les hommes Foulbé en Côte d'Ivoire' (ResearchGate 2023)
African Commission on Human and Peoples' Rights, 'The Right to Nationality in Africa' (African Comm 2014)
Alexander H, 'Report on Citizenship Law: Mali' (GlobalCit, Euro U 2020)
Beyene S, 'Securing, Protecting and Improving the Lives, Livelihoods and Rights of Pastoralist Communities' (African Union Dept of Rural Economy and Agr 2010)Committee on the Rights of the Child, 'Item 4 of the Provisional Agenda: Consideration of Reports of States parties: List of Issues in relation to the Second Periodic Report of Kuwait' (Comm on the Rights of the Child, Sixty-fourth session 2013)
De Chickera A, 'Unravelling Anomaly: Detention, Discrimination and the Protection Needs of Stateless Persons' (Equal Rights Trust 2010)
Dembele O, 'Migration, Emploi, Pression Foncière et Cohésion Sociale en Côte d'Ivoire' (Intl Org for Migration 2009)

Duraisingam T, 'Chronology of Policies Affecting Potentially Stateless Persons and Refugees in Malaysia' (2016) Statelessness Working Paper Series No (Inst on Statelessness and Inclusion2016/07)

Economic Community of West African States (ECOWAS), 'Plan of Action on Eradication of Statelessness 2017–2024 (Banjul Plan of Action)' (ECOWAS 2017)

European Committee of Ministers, 'Recommendation No. R (83) 1 of the Committee of Ministers to Member States on Statelessness Nomadic Peoples and Nomadic Peoples of Undetermined Nationality' (Council of Eur 1983)

European Network on Statelessness (ENS), 'Statelessness Determination and the Protection Status of Stateless Individuals' (ENS 2013)

Fernandez E S, 'Philippine-Malaysia Dispute over Sabah: A Bibliographic Survey' (Philippine E-J 2007)

Frank A, 'Negotiation Borders: Everyday Corruption and Immigration Policing in Malaysia' (ISA Working Paper 2014)

Gary J and Rubin N, 'UN Matters: Are LGBT Rights Human Rights? Recent Developments at the United Nations' (Psychology Intl 2012)

Global COVID19 Consortium and Institute on Statelessness and Inclusion (ISI), 'Malaysia, Together We Can: The COVID-19 Impact on Stateless People and a Roadmap for Change' (ISI 2023)

Greenwood C, 'Tun Mustapha Park: The Creation of a Marine Protected Area: A Case Study on Malaysia' (World Wildlife Fund 2017)

High Commissioner for Human Rights (OHCHR), 'Minority Rights: International Standards and Guidance for Implementation' (OHCHR HR/PUB/10/3 2010)

Human Rights Commission of Malaysia, 'Human Rights and Statelessness in Peninsular Malaysia' (HR Com of Malaysia 2023)

Human Rights Committee (HRC), 'CCPR General Comment No. 18: Non-discrimination' (HRC 1989)

Human Rights Committee (HRC), 'General Comments Adopted by the Human Rights Committee Under Article 40' Addendum General Comment No. 27(67): Freedom of Movement (HRC 1994)

Human Rights Committee (HRC), 'General Comment on Article 6 of the African Charter on the Rights and Welfare of the Child' (HRC 2014)

Human Rights Council, 'Birth Registration and the Right of Everyone to Recognition Everywhere as a Person before the Law: Report of the Office of the United Nations High Commissioner for Human Rights' (HR Council Twenty-seventh ses A/HRC/27/22 2014)

Human Rights Council 'Report on Discrimination against Women on Nationality-Related Matters, including the Impact on Children' (HR Council Twenty-third ses 2013)

Human Rights Council 'Report of the Special Rapporteur on Contemporary Forms of Racism Racial Discrimination Xenophobia and related Intolerance' (HR Council Thirty-eighth ses 2018)

Immigration and Refugee Board of Canada, 'Mali: NINA Card, including Date and Circumstances of Its Introduction; Method Used to Collect Data on Future Cardholders, including Data Collection Period; Opportunity to Correct or Update Card Information, such as Place of Residence and Occupation; Procedure to Correct or Update Card Information (2009-September 2016)' (Imm and Ref Board of Canada 2016)

Immigration and Refugee Board of Canada, 'Malaysian Nationality Law, and the Case of M. Navin, Goh Siu Lin, "In the Case of M. Navin, the Guiding Criteria for Article 15A" Association of Women Lawyers' (Imm and Ref Board of Canada 2016)

International Displacement Monitoring Centre, '2016 Africa Report on Internal Displacement' (Intl Displacement Monitoring Centre 2016)

International Business Publications, 'Mali Mineral & Mining Sector Investment and Business Guide' (Intl Business Pub 2007)

International Criminal Court, 'Public Registry's Report on Proof of Identity Documents Available in Mali and Transmission of Proposed Application Forms for Rule 85(b) RPE Victims and Groups of Victims' (ICC-01/12-01/18 2018)

Kassim A and Haji Mat Z R, 'Policy on Irregular Migrants in Malaysia: An Analysis of its Implementation and Effectiveness' (Philippine Inst for Dev Stud 2011)

Leonhardt M, 'Regional Policies and Response to Manage Pastoral Movements within the ECOWAS Region Study on behalf of the International Organization for Migration (IOM), within the framework of the Support to Free Movement of Persons and Migration in West Africa' (FMM West Africa Proj 2019)

Manby B, 'Who Belongs? Statelessness and Nationality in West Africa' (Migration Policy Inst 2016)

North Borneo and Sarawak Commission of Enquiry, 1961-1962, 'Report of the Commission of Enquiry, North Borneo and Sarawak, 1962 (Cobbold Commission)' (Comm of Enquiry 1962)

Offermann M, 'Les risques d'apatridie au Mali et pour les Maliens vivant à l'étranger en application des législations et pratiques relatives à la nationalité, au Mali et dans les pays d'accueil de Maliens' (UNHCR 2020)

Poling G, 'The South China Sea in Focus: Clarifying the Limits of Maritime Dispute' (Center for Strategic and Intl Stud 2013)

Regino Montes, A and Torres Cisneros, G 'The United Nations Declaration on the Rights of Indigenous Peoples: The Foundation of a New Relationship between Indigenous Peoples, States and Societies' Charters C, and Stavenhagen, R (eds)., Making the Declaration Work: The United Nations Declaration on the Rights of Indigenous Peoples (Copenhagen: International Work Group for Indigenous Affairs, 2009)

Razali R, 'Addressing Statelessness in Malaysia: New Hopes and Remaining Challenges' (2017) ISI Statelessness Working Paper Series No 2017/9

Salam for Democracy and Human Rights and Institute on Statelessness and Inclusion, 'Nothing but a Pen and a Word: Voices From the Stateless Bidoon Community in Kuwait During the COVID-19 Pandemic' (ISI 2023)

Sather C, 'Sulu's Political Jurisdiction over the Bajau Laut' (1971) 3 Borneo Res Bulletin 43

Semporna Islands Project, 'Management Plan for the Semporna Islands Park (Draft: 1-2001) Part 10: Legal Aspects and Regulations' (Semporna Islands Pro 2010)

Saleeby N M, 'Studies in Moro History, Law and Religion' (Proj Gutenberg Ebook 2013, Philippines Dept of the Int 1905)

Sperfeldt C, 'Digital Exclusions: Legal Identity, Identification, and the Sustainable Development Goals in Southeast Asia' (2023) Copenhagen UP MOBILE Working Paper Series

Stewart D J, 'What's Next for Mali? The Roots of Conflict and Challenges to Stability' (US Army War College Strategic Stud Inst 2013) <https://press.armywarcollege.edu/monographs/514>

Tan Sri Datuk Amar Steve Shim Lip Kiong (Chairman) and Commissioners, Royal Commission of Enquiry, 'Report of the Commission of Enquiry on Immigrants in Sabah' (Royal Comm of Enquiry 2012)

UN Ad Hoc Committee on Refugees and Stateless Persons, 'A Study of Statelessness' (Lake Success, New York) (1949) UN Docs E/1112 and E/1112/Add.1

UN Committee on the Elimination of Discrimination Against Women (CEDAW) 'General Recommendation No. 32 on the Gender-Related Dimensions of Refugee Status, Asylum, Nationality and Statelessness of Women' (2014) CEDAW/C/GC/32

UN Development Group, 'Guidelines on Indigenous Peoples' Issues' (UN Dev Group 2009)

UN Dept of Economic and Social Affairs, 'Principles and Recommendations for a Vital Statistics System, Statistical Papers' (2014) UNDESA Series M No. 19/Rev.3

UNHCR, 'Guidelines on Statelessness No. 4: Ensuring Every Child's Right to Acquire a Nationality through Articles 1-4 of the 1961 Convention on the Reduction of Statelessness' (UNHCR 2012)

UNHCR, 'Global Report 2013, Mauritania' (UNHCR 2013)
UNHCR, 'Global Action Plan to End Statelessness 2014-2024' (UNHCR, Div of Intl Protection 2014)
UNHCR, 'Handbook on the Protection of Stateless Persons Under the 1954 Convention Relating to the Status of Stateless Persons' (UNHCR 2014)
UNHCR IBelong Campaign, 'This Is Our Home: Stateless Minorities and Their Search for Citizenship' (UNHCR 2017)
UN Childrens Fund (UNICEF), 'Strengthening Birth Registration in Africa: Opportunities and Partnerships Technical Paper: Opportunities and Partnerships Technical Paper' (UNICEF 2012)
US Department of State, 'US Country Reports on Human Rights Practices for 2013, Libya' (US Dept of State 2013)
World Bank, 'ID4D: Country Diagnostic: Côte d'Ivoire' (World Bank Group 2016)

Dissertations, Theses, and Lecture Notes

Beaugrand C, 'Statelessness and Transnationalism in Northern Arabia: Biduns and State Building in Kuwait, 1959-2009' (PhD thesis, London Sch of Econ 2010)
Benetti T, 'Entwicklung des Verhältnisses zwischen Tuareg und staatlichen Strukturen in Mali' (masters thesis, U of Vienna 2008)
Brunt H, 'Stateless Stakeholders: Seen but Not Heard? The Case of the Sama Dilaut in Sabah, Malaysia' (masters thesis, U Sussex 2013)
Dickens R, 'Defining French Citizenship Policy in West Africa' (PhD thesis, Emory U 2001)
Guinee W, 'Race, Ethnicity, and Ethnic Relations: A Malaysian Case Study: A Curriculum Project for the Fulbright-Hays Seminar Abroad: Malaysia and Singapore' (Westminster C 2005)
Lecocq B, *That Desert Is Our Country: Tuareg Rebellions and Competing Nationalisms in Contemporary Mali (1946-1996)* (PhD, Amsterdam Inst for Soc Sci Res 2002)
Lund-Johansen M, 'Fighting for Citizenship in Kuwait' (thesis, Oslo U 2014)

Works Consulted

Books and Book Chapters

Al-Ashker A and Wilson R, *Islamic Economics: A Short History* (Brill 2006)
Alexander H, 'The Ethics of Counting Statelessness' in Bloom T and Kingston L, *Statelessness, Governance, and the Problem of Citizenship* (Manchester UP 2021)
Alghanim S, *The Reign of Mubarak-Al-Sabah: Shaikh of Kuwait 1896-1915* (I B Tauris 1998)
Al-Mughni H and Tetreault M A, 'Political Actors without the Franchise' in Dresch P and Piscatori J (eds), *Monarchies and Nations: Globalisation and Identity in the Arab States of the Gulf* (I B Tauris 2005)
Alon Y, *The Making of Jordan: Tribes, Colonialism and the Modern State* (I B Tauris 2007)
Azarya V, 'The Nomadic Factor in Africa: Dominance or Marginality' in Khazanov A M and Wink A (eds), *Nomads in the Sedentary World* (Curzon 2001)
Babar Z, 'Citizenship in the Gulf States: Conceptualization and Practice' in Butenschon N A, Davis U and Hassassian M (eds), *Citizenship and the State in the Middle East: Approaches and Applications* (Syracuse 2000)
Bader V, 'Introduction' in Bader V (ed), *Citizenship and Exclusion* (Universiteit van Amsterdam 1997)
Banegas R and Cutolo A, *ID Wars in Côte d'Ivoire: A Political Ethnography of Identification and Citizenship* (OUP 2024)

Banégas R, Cutolo A and Kouyaté S, 'General Amnesty for All 'René Caillés'! Falsifying Birth Certificates and Reforming Legal Identification in Côte d'Ivoire' in Banégas R Cutolo A and Souleymane K (eds) *Identification and Citizenship in Africa Biometrics, the Documentary State and Bureaucratic Writings of the Self* (Routledge 2021)

Barfield T, 'Nomads and States in Comparative Perspective' in Levin J (ed), *Nomad-State Relationships in International Relations* (Palgrave 2020)

Bates R, 'Modernization, Ethnic Competition, and the Rationality of Politics in Contemporary Africa' in Rothchild D and Olorunsola V (eds), *State versus Ethnic Claims: African Policy Dilemmas* (Westview 1982)

Bauböck R, 'The Trade-Off Between Transnational Citizenship and Political Autonomy' in Faiset T and Kivisto P (eds), *Dual Citizenship in Global Perspective: From Unitary to Multiple Citizenship* (Palgrave 2007)

Beckman L, 'Is Residence Special? Democracy in the Age of Migration and Human Mobility' in Beckman L and Erman E (eds), *Territories of Citizenship* (Palgrave 2012)

Belton K, 'Statelessness: A Matter of Human Rights' in Howard-Hassmann R and Walton-Roberts M (eds), *The Human Right to Citizenship: A Slippery Concept* (Pennsylvania UP 2015)

Benhabib S, 'Twilight of Sovereignty or the Emergence of Cosmopolitan Norms? Rethinking Citizenship in Volatile Times' in Isin E Nyers P and Turner B (eds), *Citizenship between Past and Future* (Routledge 2008)

Benko G and Strohmayer U, *Human Geography: A History for the 21st Century* (Arnold 2004)

Benswait A, 'Language and Statelessness: The Impact of Political Discourses on the Bidoon Community in Kuwait' in Bloom T and Kingston L (eds) *Statelessness, Governance, and the Problem of Citizenship* (Manchester UP 2021)

Bermudez M S, 'Accessing Documents, Preventing Statelessness' in Institute on Statelessness and Inclusion, *The World's Stateless: Children* (Wolf 2017)

Bernarde P, 'Peuls en mouvement, Peuls en conflits en moyenne et haute Côte d'Ivoire, de 1950 à 1990' in Botte R, Boutrais J and Schmitz J (eds) *Figures peules* (Karthala 1999)

Blanche P, *Nomades de la mer, Vezos, Bajaus, Mokens* (Ibis 2008)

Blitz B, 'The State and the Stateless: The Legacy of Hannah Arendt Reconsidered' in Bloom T, Tonkiss K and Cole P (eds), *Understanding Statelessness* (Routledge 2017)

Boureima D, 'La constitution d'un réseau régional avec les communautés es pastorales d'Afrique de l'Oust : le Réseau Billital maroobe' in Jensen M W (ed), *Pasteurs Nomades et Transhumants Autochtones* (Harmattan 2010)

Brenner L, *Muslim Identity and Social Change in Sub-Saharan Africa* (Indiana UP 1993)

Brett P, 'Discrimination and Childhood Statelessness in the Work of the UN Human Rights Treaty Bodies' in Institute on Statelessness and Inclusion, *The World's Stateless: Children* (Wolf 2017)

Brown T C, *Statelessness: On Almost Not Existing* (Minnesota UP 2019)

Buckle S, *Natural Law and the Theory of Property: Grotius to Hume* (Clarendon 1991)

Chatty D, *Adapting to Multinational Oil Exploration: The Mobile Pastoralists of Oman* (Halle-Wittenberg UP 2002)

Chatty D, 'Multinational Oil Exploitation and Social Investment: Mobile Pastoralists in the Sultanate of Oman' in Chatty D (ed), *Nomadic Societies in the Middle East and North Africa: Entering the 21st Century* (Brill 2006)

Chou C, *Indonesian Sea Nomads; Money Magic and Fear of the Orang Suku Laut* (Routledge 2003)

Chou C, *The Orang Suku Laut of Riau, Indonesia: The Inalienable Gift of Territory* (Routledge 2010)

Clarke P (ed), *The Oxford Handbook of the Sociology of Religion* (OUP 2009)

Claudot-Hawad H, 'A Nomadic Fight against Immobility: the Tuareg in the Modern State' in Chatty D (ed), *Nomadic Societies in The Middle East and North Africa: Entering the 21st Century* (Brill 2006)

Coquery-Vidrovitch C, 'The Transfer of Economic Power in French-Speaking West Africa' in Proser G and Louis W M Roger (eds), *Decolonization and African Independence: The Transfers of Power, 1960-1980* (Yale UP 1988)

Courbe P, *Le nouveau droit de la nationalité* (Dalloz 1994)

Diallo Y, 'Processes and types of pastoral migration in northern Côte d'Ivoire' in De Bruijn M and Van Dijk H (eds), *Mobile Africa* (Brill 2001)

Durand F and Curtis R, *Maps of Malaysia and Borneo: Discovery, Statehood and Progress* (Didier Millet 2014)

Ehrlich E, *Fundamental Principles of the Sociology of Law* (Transaction 1936)

Elias N, *The Civilizing Process: State Formation and Civilization* (Basil Blackwell 1994)

Fabietti U, 'Facing Change in Arabia: The Bedouin Community and the Notion of Development' in Chatty D (ed), *Nomadic Societies in the Middle East and North Africa: Entering the 21st Century* (Brill 2006)

Fischer A and Kohl I, 'Tuareg Moving Global: An Introduction' in Fischer A and Kohl I (eds), *Tuareg Society within a Globalized World: Saharan Life in Transition* (I B Tauris 2010)

Fisher A, 'Research and Nomads in the Age of Globalization' in Fischer A and Kohl I (eds), *Tuareg Society within a Globalized World: Saharan Life in Transition* (I B Tauris 2010)

Fouberg E, Murphy A and De Blij H, *Human Geography: People, Place and Culture* (9th edn, Wiley 2009)

Fripp E, *Nationality and Statelessness in the International Law of Refugee Status* (Hart 2016)

Galaty J, 'The Maasai Group-Ranch: Politics and Development in an African Pastoral Society' in Salzman P C and Sadala E, *When Nomads Settle: Processes of Sedentarization as Adaptation and Response* (Praeger 1980)

Gibney M, 'Statelessness and Citizenship in Ethical and Political Perspective' in Edwards A and van Waas L (eds), *Nationality and Statelessness Under International Law* (CUP 2014)

Giurida A, 'Tuareg Networks: An Integrated Approach to Mobility and Stasis' in Kohl I and Fischer A (eds), *Tuareg Society within a Globalized World: Saharan Life in Transition* (I B Tauris 2010)

Goh B, 'Dilemma of Progressive Politics in Malaysia: Islamic Orthodoxy versus Human Rights' in Mee W and Kahn J (eds), *Questioning Modernity in Indonesia and Malaysia* (NUS Press 2012)

Gorman D, *Imperial Citizenship: Empire and the Question of Belonging* (Manchester UP 2006)

Govil R and Edwards A, 'Women, Nationality and Statelessness: The Problem of Unequal Rights' in Institute on Statelessness and Inclusion, *The World's Stateless: Children* (Wolf 2017)

Grégoire E and Schmitz J, 'Monde arabe et Afrique noire: permanences et nouveaux liens' in Grégoire E and Schmitz J, *Afrique noire et monde arabe: continuités et ruptures* (Aube IRD 2000)

Gulalp H, 'Introduction: Citizenship vs. Nationality?' in Gulalp H (ed), *Citizenship and Ethnic Conflict: Challenging the nation-state* (Routledge 2009)

Gyulai G, 'The Long-Overlooked Mystery of Refugee Children's Nationality' in Institute on Statelessness and Inclusion, *The World's Stateless: Children* (Wolf 2017)

Hampshire J, *Citizenship and Belonging: Immigration and the Politics of Demographic Governance in Postwar Britain* (Palgrave Macmillan 2005)

Hanjian C, *The Sovrien: An Exploration of the Right to Be Stateless* (Polyspire 2003)

Hansen R, *Citizenship and Immigration in Post-war Britain* (OUP 2000)

Hesse C, 'La création de richesses grâce à la variabilité de l'environnement : l'économie du pastoralisme dans les zones arides d'Afrique orientale' in Wiben Jensen M (ed) *Pasteurs Nomades et Transhumants Autochtones* (Harmattan 2010)

Holst F, *Ethnicization and Identity Construction in Malaysia* (Routledge 2012)

Howard-Hassmann R, 'Introduction: The Human Right to Citizenship' in Howard-Hassmann R and Walton-Roberts M (eds), *The Human Right to Citizenship: A Slippery Concept* (Pennsylvania UP 2015)

Isin E Nyers P and Turner B (eds), *Citizenship between Past and Future* (Routledge 2008)

Jackson M and Smith I, 'Ownership or Tenure? A Case Study' in Relaki M and Catapoti D (eds), *An Archaeology of Land Ownership* (Taylor and Francis 2013)

Janzen J, *Nomads in the Sultanate of Oman* (Westview 1986)

Jones A, *Human Geography: The Basics* (Routledge 2012)

Jordan A, *The Making of a Modern Kingdom: Globalization and Change in Saudi Arabia* (Waveland 2011)

Kahn J, 'Islam and Capitalism in the Frontiers and Borderlands' in Mee W and Kahn J (eds.), *Questioning Modernity in Indonesia and Malaysia* (NUS Press 2012)

Kamian B, 'La dynamique des intégrations, de la période coloniale à nos jours' in Sanankoua B (ed), *Les États-nations face à l'intégration régionale en Afrique de l'Ouest—Le cas du Mali* (Karthala 2007)

Kasaba R, *A Movable Empire: Ottoman Nomads, Migrants and Refugees* (Washington UP 2009)

Keenan J, 'Sedentarization and Changing Patterns of Social Organization amongst the Tuareg of Algeria' in Chatty D (ed) *Nomadic Societies in the Middle East and North Africa: Entering the 21st Century* (Brill 2006)

Keller, E 'The State, Public Policy and the Mediation of Ethnic Conflict in Africa' in Rothchild D and Olorunsola V A (eds) *State Versus Ethnic Claims: African Policy Dilemmas* (Routledge 1983)

Klar M, *Resource Wars: The New Landscape of Global Conflict* (Holt 2002)

Kohl I and Fischer A (eds), *Tuareg Society within a Globalized World: Saharan Life in Transition* (I B Tauris 2010)

Kymlicka W, *Multicultural Citizenship: A Liberal Theory of Minority Rights* (OUP 1995)

Lagarde J, 'La nomadisation des Ifoghas et son contrôle (1943-1944-1945)' in Bernus E and others (eds), *Nomades et commandants: Administration et sociétés nomades dans l'ancienne A.O.F.* (Karthala 1993)

Lancaster W and Lancaster F, 'Integration into Modernity: Some Tribal Rural Societies in the Bilad Ash-Sham' in Chatty D (ed), *Nomadic Societies in the Middle East and North Africa: Entering the 21st Century* (Brill 2006)

Larkins J, *From Hierarchy to Anarchy; Territory and Politics before Westphalia* (Palgrave Macmillan 2010)

Lim H, 'Electoral Politics in Malaysia: `Managing' Elections in a Plural Society' in Bruns G, Croissant A and John M (eds), *Electoral Politics in Southeast & East Asia* (Friedrich-Ebert-Stiftung 2002)

Loiseau P, 'L'administration et les rapports nomades/sédentaires' in Bernus E and others (eds), *Nomades et commandants: Administration et sociétés nomades dans l'ancienne A.O.F.* (Karthala 1993)

Longva A N, 'Neither Autocracy nor Democracy' in Dresch P and Piscatori J (eds), *Monarchies and Nations: Globalisation and Identity in the Arab States of the Gulf* (I B Tauris 2005)

Lowe V, *International Law* (OUP 2007)

Maiga M, *Le Mali : de la sécheresse a la rébellion nomade : Chronique et analyse d'un double phénomène du contre développement en Afrique sahélienne* (Harmattan 1997)

Manby B, *Struggles for Nationality in Africa* (Zed Books 2009)

Marek K, *Identity and Continuity of States in Public International Law* (Librairie Droz 1968)

Marnham P, *Nomads of the Sahel* (Minority Rights International 1979)

Martignoni M and Papadopoulos D, 'Genealogies of Autonomous Mobility' in Isin E and Nyers P (eds), *Routledge Handbook of Global Citizenship Studies* (Routledge 2014)

Marushiakova E and Popov V, 'The Roma: A Nation without a State? Historical Background and Contemporary Tendencies' in Streck B (ed), *Segmentation und Komplementarität. Organisatorische, okonomische und kulturelle Aspekte der Interaktion von Nomaden und Sesshaften 6 Orientwissenschaftliche* (Hefte 2004)

Masters B, *The Arabs of the Ottoman Empire 1516-1918: A Social and Cultural History* (CUP 2013)

Maunati Y, 'Networking the Pan-Dayak' in Mee W and Kahn J S, *Questioning Modernity in Indonesia and Malaysia* (NUS Press 2012)
McAdam J, 'Disappearing States, Statelessness and the Boundaries of International Law' in McAdam J (ed), *Climate Change and Displacement: Multidisciplinary Perspectives* (OUP 2010)
Meijer R, Sater J, Babar Z, *Routledge Handbook of Citizenship in the Middle East and North Africa* (Routledge 2021)
Meir A, 'Delivering Essential Public Services to Arid Zone Nomads' in *Desert Development: Man and Technology in Sparselands* (Springer Nature 1985) Nicolaisen J and Nicolaisen I, *The Pastoral Tuareg; Ecology, Culture and Society, Volume Two* (Thames and Hudson 1997)
O'Fahey R, 'Islamic Hegemonies in the Sudan: Sufism, Mahdism and Islamism' in Brenner L (ed), *Muslim Identity and Social Change in Subsaharan Africa* (Indiana UP 1993)
Panter-Brick K, 'Independence, French Style' in Gifford P and Louis R W, *Decolonization and African Independence* (Yale UP 1988)
Pezard S and Shurkin M, *Toward a Secure and Stable Northern Mali: Approaches to Engaging Local Actors* (Rand Corporation 2013)
Rajan S, Varghese V and Jayakumar M, *Dreaming Mobility and Buying Vulnerability: Overseas Recruitment Practices in India* (Routledge 2011)
Rana S, 'Nomads' in Ray S and Schwarz H (eds), *The Encyclopedia of Postcolonial Studies* Wiley 2016)
Rocaboy J, 'Le cas hamallist' in Bernus E and others (eds), *Nomades et commandants: Administration et sociétés nomades dans l'ancienne A.O.F.* (Karthala 1993)
Rodet M, *Les migrantes ignorées du Haut-Sénégal: 1900-1946* (Karthala 2009)
Rothchild D and Olorunsola V, 'Managing Competing State and Ethnic Claims' in Rothchild D and Olorunsola V (eds), *State Versus Ethnic Claims: African Policy Dilemmas* (Westview Press 1983)
Rush A, *Al-Sabah: History and Genealogy of Kuwait's Ruling Family, 1752-1987* (Ithaca UP 1997)
Ryser R, *Indigenous Nations and Modern States; The Political Emergence of Nations Challenging State Power* (Routledge 2012)
Salmond J, *Jurisprudence, or the theory of law* (7th edn, Sweet and Maxwell 1924)
Salzman P, *Pastoralists: Equality, Hierarchy and the State* (Westview 2004)
Scheele J, *Smugglers and Saints of the Sahara: Regional Connectivity in the 20th Century* (CUP 2012)
Shachar A, *The Birthright Lottery* (Harvard UP 2009)
Simel J, 'Le pastoralisme et les dés du changement climatique' in Jensen M (ed), *Pasteurs Nomades et Transhumants Autochtones* (Harmattan 2010)
Smith A, *National Identity* (Nevada UP 1991)
Smith L, *Making Citizens in Africa: Ethnicity, Gender, and National Identity in Ethiopia* (CUP 2013)
Spiro P, *At Home in Two Countries: The Past and Future of Dual Citizenship* (New York UP 2016)
Stolcke V, 'The "Nature" of Nationality' in Bader V (ed), *Citizenship and Exclusion* (Universiteit van Amsterdam 1997)
Tamarkin N and Giaudo R, 'African Indigenous Citizenship' in Isin E and Nyers P (eds), *Routledge Handbook of Global Citizenship* (Routledge 2014)
Tarling N, *Sulu and Sabah; A Study of British Policy Towards the Philippines and North Borneo from the Late 18th Century* (OUP 1978)
UNHCR, 'Statelessness and Citizenship' in UNHCR (ed), *The State of the World's Refugees—A Humanitarian Agenda* (OUP 1997)
van Waas L and De Chickera A, 'Forward' in Institute on Statelessness and Inclusion, *The World's Stateless: Children* (Wolf 2017)

VerEecke C, *Nigeria's Experiment with a National Program for Nomadic Education* (Ohio State U 1989)
Warren J, 'Trade for Bullion to Trade for Commodities and "Piracy": Cina, the West and the Sulu Zone, 1768-1898' in Amirell S and Muller L (eds), *Persistent Piracy: Maritime Violence and State-Formation in Global Historical Perspective* (Palgrave Macmillan 2014)
Weber M, 'Politics as a Vocation' in Gerth H H and Mills C W (eds), *From Max Weber: Essays in Sociology* (Routledge 1970)
Wehrey F, *Sectarian Politics in the Gulf: From the Iraq War to the Arab Uprisings* (Columbia UP 2014)
White W, *Sea Gypsies of Malaysia* (Ams Pri 1981)
Wink A, *Indo-Islamic Society: 14th-15th Centuries* (Brill 2004)
Wondji C, 'Symbolismes Culturels Traditionnels et Indépendances Africaines' in Ageron C-R and Michel M (eds), *L'Afrique noire française: l'heure des indépendances* (CNRS Éditions 2015)
Yanai S, *The Political Transformation of Gulf Tribal States: Elitism and the Social Contract in Kuwait, Bahrain and Dubai: 1918-1970s* (Sussex 2014)
Yizraeli S, *Politics and Society in Saudi Arabia: The Crucial Years of Development 1960-1982* (OUP 2012)
Young C, 'The Colonial State and Post-Colonial Crisis' in Gifford P and Roger Louis WM (eds), *Decolonization and African Independence: The Transfers of Power, 1960-1980* (Yale UP 1988)
Young K, Bussink W and Hasan P (eds), *Malaysia: Growth and Equity in a Multiracial Society* (Johns Hopkins UP 1980)
Zeineddin C, 'State-Religion-Minorities Tensions in the Arab Gulf' in Al-Zoby M and Baskan B (eds.), *State-Society Relations in the Arab Gulf States* (Gerlach 2014)

Journal Articles

Alexander H and Simon J, 'Sinking into Statelessness' (2014) 19 Tilburg L Rev 20
Ali I, 'Since Birth till Death, What Is Their Status? A Case Study of the Sea Bajau in Pulau Mabul, Semporna,' (2010) 1 J Arts, Sci Com 156
Allerton C, 'Statelessness and the lives of the children of migrants in Sabah, East Malaysia' (2014) 19 Tilburg L Rev: J Intl Eur L 26
Allerton C, 'Impossible Children: Illegality and Excluded Belonging among Children of Migrants in Sabah, East Malaysia' (2018) 44 J Ethnic Migration Stud 1081
Barnard T P, 'Celates, Rayat-Laut, Pirates: The Orang Laut and Their Decline in History' (2007) 80 J Malaysian Branch Royal Asiatic Soc 33
Barral H, 'Mobilité et cloisonnement chez les éleveurs du nord de la Haute-Volta : les zones dites "d'endodromie pastorale"' (1974) 11 Cahiers ORSTOM, Série Sciences Humaines 127
Bassett T J, 'Bergers salariés et gestion du troupeau chez les éleveurs peuls du Nord de la Côte-d'Ivoire' (1994) 34 Cahiers d'Études Africaines 147
Baynes K, 'Kant on Property Rights and the Social Contract' (1989) 72 The Monist 433
Benoit M, 'Pastoralisme et migration : Les Peuhls de Barani et de Dokui (Haute-Volta)' (1978) 70 Études Rurales 9
Bloom T, 'Citizenship and Colonization: Liberal Concepts of Citizenship Are Not Adequate for Understanding Contemporary Individual-State Relationships' (2018) 67 Soundings 114
Boutrais J, 'Pour une nouvelle cartographie des Peuls' (1994) 34 Cahiers d'Études Africaines 137
Büssow J, 'Negotiating the Future of a Bedouin Polity in Mandatory Syria: Political Dynamics of the Sba'a 'Abada During the 1930s' (2011) 15 Nom Peoples 70
Caselliy F, Morelli M and Rohnerx D, 'The Geography of Inter-State Resource Wars' (2015) 130 Q J Econ 267

Chatty D, 'The Persistence of Bedouin Identity and Increasing Political Self-Representation in Lebanon and Syria' 18 Nom Peoples 16 (2014).
Cheva-Isarakul J and Sperfeldt C 'Citizenship and Statelessness among Mobile Maritime Populations: The Case of the Moken in Thailand' (2023) 27 Citizenship Stud 530
Clifton J, Acciaoli G, Brunt H, Dressler W, Fabinyi M and Singh S, 'Statelessness and Conservation: Exploring the Implications of an International Governance Agenda' (2014) 19 Tilburg L Rev 81
Clifton J and Majors C, 'Culture, Conservation, and Conflict: Perspectives on Marine Protection among the Bajau of Southeast Asia' (2011) 25 Soc Nat Res 716
Cohen E, 'Tourism and Land Grab in the Aftermath of the Indian Ocean Tsunami' (2011) 11 Scandinavian J Hospitality Tourism 224
Cowen Z, 'The Emergence of a New Federation in Malaya' (1958) 1 Tasmanian U L Rev 53
Craig S, 'Indigenous Self-Determination and Decolonization of the International Imagination: A Plea,' (1996) 18 Hum R Q 814
De Bruijn M and Pelckmans L, 'Facing Dilemmas: Former Fulbe Slaves in Modern Mali' (2005) 39 Canadian J Afr Stud [Revue Canadienne des Études Africaines] 69
Diallo Y, 'Les Peuls, les Sénoufo et l'État au nord de la Côte d'Ivoire. Problèmes fonciers et gestion du pastoralisme' (1995) 10 Bulletin d'APAD 1
Elias B, Busby K and Martins P, 'One Little, too Little: Counting Canada's Indigenous People for Improved Health Reporting' (2015) 138 Social Sci Med 179
Fry J and Loj M, 'The Roots of Historic Title: Non-Western Pre-Colonial Normative Systems and Legal Resolution of Territorial Disputes' (2014) 27 Leiden J Intl L 727
Hagburg S, 'À l'ombre du conflit violent. Règlement et gestion des conflits entre agriculteurs karaboro et agro-pasteurs peuls au Burkina Faso' (2001) 41 Cahiers d'Études Africaines 161, 45
Hampshire K, 'Fulani on the Move: Seasonal Economic Migration in the Sahel as a Social Process' (2002) 38 J Development Stud 15
Heikkil L, 'Welfare Services in Enhancing Good Life for the Sami: A Reflection on conducting Ethically Responsible Research and Developing an Improved Sense of Culture' (2016) 59 Intl Social Work 653
Holbrook J, 'Legal Hybridity in the Philippines: Lessons in Legal Pluralism from Mindanao and the Sulu Archipelago' (2010) 18 Tulane J Intl Comp L
Howarth A Heiskanen J Steglich S and Manchanda N, 'Nomads' Land: Exploring the Social and Political Life of the Nomad Category' (2024) 18 Intl Pol Soc 34
Jaghai S, 'Statelessness at Home: The Story of a Stateless Student at Tilburg Law School' (2014) 19 Tilburg L Rev 108
Kubben R, 'To Belong or Not Belong' (2014) 19 Tilburg Spec Issue on Statelessness 136
Kuntz J, 'The Nottebohm Case (Second Phase)' (1960) 54 Am J Intl L 536
Lenhart L, 'Orang Suku Laut Ethnicity and Acculturation' in (1997) 153 Bijdragen tot de Taal-, Land- en Volkenkunde Deel, Riau in Transition 577
Lenhart L, 'Orang Suku Laut Communities at Risk: Effects of Modernization on the Resource Base, Livelihood and Culture of the "Sea Tribe People" of the Riau Islands (Indonesia)' (2002) 5 Nom Peoples 67
Liu H, 'The Right to be Nomadic? Freedom of Movement in the Aspect of Mokens' (2017) 8 Assumption U L J 2560
Marx E, 'The Tribe as Unit of Subsistence: Nomadic Pastoralism in the Middle East' (2009) 79 Am Anthropologist 346
McGovney D, 'French Nationality Laws Imposing Nationality at Birth,' (1911) 5 Am J Intl L 325
Meir A, 'Nomads, Development and Health: Delivering Public Health Services to the Bedouin in Israel' (1987) 69 Geograska Annaler 115
Mervyn J, 'The Nottebohm Case' (1956) 5 Intl Comp L Q 230
Morris D and Francombe J, 'The Ngisipet and Trachoma Prevention: Solving the Latrine Problem in Nomadic Tribes' (2007) 20 Community Eye Health J 70

Nadasdy P, '"Property" and Aboriginal Land Claims in the Canadian Subarctic: Some Theoretical Considerations' (2002) 104 Am Anthol 247
Pratt A, McDonald D, 'Aboriginal Self-determination: Fine Words and Crocodile Tears' (1999) 11 Curr Issues Crim Just 349
Pribadi M, 'Ibn Khaldun's Social Thought on Bedouin and Hadar' (2014) 52 Al-Jami'ah J Islamic Stud 417
Sanders D, 'Indigenous Land Rights in Malaysia: Nor Nyawai & 3 Ors v Borneo Pulp Plantation Sdn Bhd and 2 Ors' 5(14) (2002) Indigenous L Bull 21
Sanderson M, 'Statelessness and Mass Expulsion in Sudan: A Reassessment of the International Law' (2014) 12 Nw J Intl Hum Rts 74
Sarkin J and Cook A, 'The Human Rights of the San (Bushmen) of Botswana' (2010) 20 Fla St J Transnat L Pol 1
Sigona N, 'How Can a Nomad Be a Refugee? Kosovo Roma and Labelling Policy in Italy' (2003) 37 Socio 69
Slone R, 'Breaking the Genuine Link: The Contemporary International Legal Regulation of Nationality' (2009) 50 Harvard Intl L J 1
Stewart F, 'The Contract with Surety in Bedouin Customary Law' (2003) 2 UCLA J Islam 163
Stilz A, 'Nation, States and Territory' (2011) 121 Ethics 572
Toth A, 'Tribes and Tribulations: Bedouin Losses in the Saudi and Iraqi Struggles over Kuwait's Frontiers, 1918-1943' (2005) 32 Brit J Middle E Stud 145
Toth A, 'Control and Allegiance at the Dawn of the Oil Age: Bedouin, Zakat and Struggles for Sovereignty in Arabia, 1916-1955' (2012) 21 Middle E Critique 57
Tucker J, 'Questioning de facto Statelessness' (2014) 19 Tilburg L Rev 276
Turner M, 'Political Ecology and the Moral Dimensions of 'Resource Conflicts': The Case of Farmer–Herder Conflicts in the Sahel' (2004) 23 Pol Geo 863
Whaley J, 'Mali: A Country on the Cusp?' (2008) 5 GeoExpro 4
Wright L, 'Historical Notes on the North Borneo Dispute' (1966) 25 J Asian Stud 471

Reports, Policy Papers, Dissertations, and Handbooks

African Commission on Human and Peoples' Rights, 28th ordinary session, 'Report of the ACHPR Working Group of Experts on Indigenous Populations/ Communities' (2005)
Akamine J, 'The Role of Sama/Bajaus in Sea Cucumber Trades in the Sulu Sultanate Economy: Towards a Reconstruction of Dynamic Maritime History in Southeast Asia' (Hitotsubashi University, Conference Paper 2017)
Al Barazi Z and van Waas L, 'Statelessness and Displacement Scoping Paper' (Norwegian Refugee Council and Tilburg University, July 2018)
Aly, Lahyerou AG, The rights of the indigenous peoples to self-determination: Attempts to address the violation of human rights with specific reference to Mali (University of Pretoria Faculty of Law 2010)
Amnesty International, 'The withouts of Kuwait: Nationality for Stateless Bidun Now' (September 16, 2013)
Asia Pacific Refugee Rights Network, 'The Vulnerability of Sama Dilaut (Sama Dilaut) Children in Sabah, Malaysia' (2015)
Bingham L Reddy J H and Kohn S, 'De Jure Statelessness in the Real World: Applying the Prato Summary Conclusion' (Open Society Justice Initiative 2011)
Brown N J, 'Pushing Towards Party Politics? Kuwait's Islamic Constitutional Movement' (Carnegie Endowment for International Peace 2007)
Brunt H, 'Stateless Stakeholders: Seen but Not Heard? The Case of the Sama Dilaut in Sabah, Malaysia' (University of Sussex 2013)
Carnegie Endowment for International Peace, 'Uranium in Sahara Sands' (2013)

Carruthers N, 'Sabah ICs for Sabahans: Will It Help? Executive Summary' (Yusof Ishak Institute 2016)
Chatty D, 'Adapting to Multinational Oil Exploration: The Mobile Pastoralists of Oman' in Leder S and Streck B (eds) Akkulturation und Selbstbehauptung. Beiträge des Kolloquiums am 14.12.2001. Halle 2002 (Orientwissenschaftliche Hefte 4; Mitteilungen des SFB 'Dierenz und Integration')
Chatty D, 'Nomadic Peoples, Migration and Biodiversity' SGI Q (October 2003)
Claiming Human Rights, 'Guide to International Procedures Available in Cases of Human Rights Violations in Africa' (2010)
Committee on the Elimination of Racial Discrimination, Consideration of Reports Submitted by States Parties under Article 9 of the Convention, Fourteenth periodic reports of States parties due in 2001, Addendum MALI* (CERD/C/407/Add.2)
Committee on the Rights of the Child, Consideration of the Reports Submitted by States Parties under Article 44 of the Convention: Concluding Observations: Mali, CRC/C/MLI/CO/2 (3 May 2007).
Congrès constitutif du parti de la fédération africaine, 'Proceedings' Afrique Nouvelle (3 July 1959)
Coordinating Committee for Geoscience Programs in East and Southeast Asia, 'Petroleum Potential of West Palawan Basins and Sulu Sea Region' (8 August 2002)
Council of Europe: Committee of Ministers, Recommendation No R (83) 1 of the Committee of Ministers to Member States on Statelessness Nomads and Nomads of Undetermined Nationality (22 February 1983)
De Schutter O, 'Interim report of the Special Rapporteur on the right to food' (UN General Assembly submitted in accordance with General Assembly resolution 64/15 11 August 2010)
Development of Human Resources in Rural Areas (DHRRA), 'Citizenship and Statelessness Fact Sheet 2' (January 2015)
Djire M, 'Land Registration in Mali; No Land Ownership for Farmers?' (International Institute for Environment and Development 2007)
Donini A and Scalettaris G, 'Planning from the Future: Component 2: The Contemporary Humanitarian Landscape: Malaise, Blockages and Game Changers; Case Study: Regional Humanitarian Challenges in the Sahel' (Feinstein International Center, Humanitarian Policy Group, Kings College London April 2016)
ECOWAS, Forty-ninth Session of the Council of Ministers, Regulation C/REG.3/01/03 Relating to the implementation of the regulations on Transhumance between the ECOWAS Member States (Dakar 26–28 January 2003)
European Network on Statelessness, 'Protecting Stateless Persons from Arbitrary Detention: An Agenda for Change' (April 2017)
Ewing W A, Martinez D E and Rumbaut R G, 'The Criminalization of Immigration in the United States' (American Immigration Council Special Report 2015)
Government of the Philippines, 'Petroleum Potential of the Sulu Sea Region, Philippines' (2020)
Gregoire E and Schmit J, 'Afrique noire et monde arabe: continuités et ruptures' (Institut de recherche pour le développement 2000)
Haller-Tros R, 'The Territorial Dispute between Indonesia and Malaysia over Pulau Sipadan' (International Boundaries Research Unit, Boundary and Territory Briefing, Durham University 1995)
Human Rights Council, Thirty-first session, 'Impact of the Arbitrary Deprivation of Nationality on the Enjoyment of the Rights of Children concerned, and Existing Laws and Practices on Accessibility for Children to Acquire Nationality, inter alia, of the Country in which They Are Born, if they Otherwise Would Be Stateless' A/HRC/31/29 (16 December 2015)
Human Rights Council, Twenty-fifth session, 'Human Rights and Arbitrary Deprivation of Nationality' Report of the Secretary-General (19 December 2013)
Human Rights Watch, 'Mali: New Abuses by Tuareg Rebels, Soldiers' (7 June 2013)

Human Rights Watch, 'Prisoners of the Past, Kuwaiti Bidun and the Burden of Statelessness' (13 June 2011)

Human Rights Watch, 'Stateless at Sea: The Moken of Burma and Thailand' (25 June 2015)

Human Rights Watch, 'The Bedoons of Kuwait: Citizens without Citizenship' (1 August 1995)

Imai S and Buttery K, 'Indigenous Belonging: A Commentary on Membership and Identity in the United Nations Declaration on the Rights of Indigenous People' (2013) 49 York UP Working Paper

Institute on Statelessness and Inclusion, 'Universal Periodic Review, 27th session: Overview and analysis of recommendations on nationality and statelessness' (May 2017)

Institute on Statelessness and Inclusion and NYU Center for Global Affairs and Open Society Foundations, 'Statelessness, Citizenship & Inclusion: Highlights of the Dedicated programme for Academics' (5–9 June 2017 New York)

Interights, 'Non-Discrimination in International Law: A Handbook for Practitioners' (2011)

International Law Commission, sixth session, (1954), submitted to the General Assembly, para 25, YB Intl Law Commission, 1954, vol. II

Jessup P C, US Ambassador to the UN 'Remarks at UNSCOR, 383d mtg. at 9-11, Supp No 128' (2 December 1948) UN Doc S/P.V. 383

Jumin S R and Kassem K, 'Ecosystem-based Management in a Proposed Marine Protected Area: Tun Mustapha Park' (World Wildlife Fund Malaysia January 2011)

Kerno I S, 'Nationality, including Statelessness: Analysis of Changes in Nationality Legislation of States since 1930' (1953) International Law Commission A/CN.4/67

Kuwaiti National Assembly, 'The Progress of Democracy in the State of Kuwait' (October 2011)

Lee E T H, 'Scope for Improvement: Malaysia's Oil and Gas Sector' (Research for Social Advancement 2013)

Lyons Y, 'Offshore Oil and Gas in the SCS and the Protection of the Marine Environment, Part 1, A Review of the Context and a Profile of Offshore Activities' (Center for International Law, NUS Press 2011)

Macalandag R, 'Recognition and the Mobile Indigene: Periphery and Possibility The Badjao of the Philippines' (thesis, Austral Natl U 2021)

Malaysia National Gas Association, 'Malaysia: Natural Gas Industry Annual Review—2014 Edition' (2014)

Manby B, 'Nationality, Migration and Statelessness in West Africa: A study for UNHCR and IOM' (UNHCR and IOM June 2015)

Massey H, 'UNHCR and de facto Statelessness' (April 2010) UNHCR LPPR/2010/01

Maze K, 'Land Conflict, Migration, and Citizenship in West Africa: Complex Diversity and Recurring Challenges: A Desk Study' (2017) World Bank

McAdam J, 'The Refugee Convention as a Rights Blueprint for Persons in Need of International Protection' (2006)UNHCR Research Paper No. 125

Minority Rights Group International, 'State of the World's Minorities and Indigenous Peoples' (2016)

Minority Rights Group International, 'World Directory of Minorities and Indigenous Peoples - Mali: Overview' (May 2013)

Navallo K, 'Filipino Migrants in Sabah: Marginalized Citizens in the Midst of Interstate Disputes' (Kyoto U)

Norwegian Refugee Council/Internal Displacement Monitoring Centre (NRC/IDMC) 'Mali: Ongoing pursuit of durable solutions' (19 May 2014)

Office of the Commissioner General for Refugees and Stateless Persons, 'Libya: Nationality, Registration and Documents' (December 2014)

Ogbuitepu F, Consultancy Africa Intelligence, 'Realising Indigenous Peoples' Rights: The Case of the Kalahari Bushmen of Botswana' (2011)

Open Society Justice Initiative, 'Strategic Litigation Impacts: Roma School Desegregation' (Open Society Foundations 2016)

Parry C, 'Commonwealth Citizenship with Special Reference to India' (Indian Council of World Affairs 1954)
Pilgram L, 'International Law and European Nationality Laws' (EUDO Citizenship Observatory 2011)
President Jackson's Message to Congress, 'On Indian Removal,' (December 6, 1830); Records of the United States Senate, 1789-1990; Record Group 46; Records of the United States Senate, 1789-1990; National Archives
Pudar G, 'Persons at Risk of Statelessness in Serbia' (June 2011)
Refugees International, 'Without Citizenship, Statelessness, Discrimination and Repression in Kuwait' (2012)
Regional Bureau for Europe (RBE) 'Nationality Laws of the Former Soviet Republics' (1 July 1993)
Report of the Commission to the General Assembly on the work of its forty-ninth session, Commentary to Art. 2., YB Intl Law Commission 1997, vol II, pt 2 (1997)
Reynolds S, 'Kuwait's Stateless: Not Giving Up the Fight' (Refugees International March 19, 2014)
Sahel and West Africa Club, 'Vulnerabilities and factors of insecurity in the Sahel, West African Challenges' (2010)
Semporna Islands Project, 'Management Plan for the Semporna Islands Park, Part 10: Legal Aspects and Regulations' (2001)
Senate of Canada, Standing Senate Committee on Aboriginal Peoples 'Border Crossing Issues and the Jay Treaty' (June 2016)
Simperingham E, 'The International Protection of Stateless Individuals: A Call for Change' (masters thesis, U of Auckland 2003)
Straus S, 'Mali and Its Sahelian Neighbors' (World Development Report, World Bank 2011)
UNHCR, 'Expert Meeting—The Concept of Stateless Persons under International Law' (Prato Conclusions May 2010)
UNHCR, 'Global Appeal 2014-2015: Malaysia' (2013)
UNHCR, 'Submission by the United Nations High Commissioner for Refugees for the Office of the High Commissioner for Human Rights' Compilation Report: Universal Periodic Review: Malaysia,' (March 2013)
UNHCR, 'I Am Here, I Belong: The Urgent Need to End Childhood Statelessness' (2015)
UNHCR, 'Statelessness in West Africa Newsletter #9' (April–June 2016)
UNICEF, 'Every Child's Birth Right: Inequalities and Trends in Birth Registration' (2013)
United Kingdom Home Office, 'Country Information and Guidance Kuwaiti Bidoon' (3 February 2014)
United Nations, 'Our Common Future' (1987)
USAID, 'Property Rights and Resource Governance Program: Mali' (2010)
US Committee for Refugees and Immigrants, 'U.S. Committee for Refugees World Refugee Survey 1997–Mali' (1 January 1997)
US Dept of Commerce Intl Trade Administration, 'Malaysia—Oil and Gas' (18 June 2017)
US Dept of State, '2010 Country Reports on Human Rights Practices–Mali' (8 April 2011)
US Dept of State, 'Limits in the Seas: No. 142 Philippines' (2014)
US Energy Information Administration, 'Malaysia: International Energy Data and Analysis' (April 2017)
Van der Baaren L J, 'Emigrant Nationality. A Comparative Analysis of the Toleration of Dual Nationality from an (Maastricht 2020)
van Waas L, 'The Situation of Stateless Persons in the Middle East and North Africa' (UNHCR October 2010)
van Waas L, 'The Stateless Tebu of Libya?' (2013) (Tilburg University No. 010/)
Vela M J R, Institute on Statelessness and Inclusion, 'An Interview with Benyam Dawit Mezmur, Chairperson of the United Nations Committee on the Rights of the Children Voice of the Children, 'Birth Registration, Briefing Paper for UPR, Malaysia' (2013)

Index

For the benefit of digital users, indexed terms that span two pages (e.g., 52–53) may, on occasion, appear on only one of those pages.

Figures are indicated by an italic *f* following the page number.